"*The Fear* . . . by Peter Godwin — the Rhodesia-born correspondent who has become the most intrepid chronicler of Zimbabwe's last decade — describes in chilling detail the beatings, tortures, and murders that ZANU-PF mobs inflicted on MDC supporters in the spring and summer of 2008, after Tsvangirai defeated Mugabe in the presidential election and was subsequently forced to compete in a run-off."   —Joshua Hammer, *The New Republic*

"Godwin's *The Fear*, a powerful — and often achingly personal — account of recent events in Zimbabwe, is a necessary book. I can't recommend it more highly to anyone seeking to understand the current, and historical, situation in this troubled, beautiful country."
                              —Peter Orner, author of *The Second
                                       Coming of Mavala Shikongo*

"*The Fear* is a thoughtful, brave, and gripping book. Scenes from it will remain in a reader's mind with the force of real memories."
                  —Alec Wilkinson, author of *The Protest Singer*

"Peter Godwin's passionate and courageous memoir catalogues Zimbabwe's descent into horror with such vivid detail. . . . But this is not just a book about the savagery of Mugabe's goons. It is a testament to the courage and resilience of my fellow countrymen and women. . . . Godwin's heroes refuse to back down. Again and again they find ways to resist. This remarkable courage runs a thread of hope through the book."   —Wilf Mbanga, *The Guardian*

"Godwin, a white Zimbabwean journalist schooled in and relocated to England, bears brave witness to the last brutal days of Robert Mugabe's dictatorship. The author managed to infiltrate his devastated homeland during several months in 2008, when the eighty-four-year-old dictator was finally voted out of power yet held on by a savage reign of terror and violence. . . . Godwin's work serves as an invaluable, urgent dispatch from a country in the throes of an international humanitarian crisis. The author's return to his beloved homeland transformed by violence and no longer familiar proves heart-wrenching and extremely moving."   —*Kirkus Reviews*

THE FEAR

THE FEAR

ROBERT MUGABE AND THE MARTYRDOM OF ZIMBABWE

Peter Godwin

LITTLE, BROWN AND COMPANY

New York · Boston · London

LITTLE, BROWN AND COMPANY
HACHETTE BOOK GROUP
237 PARK AVENUE, NEW YORK, NY 10017
WWW.HACHETTEBOOKGROUP.COM

FIRST U.S. EDITION: MARCH 2011
ORIGINALLY PUBLISHED IN GREAT BRITAIN BY PICADOR, 2010

LITTLE, BROWN AND COMPANY IS A DIVISION OF HACHETTE BOOK GROUP, INC. THE LITTLE, BROWN NAME AND LOGO ARE TRADEMARKS OF HACHETTE BOOK GROUP, INC.

THE PUBLISHER IS NOT RESPONSIBLE FOR WEBSITES (OR THEIR CONTENT) THAT ARE NOT OWNED BY THE PUBLISHER.

MAP BY GEORGE W. WARD

LIBRARY OF CONGRESS CATALOGING-IN-PUBLICATION DATA
GODWIN, PETER.
THE FEAR : ROBERT MUGABE AND THE MARTYRDOM OF ZIMBABWE / BY PETER GODWIN.— 1ST US ED.
   P. CM.
  ISBN 978-0-316-05173-6
  1. ZIMBABWE—POLITICS AND GOVERNMENT—1980– 2. ZIMBABWE—ECONOMIC CONDITIONS—1980– 3. ZIMBABWE—SOCIAL CONDITIONS—1980– 4. MUGABE, ROBERT GABRIEL, 1924– I. TITLE.
  DT2996.G64 2011
  968.9105'1—DC22   2010041557

10 9 8 7 6 5 4 3 2 1

RRD-IN

PRINTED IN THE UNITED STATES OF AMERICA

This book is dedicated to the many Zimbabweans
who have been threatened, hurt or killed
in the struggle to be free from the dictatorship.
May their sacrifice not be forgotten.

"I learned that courage was not
the absence of fear, but the triumph over it.
The brave man is not he who does not feel afraid,
but he who conquers that fear."
Nelson Mandela

CONTENTS

CONTENTS

THE FEAR

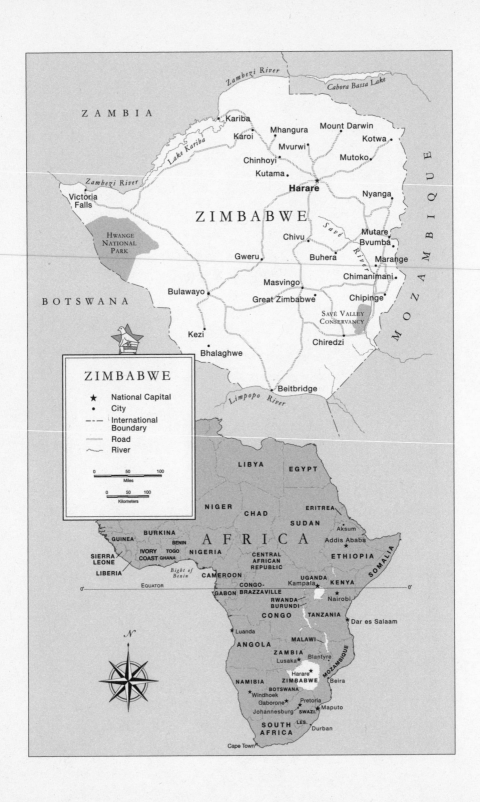

SEARCHING FOR SKY

M Y MOTHER LIES ON HER BED and tries to see the sky. If she cranes her head at a certain angle, she thinks she might just catch a sliver of it, through the high, narrow strip of window. But all she can see is the red brick of the house next door, a few feet away. She falls back on her pillow, defeated, and listens to the densely stacked planes banking over North London on their final approach to Heathrow. It doesn't really matter — it's a cheerless, iron-dull sky anyway, more of a lid, a manhole cover, than a sky. Not like the African sky she has been used to these last fifty years. That sky, she remembers, was a soaring cathedral of cerulean. At night, it turned into a star-sprayed window on the universe. And in the rainy season, soft churning anvils of cumulonimbus reared up for the drama of rain. Rain wasn't such a drama here. Generally you couldn't quite tell where it came from, even when you *could* see the sky. But she knows it is raining again now, from the wet swish of the car tires on the street.

She misses Africa acutely, but she is grateful to be here. She is grateful for Radio 4, where people even disagree in such reasonable tones. She's grateful for the nice people from Camden Library home-delivery service who keep her supplied with library books (her taste runs to biographies and history, mostly). She's grateful for the Association of Jewish Refugees, who deliver meals to her, even though she's a parson's daughter, and only the widow of a Jew. She especially likes the lamb hotpot, and the chocolate cake, which reminds her of the one her mother used to make.

She is grateful not to be parked in some institutional home for the elderly, inhaling the odor of boiled cabbage and bleach, cared for by indifferent staff on minimum wages. She is grateful to be living with her own blood-line, her daughter Georgina, and her seven-year-old granddaughter, Xanthe—three generations of Godwin women, together in this small apartment, making the best of their radically altered circumstances.

She has lived a long and surprising life. As a girl in Kent, she watched the Battle of Britain in the skies overhead. As a rating in the Royal Navy, stationed in Dover, she was frequently under shell-fire from the German "big guns" at Calais. As a doctor in Zimbabwe, she has run leper colonies and tuberculosis hospitals; she has vaccinated thousands, saved second twins, held the hands of patients dying of a new disease called AIDS, even as others shrank from them.

She has lived through a guerrilla war, seen her oldest daughter killed in it. In her old age, she has felt her heart break again. The health-care system she dedicated her life to building lies shattered. She has lost her house and her savings and her friends and her dogs. And she has watched her husband die a difficult death. Now she is determined that death will not cheat her.

She shows me a document she has been working on. It is called a living will or, now rebranded, like a fickle pop star, "Advance Decision—formerly a Living Will," a form provided by Dignity in Dying, motto—*Your Life, Your Choice*. She has ticked all the boxes to decline treatment if she has an imminently life-threatening illness, if she suffers serious mental impairment together with a physical need for life-sustaining treatment, or if she is persistently unconscious.

But in addition to the pro-forma options, my mother has added a section of her own, carefully written out in her spidery doctor's hand. Culled from her extensive medical experience in palliative care in Africa, she has tried to recall, and refuse treatment for, all the awful ways that the elderly wear out: "Degenerative disease of the Central Nervous System including multiple sclerosis, motor neuron disease and Parkinson's disease. Dementia or brain damage from any other cause including Alzheimer's disease or head injury or stroke. Advanced cancers, diseases linked to those cancers. Severe difficulty in breathing (Dypnoea) that cannot be cured. Incurable double incontinence. Uncontrollable vomiting and nausea."

Later we inch up Church Row on an outing to Hampstead High Street. She leans over her aluminum walker, choosing its next landfall with all the care of a rapeller placing a piton into a cliff face, and scrutinizing the pavement for the lethal bumps and ridges which can so easily fell her now.

We pass the historic St. John's parish cemetery, with its towering cedars of Lebanon, creeping buttercup and hart's tongue fern, and its leaning mossy headstones. The landscape painter John Constable is buried here. So is the former Labor Party leader Hugh Gaitskell, and John Harrison, inventor of the marine chronometer for measuring longitude. "Where would you like to be buried when *you* die?" I ask her. "At home," she says, without breaking stride. "In Africa. Next to your father."

one

The Fist of Empowerment

2 April 2008

DEEP INTO THE NIGHT, in pursuit of the westward escaping sun, we fly into a fogbank, where the cold Atlantic breakers curdle upon the warm West African shore below. Consoled, somehow, to have reached the continent of my birth, I lay down my book and fall uncomfortably asleep, my head wedged against the buzzing fuselage.

I am on my way home to Zimbabwe, to dance on Robert Mugabe's political grave. The crooked elections he has just held have spun out of his control, and after twenty-eight years the world's oldest leader is about to be toppled.

When I arrive the next evening in Harare, the capital, his portrait is everywhere still, staring balefully down at us. From the walls of the airport, as the immigration officer harvests my U.S. dollars, sweeping them across his worn wooden counter, and softly thumping a smudged blue visa into my passport. From the campaign placards pasted to the posts of the broken street lights, during our bumpy ride into the reproachfully silent city. Watched only by the feral packs of hollow-chested dogs, he raises his fist into the sultry dome of night, as though blaming the fates for his mutinous subjects. *The Fist of Empowerment,* his caption fleetingly promises our insect-flecked beams.

Somehow, though, his large gold-rimmed spectacles, the little tuft of starched white handkerchief that winks from his brandished clench, and his toothbrush mustache tell a different story. The story of the prissy schoolmaster he once was, a slight, almost effeminate figure, his small, manicured hands given to birdlike gestures. And indeed, if you were casting the role of "homicidal African dictator who fights his way to power and stays there against the odds for nearly three decades," Robert Mugabe wouldn't even rate a callback. This is no swaggering askari, no Idi Amin Dada, heavyweight boxing champion of the King's African Rifles, nor some wide-shouldered, medal-strewn Nigerian general. This is an altogether more dangerous dictator — an intellectual, a spiteful African Robespierre who has outlasted them all. Eighty-four years old now, with his dyed black hair and his blood transfusions, his Botox and vitamin-cocktail shots, he has querulously dominated his country for a generation.

But now he is on the verge of an exit. Five days ago, presidential elections, which he has fixed with ease in the past, using a combination of rigging, fraud and intimidation, have gone wrong. Zimbabweans have rejected him in such overwhelming numbers that he will finally be forced to accept their verdict.

They have many reasons to reject him. Once they enjoyed the highest standard of living in Africa. Now their money is nearly worthless, halving in value every twenty-four hours. Only 6 percent of workers have jobs. Their incomes have sunk to pre-1950 levels. They are starving. Their schools are closed, their hospitals collapsed. Their life expectancy has crashed from sixty to thirty-six. They have the world's highest ratio of orphans. They are officially the unhappiest people on earth, and they are fleeing the shattered country in their millions — an exodus of up to a third of the population.

But throughout this election campaign, Mugabe has remained

belligerently unrepentant, blaming the country's ills on the West—Britain, the former colonizer, in particular—and using the tiny number of whites remaining in Zimbabwe as political piñatas. He thwacks them and out pour the stale bonbons of historic blame to excuse his own shattering failure of leadership, his own rampant megalomania.

In a few days, he will meet with his politburo to contemplate his own farewell. I've been anticipating this moment for so long.

On my flights across the world to get here, I have reread Gabriel García Márquez's *The Autumn of the Patriarch,* and relished the scene in which sharp-beaked vultures, maddened by the stink of human carrion, tear their way through the mosquito screens of the imperial palace, alerting the citizens in the city below to the death of the dictator, and allowing their future to begin.

MY YOUNGER SISTER, Georgina, a broadcaster who now lives in London, is joining me here. We are supposed to be staying at York Lodge, a small pension in Harare's northern suburbs, but when Georgina calls to confirm, the manager brusquely informs her that our rooms are no longer available, and hangs up. Later we find out that the lodge is being raided by the police looking for Western journalists, who are banned from reporting in this country. As Georgina is on the line, the police are arresting the correspondents from the *New York Times* and the *Daily Telegraph.*

Instead, Georgina has booked rooms under her ex-husband's surname at the Meikles Hotel, in the city center. Once, all the journalists stayed there. Now none do. Neither of us is really supposed to be here. We are in double jeopardy: not only from Mugabe's banning of Western journalists, but also because I was once declared an enemy of the state, accused of spying, and Georgina worked for an anti-Mugabe radio station, in London, and she also featured on a list of undesirables, excluded from the country.

Beneath my window is a park, African Unity Square. The concrete tables which used to teem with vivid flowers are empty now, their sellers chased away as part of Operation Murambatsvina,

"Clear Out the Dirt," three years ago, when Mugabe—scared by growing hostility toward him in the urban areas—forcibly cleared out "informal housing" and street markets, leaving the cities dull and quiet. His police demolished the shops and dwellings (many of them quite substantial) of more than seven hundred thousand people, whom they dumped on barren land miles away, at the onset of winter, without water or sanitation. In all, this sham "slum clearance" operation devastated the lives of more than three million people.

In the other direction, my view is over a busy intersection, commanded by wildly erratic traffic lights. Sometimes they are resolutely blank. Sometimes they show red or flashing amber to all roads. Oncoming vehicles play a game of chicken, using pedestrians as shields, and auditing a number of factors to determine who goes next. Big scores over small, fast over slow, old over new, dilapidated over luxury, man over woman, black over white. It gets most interesting when the lights, as they quite often do, summon traffic from all directions simultaneously, with a cheery green come-on. Quite regularly, the crunch of metal, the jangle of glass, and the squall of argument summon me to my window to view another accident.

Everyone gives way to the frequently passing police pick-up trucks overloaded with riot-squad officers. The men are terribly young, riot interns really, not yet fully adult, pupas with brand-new blue fatigues and helmets. They remind me of myself at eighteen, still at police training depot, in the same uniform, "riot blues," drafted into service of an earlier regime. I wonder, as we all do, whether these underage gladiators will fire at their own people when ordered.

The atmosphere in the capital is tense with anticipation. How will this end? It's a state of mind I recognize now, a state I'm prone to myself, a wild swing between the tantalizing taste of change and the dull recognition of continued dictatorship. We call it euphoric despair.

THE BAR AT AMANZI (it means "water" in siNdebele, the language spoken in the country's south) is one of the few places in town that's heaving—here, where people have money in common, euphoria is at least temporarily vanquishing despair. Charles Summerfield and his band, the URJ, pump out electrified Afro fusion. Between sets, Summerfield tells me how he was recently tied up and badly beaten when his house was robbed, but tonight he's "loose, man, loose."

"*URJ*, like urge?" I ask.

"Nah." He shakes his matted dreads.

"Union of Reformed Judaism?" It's less of a reach than you might think—he is actually Jewish.

"Unlimited Resources of Joy," he says.

His band plays to a clientele so bizarrely disparate, it could grace *Star Wars*' Chalmun's Cantina, the intergalactic pirates' water hole. The Cypriot honorary consul presses his embossed card into my palm, *Nestoras P. Nestoras* (so good, they named him twice), and a gay carpenter who once made me a bed from the carved doors of Tonga tribal huts, high-fives. At the corner of the teak bar, where a Zambezi lager now costs 200 million Zimbabwean dollars (about $4 U.S. in illegal hard currency, on the black market), the average monthly income, some Ukrainian girls with platinum-blond hair cross and re-cross their lotioned legs below black Lycra microskirts. And spilling outside, toward the ornamental waterfall, where the musasa trees rustle in a cool evening breeze, aid workers and evicted tobacco farmers, black-market currency dealers and illegal diamond traders, ruling party fat cats, cell-phone magnates and opposition activists mingle.

We're on the brink of something historic here. Everyone is waiting for it.

Robert Mugabe and his generals are being lured with plump exit packages. I discuss them the next day with Andrew Pocock, the British ambassador, at his residence. As representative of the former colonial power, Pocock has a starring role in Mugabe's demonology—chief imperial agent of "regime change"—and he is shunned and excoriated in the state media. He exists in a kind of enforced political purdah. Here but not here, isolated from high-level contact with the host government, even though the UK provides food aid to many of Zimbabwe's starving.

Pocock knows well the feel of the ex-colonial outpost—he is Trinidadian born and raised. His clipped elocution hints at exfoliated traces of a West Indian lilt, and his mufti dress-code, short sleeves and thonged sandals, is more Caribbean than Cotswolds. He handles the heat better than most British envoys I've encountered. He's far from the archetypal Morgan Leafy, William Boyd's pudgy Britlomat abroad, whose ham-pink brow beads sweat at the first solar glance, whose taupe "tropical" linen suit is contoured with damp creases.

Under the gentle pealing of gamelan wind chimes on the cool, colonnaded veranda of the official residence, looking north toward Lunar Ridge across the green pelt of lawn, Pocock seems in his element, his hair immaculately coifed, brushed sharply back off his brow.

As a newly minted diplomat on his first posting, to Lagos in the early 1980s, Pocock was finishing an Oxford doctoral thesis on his Trinidadian compatriot, V. S. Naipaul, whose novel *A Bend in the River* portrays the cultural confusion of post-colonial Africa.

The Big Man in that book stays just offstage, cultivating an isolation that feeds his mystique and adds to his power. His ubiquitous photographs grow ever larger in the course of the book, says Pocock, like lengthening shadows. And they morph, from soldier to statesman to king. And so it has been with our own Big Man, Mugabe, who sheds his skins for the times. The olive military fatigues in his early official portraits have given way to Italian suits, now accessorized with an operatically pompous green silk sash, and the ludicrous mustache that begs for Adolfian allusions, ones he is not averse to making himself.

"I am still the Hitler of the time," he once boasted, when criticized for land takeovers. "This Hitler has only one objective, justice for his own people, sovereignty for his people, recognition of the independence of his people, and their right to their resources. If that is Hitler, then let me be a Hitler tenfold."

Pocock and I have heard that the opposition leader and presidential rival, Morgan Tsvangirai, has lured Mugabe's top brass with generous index-linked pensions, immunity from prosecution for human-rights abuses, continued ownership of one farm each of those they have recently confiscated from white settlers—if only they will accept their defeat. Mugabe himself is reliably reported to be tired and tempted. His young wife, Grace, a woman of prodigious retail appetite, the Imelda Marcos of Africa, known unaffectionately by her people as the First Shopper, is said to be keen for a negotiated exit too.

I wonder if we can dare to hope. It's been so, so long and Zimbabwe has known no other leader. The ambassador is telling me he has just converted his squash court (built to the wrong dimensions by a previous owner—interior dimensions mistaken for exterior ones) into a crisis command center. It is equipped with its own generator and communications systems, in case it "all goes up in flames here," and he has to supervise an evacuation of Britons. What his Foreign Secretary, David Miliband, has just called "a doomsday scenario." Pocock reckons there are about ten thousand Brits left here. And for those who don't make it out alive, the residence has a new addition, a large walk-in cold room, which could serve as a morgue.

After hooking his three phones to his belt—a local cell, a UK BlackBerry and a satellite phone—Pocock drives me back in his wife's acid-green Prado. Strangely, for the wheels of an ambassador's wife, it has silver hotrod flames painted along the hood.

"There was a scratch on it when we got it, so Raj, the best Indian detailer in Harare, said he would deal with it." He grins. "This was his solution."

Opposite the university, which is on strike, ragged men are repairing jagged potholes so big they look like shell holes. The men have propped a cardboard sign in the middle of the road, which reads: "Voluntary work. Pliz help."

"Isn't it impressive," murmurs Pocock, almost to himself, as we lurch through the graceful avenues of overhanging boughs that still line the dilapidated streets, "how the original arboreal architecture of the city's planners has confounded even the urban decay."

FOR MUCH OF FRIDAY 4 APRIL Mugabe is locked in a meeting with his politburo. We know he's up there, on the top floor of the party headquarters, "Shake-Shake" House, because the gold-bereted soldiers of the Presidential Guard, garlanded with bandoliers, machine guns, and grenades, are lolling outside. And several hundred "war veterans," bussed in from the provinces, are assembled in the car park. They are mostly young peasant boys (unborn in the independence war) in coarse woollen sweaters, the bedrolls on their backs snagged with grass seeds from sleeping outside.

Mugabe's party HQ is really called Jongwe House, "cockerel" in Shona, which is his party's motif. But the pitched pediment at the top of the building (complete with a crowing cockerel) reminds us of the wax cartons of thick millet beer, Chibuku, which you must shake before drinking, to mix the sediment. Repeated urgently in red on each eave of the carton's pediment is the instruction that gave the beer and now Mugabe's party HQ their names. Shake-Shake. In a dictatorship that diminishes us all, a subversive nickname is meant to mollify. When we mention Mugabe's draconian spying agency, the Central Intelligence Organization (CIO), we often call it Charlie Ten. And instead of referring to Robert Mugabe by any of his many official titles — His Excellency, Supreme Leader of ZANU-PF, Commander in Chief, Comrade — most Zimbabweans call him, simply, Bob. After all, how can you be scared of a dictator called Bob?

Later, after waiting in vain for the President to address them, the war vets march through town, chanting his praises. Political demonstrations are illegal here, but only if they are attempted by the opposition.

The meeting goes on for more than five hours. The fate of the country hangs on its outcome. Although the election results have still not been announced, six days after the vote, the party now knows what they are. And despite the gerrymandering and the intimidation, the rigging and the "ghost voters," Mugabe has lost resoundingly to his nemesis, Morgan Tsvangirai, who, according to the constitution, should now be declared the new President.

But it is here, in this meeting chaired by Mugabe himself, that his own tenure will actually be decided. And his four dozen or so politburo members, many of them comrades from the war of independence to overturn white rule (fought from 1972 to 1980), now divided between hawks and doves, between hardliners and conciliators, between rivals for the succession, must decide whether to concede power, drawing the twenty-eight-year reign of the dictator to a close, or to fight on.

The state-controlled broadcaster, ZTV, shows the scene inside. Mugabe, in a well-cut dark suit and polka-dotted tie, moves slowly around the large flower-topped horseshoe table, shaking hands with each person. What's noticeable is the way, even now, in his hour of humiliation, they all seem to revere him, bowing their heads as he approaches and, in the case of the few women, curtseying, as though to a king.

My ears in the room come via James Mushore. I have known him since we were thirteen, boarding in the same granite-walled dormitory at the local Jesuit College, St. George's. He is a prominent investment banker, straight-backed and tall, with gold-rimmed glasses, a connoisseur of single malts and Cuban cigars.

James is also the nephew of retired General Solomon Mujuru — now trying to position himself as a "moderate" within Mugabe's party, though he was not ever thus. Years ago, not long after the end of the independence war, when he still used his guerrilla name, Rex Nhongo (his wife, Joice, who today serves as Mugabe's deputy, called herself Teurai Ropa — "Spill Blood"), the general had put the barrel of his pistol to my heart and threatened to shoot me. It was a Russian-made Tokarev, with an iridescent mother-of-pearl handle. Odd, how you remember such details. He had worked his way through most of a liter bottle of Johnny Walker Red Label at the time, but his grip remained remarkably steady.

That was back in 1983, during the Matabeleland massacres,

when Mugabe unleashed his fearsome North-Korean-trained Fifth Brigade on the southern province to crush the "dissidents" there from the Joshua Nkomo's Ndebele opposition party, ZAPU (Zimbabwe African People's Union). It was a particularly brutal campaign of pacification. I had written about the massacres for the *Sunday Times,* which is what prompted the general to draw his gun when our paths crossed. He was in charge of the media junket intended to show that I had imagined it all. "You drive in front," I was told. "There may be land mines." I was subsequently accused of being a spy and forced to flee the country, threatened with death. It's a threat, I hope, that's now sufficiently antique to have lapsed.

I RECEIVE James's text on Friday evening — Georgina and I are having supper with husband and wife architects Richard and Penny Beattie. Georgina has brought a bottle of Moët from Heathrow duty-free. It stands expectantly in an ice bucket, waiting for the politburo's endorsement of Mugabe's decision to concede defeat.

Supper is an improvised affair. The power is out, and so is the water. The Beatties are cooking on gas canisters in candlelight. "It's like camping, only for longer," says Penny. They have surfed Dipleague, a sort of Craig's List for diplomats, on which only forex is accepted, to buy what was intriguingly billed as "neatly killed chicken."

Even for well-off upper-middle-class families like this, life is a struggle. Chicken is the only meat they've been able to eat for months now. "I could write a recipe book on how to cook chicken a hundred different ways," Richard mutters wearily, and thwacks his neatly killed chicken with a cleaver. Tonight he's settled on a coq au jus. Jongwe au jus — cooked in its own blood.

I read James's text aloud. The politburo has decided the presidential election results: 43.2 percent for Mugabe, and 47.9 percent for his challenger, Tsvangirai — below the crucial 50 percent threshold. This means that a second, run-off, election will now be necessary.

Mugabe has not conceded defeat after all. There is no political grave upon which to dance.

"I'm not sure how much more of this I can take," says Penny, and she slumps, deflated, onto a bar stool in the flame-flickering gloom. The Moët stands redundant in its chilled silo. The jongwe boils over. Nobody notices.

Of *course* he won't give up power—I realize that now. What were we *thinking?* The old man isn't going anywhere; he'll die in office. We'll have to carry him out in his boots, or rather in his Jermyn Street Oxfords.

two

A Nation of Gentlemen

L IKE MOST DICTATORS, Mugabe is both ubiquitous and remote; the landmarks of his life already read like an obituary, at once fixed and mythical. The boy who grew up to be our dictator, Robert Gabriel Karigamombe Mugabe, was born in 1924, at Kutama, a Jesuit mission station, sixty miles west of the capital, Harare. When he was ten, his father, Gabriel Matibili, a carpenter from Malawi, deserted the family, leaving Mugabe's mother, Bona, to raise her remaining children alone.

The young Robert, by his own admission, was awkward, unathletic, and bookish. Instead of playing with other boys when tending cattle together, he would strike out on his own to read. He hero-worshipped the Irish Jesuit principal at Kutama, Father Jerome O'Hea, and contemplated joining the priesthood himself. Instead, he trained as a teacher. He was initiated into the cause of black nationalism at Fort Hare University in South Africa, a decade after Mandela had graduated there. On his graduation, Mugabe returned to Rhodesia to teach.

Petiri was one of his pupils at Mambo School in the 1950s. (He is too afraid of his old schoolmaster to use his real name.) Georgina and I arrive at his house bearing medication from his children, who are in the diaspora. He shows us his report card filled out in Mugabe's careful cursive. He recalls him as unsmiling, rigid, aloof from the other teachers. "He was a very harsh man. We nicknamed him Hammurabi, after the Mesopotamian law-giver."

Mugabe went on to teach in Ghana, where he arrived just as it became independent, Britain's first sub-Saharan colony to be unleashed. "Ghanaians were just like the rest of us, but free!" he marveled. There he met his first wife, a Ghanaian, Sally Hayfron.

Back in Rhodesia two years later, Mugabe was drawn into the leadership of black nationalist politics. He was eventually arrested on charges of subversion, and spent eleven years in jail. While he was there, his three-year-old son, Michael Nhamodzenyika ("Suffering Country," in Shona), died of cerebral malaria in Ghana. Despite a strong recommendation by his white jailer, who vouched that Mugabe would duly return from Ghana to detention in Zimbabwe, he was not allowed to attend the funeral.

Ian Smith, the Rhodesian Prime Minister, finally freed Mugabe in 1974, as part of a détente brokered by South Africa. Aided by Sister Aquina, a Catholic nun, he soon fled over the border into Mozambique. There he joined the guerrilla war against white Rhodesian settler rule—although he was never himself a soldier.

Mugabe was a reluctant participant in the 1979 Lancaster House peace treaty that ended the Rhodesian conflict. Lord Carrington, the British Foreign Secretary, who hosted the talks, said of him, "The quietly spoken Mugabe worried me: he was secretive, seemed not to need friends, mistrusted everyone. Devious and clever, he was an archetypal cold fish."

Petiri and his friends were with Mugabe's mother, Bona, in April 1980, as the results of Zimbabwe's first democratic elections were announced. She reacted strangely, he says. "Bona was not happy he had won. We were at her house and she said, 'He is not capable of doing it. He is not the kind of person who will look after other people.'"

White Rhodesians also reacted badly to Mugabe's landslide victory. Many fled to South Africa, then still in the grip of apartheid. They feared that Mugabe was an avowed communist, committed to wide-scale nationalization and a racial vendetta.

Even my parents, "white liberals," who had opposed Ian Smith, cast around for an escape. The bizarre ark they came closest to boarding was the island nation of Nauru. My father was offered the post of chief engineer there and my mother, Nauru's sole doctor.

I had never heard of Nauru, but I'd already left home for university in England by then, so it wasn't about to become my new domicile. Georgina, though, was going to have to make the trek, and asked me for help in finding out more about it. In those pre-Google days, this wasn't so simple. Nauru was hard enough to find on a map: we scanned up and down the vast blue expanse of the south Pacific until we finally chanced upon a tiny dot in the middle of the ocean. It was one of the most isolated places in the world, an eight-square-mile pile of sea-bird droppings, rich in phosphates. A muggy equatorial island, I discovered, whose residents (there were fewer than ten thousand of them) made a living by strip-mining said phosphates, and selling it to make fertilizer and explosives, to those not fortunate enough to inhabit their own pile of bird shit.

At the time we were considering it as an alternative to the prospect of a Mugabe-led Zimbabwe, this self-excavation still paid off handsomely—and Nauruans enjoyed the world's highest per-capita income. It wasn't to last. As they dug themselves into the sea, in pursuit of dwindling bird-shit supplies, their income dwindled too, and the investments made by the Nauru Phosphates Royalties Trust were spectacularly unwise. *Leonardo, the Musical,* one of the biggest disasters in the history of the West End, was just one of their money losers.

The island wallowed in another unfortunate superlative: its people were the world's most obese. About 90 percent of the residents were overweight, and nearly half of them had type-two diabetes. As their doctor, my mother would be busy, busy, busy.

For ten-year-old Georgina, there were two other strikes against

Nauru. Her new horse, Top Ace, would not be allowed on the island, as there was an equine ban, and she would have to be sent to boarding school in Australia, nearly two thousand miles away. She took to running round the house, howling, "I don't want to go to Naurooo!"

On some level, I don't think my parents were ever serious about leaving Zimbabwe. That's why they chose such a preposterous place as Nauru. And their initial horror at Mugabe's ascent soon faded when he moderated his militancy. He quickly dropped his plans for nationalization, promising instead a free-market economy.

And in his first speech as Prime Minister, Mugabe appealed to the country's whites not to flee. "Stay with us, please remain in this country and constitute a nation based on national unity," he pleaded.

My parents gratefully accepted his offer. As did other whites, especially the farmers.

As Mugabe emerged from the carapace of Rhodesian propaganda, there was much to surprise us: his obvious Anglophilia; his Savile Row suits; his fastidious English; his penchant for Graham Greene novels; his admiration of the Queen, especially once she had knighted him in 1994, for services to Anglo-Zimbabwe relations; his love of tea and cricket, a game, he said, that "civilizes people and creates good gentlemen. I want everyone to play cricket in Zimbabwe. I want ours to be a nation of gentlemen."

Excited to get home, I bought an old Bedford truck at the British army auctions near Nottingham, and with a bunch of friends from university drove the length of the African continent. On the bumper, I proudly displayed stickers of the new Zimbabwean flag. Back in Harare, I joined thousands of compatriots, black and white, from all over the world. There was a charged atmosphere of possibility. We would show the world just what could be achieved in Africa's newest independent nation.

And initially Zimbabwe prospered, the economy grew, health care and education expanded dramatically as Western aid poured in to rebuild this nation, emancipated after eight years of war.

So what went wrong?

When I look back over the trajectory of Mugabe's life, I find it hard to identify a moment when the "liberation hero" transforms into the "tyrannical villain." I think that's because there was no "good leader turns bad" metamorphosis. Robert Mugabe has been surprisingly consistent in his modus operandi. His reaction to opposition has invariably been a violent one, inherent in his political DNA.

If you rewind to the early days of his tussles for his leadership of ZANU, the Zimbabwe African National Union, you will see ample evidence already of the bloody internal feuding by which he seized the helm of the party, and fought off challengers.

The guerrilla war itself may have been a justified struggle for democracy, but as a teenaged conscript in the Rhodesian police, I witnessed first-hand the gruesome punishment of black civilians by Mugabe's guerrillas, in order to win the "balance of fear." Mugabe learned then that the barrel of Kalashnikov underwrote success at the ballot box.

He made it clear again during the 1980 elections when—in breach of the Lancaster House peace agreement—he kept many of his guerrillas out in the field to warn the voters that the war would continue if his party didn't win. Although the scale of his victory was such that he didn't need to intimidate voters, he wasn't taking any chances.

Barely three years after independence, Mugabe ordered his troops into the southern province of Matabeleland to launch Operation Gukurahundi, "The Rains That Clear Out the Chaff." They killed around twenty thousand Ndebele civilians, most of them supporters of Joshua Nkomo's ZAPU party. No one has ever been held accountable for this political genocide. It remains the single worst moral stain on Robert Mugabe's record—although at the time international reaction was shamefully muted.

After these massacres, Mugabe coerced a shattered Joshua Nkomo, the father of black Zimbabwean nationalism, into a "Unity Accord," which effectively created a one-party state. Without real opposition, Mugabe's administration grew increasingly authoritarian, inefficient and corrupt.

Mugabe appeared irked when, in 1990, Nelson Mandela was released from prison and soon swept to power in South Africa's first democratic elections, eclipsing Mugabe's role as the colossus on the African stage. Mandela joked that Mugabe had grown accustomed to being the star, "and then the sun came out."

By 2000, after thirteen years of political monopoly, Mugabe was shocked and enraged to find that a new opposition to his rule had emerged among the younger generation, and he set out to crush them, as was his default—violently.

He also ordered his party militia onto white-owned farms to forcibly evict the owners and their workers. In Shona, it was called *jambanja*, a violent overthrow. Most of the farms were doled out as bribes to his own elite; Mugabe kept six for himself. Few of the new owners had any agricultural know-how, and commercial agriculture, the economy's foundation, quickly collapsed, bringing the rest down with it.

Mugabe's old pupil, Petiri, sees a psychological tendency, on a social level, among African leadership. He traveled widely through Africa in the 1960s. "I knew Kaunda and Banda and Kenyatta before independence, when they were still on bicycles, when we were learning. I know the leadership of Africa: a father is a figurehead. It's about masculinity. All radical fathers want to dominate their wives and kids, so in a political party, that domination is carried out too—you don't want people to answer back—you select 'yes' men. This has been a problem in our leadership. People have to listen and obey, or else. Mugabe is like that. Anyone who criticizes him is eliminated. One by one, got rid of."

three

People Smell Power and Run to Where It Is

MY OLD FRIEND Godfrey Chanetsa arrives punctually for tea. His closely shaved head gleams, and he is dressed in an immaculately pressed striped shirt, dark trousers, and tasseled loafers. Educated at Queensland University in Brisbane, Australia, Godfrey, now fifty-seven, is articulate, cosmopolitan, passionate, just the kind of person that made so many enthusiastic about this country.

We met during his days as a Zimbabwean diplomat in London in the early 1980s, when we were both still rouged with the first blush of enthusiasm for the new Zimbabwe, still enjoying *our* "rainbow nation" moment. He used to hold great parties at Zimbabwe House, the embassy on the Strand, a listed building designed originally for the British Medical Association in 1907 by Charles Holden, architect of many London Underground stations.

Godfrey had proudly showed me around the building. It had eighteen large naked statues by Jacob Epstein, representing the Ages of Man, which stood in exterior alcoves. When first erected, they had appalled conservative critics, and in 1937, after claiming that Epstein's statues were crumbling, the Rhodesian authorities hacked off their extremities, ostensibly to prevent passers-by from being struck by falling stone genitals. Now the mutilated, emasculated honor guard of statues that stands shattered sentinel around Mugabe's London outpost seems appropriate.

Chanetsa returned to London for a second posting, fresh from a diplomatic stint in Moscow, where he had just witnessed the dramatic collapse of Soviet power.

"It feels like that now here in Zimbabwe," he says, enthusiastically, "that the ancien régime is over, just its phantom limb twitching."

Chanetsa's second tour of duty in London came to an abrupt end, when he clashed with Mugabe's new wife, Grace, thirty-four years Mugabe's junior, who had been a secretary in the President's protocol office. Mugabe had her husband, Stanley Goreraza, an airforce officer, posted to China, and sired two children with her while Sally was dying of kidney failure.

"I complained that we were turning our historic embassy library into a warehouse for Grace's shopping," Chanetsa explains. "I wanted her to store it elsewhere." (When she was later challenged about her expensive taste in shoes, in a land where many now go barefoot, Grace replied: "I have very narrow feet, so I wear only Ferragamo.") He was ordered onto the next plane home, "the only diplomat to be withdrawn by Robert Mugabe personally, not by the Ministry of Foreign Affairs, because I was said to have insulted his wife."

Back in Harare, he didn't last long. "It was awful, my office was next to the toilet, which wasn't disinfected, and it *stank*. Opposite my door sat Sithole, the department messenger, whose job was to cut the *Herald* [Mugabe's mouthpiece newspaper] into squares and put them on a metal spike, as toilet paper. I had just come from the Strand to this! After six months I left, I didn't even bother to get my pension."

Chanetsa joined Coca-Cola International, running their

business in the nine southern African countries. Then, at fifty, he kept a promise he'd made himself and went back to his rural home. "That's my *musha*, that's where my father is buried, and you know African superstitions, no one can come close to my graves." He established a pig farm there, complete with export abattoir.

Before becoming a diplomat, Chanetsa had been the man at Robert Mugabe's elbow. He was his personal secretary, his amanuensis, and his spokesman both in exile in Tanzania in the 1970s, and after independence in 1980 when Mugabe took power. He saw him first thing each morning.

"I wrote speeches and letters for him. He was really impressive. He has a force in him, and even some regional heads of state, they still react to that. He doesn't talk much. He just blinks and listens. He lets *you* talk. He leans back with his head cocked to one side, resting on his hands, and listens to you.

"You had to be very careful when you briefed him. You had to be really on top of it as he would ask very penetrating questions."

Chanetsa, too, describes Mugabe as the consummate loner. "He has absolute power within the party—there's no internal democracy. He stays distant, remote. He never meets his ministers except on cabinet days, every Tuesday afternoon. He never trusted anyone enough to groom as a successor."

After Tsvangirai's opposition Movement for Democratic Change (MDC) was created in 1999, says Chanetsa, Mugabe fell under the control of his security chiefs. "He has a responsibility to them. Their guiding fear is that they'll face retribution for the Matabeleland massacres. They only want to see a successor they are confident can look after their interests.

"Their bottom line is: we fought and died for this country—they—the MDC—didn't. It's an entitlement thing. This is why I really believe Mugabe will not hand over to Morgan Tsvangirai. He will *never* do it. We will all go down. The ballot box only appears to be the final determinant, but for Mugabe it's only final if it endorses *him*. Robert Mugabe doesn't understand 'process'—power to him is raw."

To understand how Mugabe keeps his people down, says Chanetsa, you must understand "the psychology of deprivation: Zimbabweans have learned to be self-reliant. There's a deep sense of individuality—no collective sense. We've become a nation of black-marketers, crooks. Robert Mugabe has subverted the revolution by keeping people busy just managing, just getting by. There's no employment but people are busy, busy.

"Only now do we realize we've been under serious dictatorship. It has become part of our identity.

"In Eastern Europe the border guards faced in. Not here. Here, the people who would be in the front line have been allowed to go." All four of Chanetsa's grown kids have joined this Zimbabwean diaspora: one in Canada, one in Australia, and two in South Africa. "My son in Australia came back for a visit. He was born when I was working for Mugabe, and Mugabe is still here—my son has known no other leader here. During his visit, there was no electricity, no running water, and he turned to me in disgust and said, 'Dad, how can you allow this? I have options, I'm outside. But *you?*'"

In these elections, Chanetsa is serving as campaign manager for a third presidential candidate, Simba Makoni, who is offering himself as a sort of ZANU-PF-lite candidate, a reformist from within. Georgina and I find Makoni in his sparsely furnished office. On the wall is his banner: a sun rising over green tilled fields, into a clear blue sky. Underneath is his slogan—"Let's Get Zimbabwe Working Again." The young men in dark suits who guard him pace around the corridor outside, looking anxious.

Makoni knows Mugabe's court from the inside too. Armed with a Ph.D. in chemistry from Leicester, he served as a deputy minister when he was only thirty. Even now, at fifty-seven, his unlined complexion gives an impression of youth. He was in the politburo and a member of the cabinet for eight years, ending up as Mugabe's Finance Minister. But after clashing with Mugabe on monetary policy, and being shuffled away from finance in 2002, he resigned—only the second man ever to have left Mugabe's cabinet voluntarily. "People said, 'Do you have a death wish!' Fear is such a crucial part of the way he runs things."

After Makoni declared his presidential challenge, Mugabe was furious, denouncing him as "worse than a prostitute," and some inside Mugabe's ZANU-PF, like General Mujuru, who had initially promised to support him, were in the end too afraid to do so.

Such fear is well founded. Since James Mushore, the general's nephew, has been helping Simba Makoni, his phones have been monitored, and he's been trailed, and received death threats.

"Originally," says Makoni, "Mugabe was puritanical and brooked no failure. In the early days, he was intolerant of greed and corruption, sloppiness and incompetence. When he came back from a foreign trip, he would even return unused foreign currency! But that all went. Now he likes greed and incompetence in his ministers, as it gives him more control over them."

Being in the politburo, he says, "feels like you're in the court of the emperor. Earlier, he used to enjoy discussion, give and take, but then he became more and more intolerant as he concentrated power in himself. Now if you differ with him, you are his enemy.

"Mugabe's a mixture, initially he had the aura of a liberation hero—eleven years in jail, seven in the bush war, self-disciplined, he does press-ups at five thirty each morning, a teetotaller. Over the years, Mugabe and ZANU have built themselves into the lives of the people, there is a very intense fear of them. I'd come out of a cabinet meeting and colleagues would say, 'How could you argue with the President like that!' The fear factor is crucial to understanding his power."

The country is in the condition it is because of a failure of leadership, says Makoni. "The other ministers could have said, 'We're not going to invade farms...' But we didn't. He managed to do that because he had a team of jellyfish. On the surface, he is a very dominant character, but you can only do that in the face of pliancy and subservience. I saw him lose his temper many times, shouting, fist thumping the table."

Makoni says that in all his dealings with Mugabe, the President never left a paper trail. "There were no memos. Everything was done face to face.

"Many say they hide things from the old man. He doesn't want to know the nasty things. In March 2001, for instance, I told Bob that we would face a food shortage and that we needed to import food. And simultaneously Joseph Made [the Agriculture Minister] says to him, 'We will have a bumper harvest.' He knows this how? Because he's flown over the country in a helicopter 'and it's all green!' When famine indeed struck, Mugabe never acknowledged this error. He said he had a bumper harvest, when the only thing we were growing were weeds.

"Again, in September 2004, when food shortages were imminent and he was told so by his colleagues, he said, 'You can't expect me to admit that in front of the UN.'

"Many colleagues, as early as 1997, disagreed with his direction, but instead of standing up, we were expedient, greedy, we betrayed the national interest. Why have we allowed him to become the Kim Il-Sung of Africa? We are cosmopolitan and worldly-wise. The war veterans spent time in Tanzania, Mozambique, Zambia, and they said, we are never going to let our country become like them, and yet we *did*. It's a terrible indictment of us, a terrible reflection of our cowardice, our opportunism, that we have followed our narrow self-interest."

The blame for the "overwhelming, omnipresent character that Mugabe has become," Makoni attributes to three things. The departure of Mugabe's most forceful colleagues, after which there was no counter to him in cabinet, as the rest all owed their jobs to him. The death of his Ghanaian wife, the tempering Sally, and the impact of his new wife, Grace. "Under her influence, the avarice and ostentation began to show, the vast convoys, the huge shopping trips." And the "Unity Accord" in 1987, which effectively established a one-party state. The switch from a British-style prime-ministership to an executive presidency sealed Mugabe's dictatorial metamorphosis.

WHEN GODFREY CHANETSA calls later, to see how our meeting with Simba Makoni went, his election prognosis has darkened. "No more politburo members support Simba. They've tested the water and retreated," he says scornfully. "People smell power and they run to where it is."

He now fears that Mugabe is preparing to punish his subjects for their latest rejection. "Robert Mugabe will make the villagers crawl back into their huts, with low-flying jets and helicopters flying all over the place. ZANU's already sending its storm-troopers into the rural areas—they know the places they didn't do well. They'll kill the cattle of the last white farmers, send soldiers and paramilitaries in to scare the voters. We have no other way to respond to force, other than by using our vote. It's our life against Mugabe's life."

four

The Last Goats

FROM THE VERY START of his political career, the opposition leader, Morgan Richard Dzingirai Tsvangirai, Mugabe's nemesis, has had a torrid time. In 1998, Mugabe's war veterans beat him with iron bars and tried to bundle him out of a tenth-story window. Since then his bodyguards have been murdered, and he's been charged with treason three times, arrested multiple times, imprisoned, and survived two further assassination attempts.

In 2007, he was arrested on his way to a prayer meeting. When his wife, Susan, finally managed to visit him in his cell, she found that he had been so severely beaten and tortured that he had lost consciousness three times, and had to be revived. TV footage of him waiting to appear in court, his head massively swollen, one eye gashed, shocked the world. He was later hospitalized with a fractured skull and internal bleeding.

A freelance cameraman, Edward Chikombo, who distributed the footage of the badly injured Tsvangirai to the foreign media, was himself abducted. His corpse was found a few days later, dumped on waste ground outside the city.

Now, as we wait for the official election results, Tsvangirai is AWOL. The MDC's own projections, based on results recorded by their election agents at most of the nine thousand or so polling stations, show that despite all the obstacles placed in his way he has not only won the presidential elections, but has cleared the crucial 50 percent barrier that triggers a run-off poll. So he has jetted off on a hectic series of meetings with African leaders, trying to persuade them to accept him as Zimbabwe's new president.

Tsvangirai's biggest hurdle to regional acceptance is Mugabe's almost messianic reputation as a "liberation leader," Africa's oldest, at eighty-four—nearly three decades older than his fifty-six-year-old rival. Mugabe's propaganda machine portrays Tsvangirai as a sell-out, someone who watched the liberation war from the sidelines. And the hyper-educated Mugabe also derides Tsvangirai as "an ignoramus," because he isn't caped with degrees.

But Tsvangirai's story is one of considerable sacrifice. The eldest of nine children of a poor bricklayer in the southeastern district of Gutu, at sixteen, Tsvangirai had to forfeit a scholarship to a good mission school in order to support his family after his father deserted them—a paternal abandonment he shares with Mugabe. He toiled in a textile factory in Mutare, before moving to Trojan Nickel Mine in Bindura, northwest of Harare. There he rapidly climbed from plant operator to mine foreman, and became the mine's trade-union rep. Initially he revered Mugabe, joining his party.

By 1988, Tsvangirai had risen to head the country's confederation of trade unions, but he soon clashed with Mugabe's over IMF-initiated reforms, and then over huge payments that Mugabe wanted to make to the country's war vets. Tsvangirai transformed the union from a pillar of the one-party state to its main effective opposition. At the time, he said that Mugabe reminded him of his own father, "a stubborn old man."

Soon after he broke with the ruling party, over its "misrule, official corruption and dictatorship," he became the founding leader of the Movement for Democratic Change, MDC. Mugabe has done his best to portray the MDC as the bastard child of revanchist whites and neo-colonial Western governments, a Trojan horse bent on purloining the country's hard-won independence. But 99 percent of MDC supporters are black. From the start, it was more movement than party. A grab bag of opponents to Mugabe's increasingly autocratic and dysfunctional rule, it attracted support mostly from the black urban working class, but also from the educated elite, churchmen, academics, industrialists, ethnic amaNdebeles, and white farmers.

The latter only really threw in their lot with the MDC once Mugabe announced his plans to confiscate their farms without compensation. The MDC, like virtually everyone in Zimbabwe, agrees that land reform is necessary, but done in a planned, coherent way, not by the chaotic government-encouraged farm invasions that decimated agriculture and ushered in famine.

The "land issue" was about so much more than land. It was about breaking up the million-strong voting bloc of black employees who worked on the farms, and who had voted for the MDC. Mugabe wanted to shatter that bloc. And they became the main, though largely unsung, victims of the land takeovers. Many of them had originally migrated from neighboring countries, Malawi, Mozambique, and Zambia, but now, after three or four generations, they were chased off the farms, and had nowhere to go. Homeless, and reduced to dire poverty, they perished in large numbers. The farmers' organization JAG (Justice for Agriculture) claims that more than half a million displaced farm workers and their dependents have perished in the decade since their expulsion, of starvation and disease.

The farm takeovers have now entered their final, mopping-up phase. "We're in the crosshairs, straight in the firing line, we're the scapegoats, but there are fewer and fewer of us goats left." John Worsley-Worswick, who heads JAG, is talking to a couple of sun-charred white farmers in shorts and desert boots, at JAG HQ in

Harare. Worswick is the designated mourner at the protracted death rattle of the white Zimbabwean farmer.

He answers the phone and immediately begins briefing: "Masvingo's hot, Centenary's hot, there are only ten farmers left there—but all will probably be off by tomorrow. It's flaring up all over the place. Karoi, Chinhoyi are heating up—they're driving farmers off there too."

It is Monday April 7th, and it seems that Godfrey Chanetsa has correctly predicted his old boss Mugabe's next move.

"The worst scenario is a military junta, but then we've effectively been under military rule anyway," sighs Worswick. He pauses to allow a jet fighter to scream overhead. For the last few days now, they have been constantly buzzing the city. Ostensibly they're practicing for the country's twenty-eighth annual independence celebrations due in a couple of weeks, but most see it as something more sinister, a signal from the old man that he still has the big guns on his side, he can still blast his rebellious people into submission.

"They're a law unto themselves," continues Worswick. "There's bugger all you can do except document and publish what they're up to."

He hangs up and turns to me. "We've been cataloguing human-rights violations on the farms since 2000, electronically mapping them and collating them with political events, building an international case to take to the Hague, to the Southern African Development Community [SADC] Tribunal, to the African Court of Human Rights, to the International Criminal Court of Rome.

"Amendment No. 17, passed in 2005, basically says white farmers are dirt, and need to be swept away. It makes it an offense to be on a farm—your own farm—without permission, you are trespassing on state land. In a country that's starving, it basically makes it an offense to farm! An offense to grow food!

"Our commercial national herd is down from two and a half million to a hundred thousand. Maize production is the lowest ever since land reform began. Tobacco is down from two hundred and forty million kilos to fifty million.

"From six thousand five hundred productive farms in 2000,

there are now only four hundred left," says Worswick. "Seventy-eight of those have investment-guarantee protection, as foreigners. We've lost another hundred farmers off the land in the last eighteen months as Operation Maguta ['Full Stomach'] was launched, when soldiers arrived to evict farmers and replace them with military personnel, promising 'the mother of all agricultural seasons.' They pledged to put in fifty thousand plows. But still there's been a greater decline in output this year than any other. Instead of being the mother of all seasons, as they proclaimed, it turned out to be the mother of all disasters."

He leans back heavily in his chair and lights up another cigarette to give me time to catch up with his torrent.

"The party elite who take over farms have access to U.S. dollars at the official rate of thirty thousand to one when the black market rate is eighty million to one. They can get loans at 25 percent per annum when hyperinflation is 200,000 percent, so they can make huge profits on the difference, buy forex on the street, generating income without actually farming."

This is the alchemy of the famous "U.S.$500 Mercedes," where Mugabe's favored can take just U.S.$500 and, in four black-market currency deals, turn it into enough to buy a brand-new Merc.

A FEW DAYS LATER, on Thursday, Georgina and I have been invited to supper by Peter Lobel, scion of the bakery family that once produced most of Zimbabwe's bread. Lobel now lives in New York (and set up an artisanal bakery there, called Tribeca Oven), but keeps a condo in a gated complex in northern Harare. The route takes us past State House, where the presidential bodyguards strut along the pavement, thrusting their AK-47s, bayonets fixed, at the passing cars, a ballet of the bellicose, intended to scare us. Like the pupa policemen, they are young and skinny, with helmets too big for their heads, oddly vulnerable, kids dressed up. And somehow this makes them more dangerous and unpredictable. You can feel the diminutive soldiers' insecurity, and how it's all about the gun.

One (black) Zimbabwean returning on holiday from the diaspora recently complained that he happened to chortle at a joke his sister had cracked while they were in their car, waiting at these traffic lights, when suddenly a presidential bodyguard banged on his window.

"What are you laughing at?" he demanded, machine-gun at the ready.

The holidaying Zimbabwean tried to explain it was just an innocent family joke.

"You don't laugh near the President's residence!" the soldier roared. "It's against the *law*."

Georgina and I keep our eyes fixed straight ahead, our mouths downturned.

As we pass through the suburb of Gun Hill, I get, as I always do in this part of town, a frisson of revulsion. Here, on Garvin Close, is where Mengistu Haile Mariam, "the Butcher of Addis," architect of Ethiopia's Red Terror, has lived in a heavily guarded luxury home since being granted sanctuary by Mugabe in 1991, when his regime was overthrown. Mengistu also spends time on a ranch confiscated from a white farmer, and in his holiday villa on Lake Kariba. His security has been redoubled since two Eritreans tried to assassinate him here in 1995.

During Mengistu's seventeen-year rule, an estimated one million Ethiopians died in famines, exacerbated when he blocked emergency food shipments to areas sympathetic to his opponents. He had half a million more killed as "counter-revolutionaries" in his Cultural Revolution-style purge of the educated classes — especially students and their professors. Human Rights Watch described the killings as "one of the most systematic uses of mass murder ever witnessed in Africa." Before they could retrieve the bodies of their loved ones, relatives were charged "the wasted bullet" tax, to pay for the execution.

At the height of the Red Terror, it was reported by another NGO official that more than a thousand children had been killed, and "their bodies are left in the streets and are being eaten by wild hyenas...You can see the heaped-up bodies of murdered children, most of them aged eleven to thirteen, lying in the gutter, as you drive out of Addis Ababa." The city's gutters, said other observers, were choked with severed heads.

In 2007, an Ethiopian court convicted Mengistu, in absentia, of genocide. Still, Mugabe refused all appeals to extradite him. "Comrade Mengistu," insisted Mugabe, "…played a key and commendable role during our struggle for independence and no one can dispute that."

Mengistu has acted as a security adviser to his host. In particular, it was he who apparently suggested that Mugabe launch Operation Murambatsvina, driving hundreds of thousands out of the cities, and bulldozing their houses. Mengistu has good reason to fear Mugabe's overthrow—the opposition here have threatened that when they come to power they will ship him back to Addis to be executed by his compatriots.

AT LOBEL'S TABLE, I'm seated opposite Heinrich von Pezold. He is, I'm told, 1,337th in line to the British throne.

On hearing that Heinrich hails from Austria, Georgina, an ardent lover of musicals, begins to trill "The Sound of Music."

"Actually," says Heinrich, who's thirty-six, with piercing blue eyes and a prominent, vaguely Churchillian forehead from which his blond hairline is in retreat, "the singing von Trapp family are my cousins—but I'm tone-deaf."

Heinrich's grandfather farmed on the slopes of Mount Kilimanjaro. His father came to Zimbabwe to recover from meningitis, and purchased Forrester estates from the Earl of Verulam, who also held the title of Lord Forrester. In 1998, while Heinrich was working on a D.Phil. at Oxford on "communist takeovers in Eastern Europe," he came here on holiday to help with the farm. Overwhelmed by the beauty of the place, he abandoned his studies and stayed on at Forrester.

"Come and see it," he insists in a soft Austrian accent. "Visiting a working farm is now somewhat of an elitist activity. There are not many of us left!"

"Oh yes, you must come out," agrees his wife, Amanda, porcelain pale, thin and elegant, and once the lead singer of the South African band Magic Cactus.

THE DRIVE to Forrester takes you past many ex-white farms, now bedraggled and barely productive, occupied by war vets and other new settlers. We slow by one, to watch squatters hacking down a long roadside avenue of mature fir trees, for firewood. Their amateur felling has toppled several trees onto the telephone poles, and now a forlorn frizz of broken wires hangs from them. Beside me, Georgina rummages in her straw bag. Soon I hear a long intake of breath. She is inhaling on a slim crimson steel cylinder, which tapers in at the stem, a postmodern take on a Jazz Age cigarette holder. This is her latest invention— NicoPipe™, motto: *Smoke without fire*. Inside is a Nicorette capsule dispensing nicotine as you suck. Nicorette's standard white plastic dispenser, she says, "looks like a tampon applicator tube. It's a pharmaceutical appliance, embarrassing and ugly." NicoPipe™, available in a range of colors and styles, is elegant and aesthetically pleasing. And she is launching it just as smoking is banned in restaurants and bars in Europe and America. NicoPipe™, she hopes, will make her fortune.

"You might not want to suck on that thing in front of the von Pezolds," I suggest. "They *are* tobacco farmers, after all, and you're trying to put them out of business."

"Somehow I suspect they'll survive the threat posed by NicoPipe," she sighs.

Forrester's main farmhouse is traditional brick and thatch, with green cement floors. We stay in *rondavels* set in the garden of cacti and palms and frangipanis, *Albizia gummifera*, African flame tree, and cassia, which is bursting with bright yellow blossom.

Despite the land crisis, Heinrich and Amanda are building an ambitious new house on a rock ledge overlooking one of the farm's six substantial dams. We pack sundowners in a wicker picnic hamper and drive across the farm to it, followed by what Heinrich insists is the world's fastest three-legged dog, a Doberman-cross-retriever called Tommy.

"He's been officially clocked running alongside the truck at 40 m.p.h.," says Heinrich. "Of course that's how he lost his leg in the first place — car-chasing."

On the way we drive through irrigated fields of mange tout and snap peas. Other fields are being prepared, at this time of year, for tobacco, wheat, and maize. At fifty thousand acres, Forrester is one of the biggest arable farms in the country, certainly the biggest still in white hands. Technically, it is protected from land invasion by the foreign investment-guarantee code, and its invasion would put in jeopardy German aid to Zimbabwe (Heinrich has German citizenship too). Though one section of Forrester has already been jambanja'd, Heinrich tells us, he still has over eighteen hundred acres of tobacco under cultivation.

One of the reasons that the squatters are only on one section of the farm — apart from the notional foreign investment-guarantee code — is that Forrester is the biggest employer of people from the adjacent Chiweshe Communal area. Heinrich employs between two and a half and three and a half thousand people, depending on the season, and he estimates that there are as many as twenty thousand living on the farm, as each employee has up to eight dependents living with him.

The squatters on one section of the farm live, for the time being, in uneasy coexistence. Heinrich's manager cures their tobacco, for example, though he charges them for the service.

The view from the site of the new house is sublime — the lake, and past it over a broken landscape dotted with steep kopjes, granite *dwala*s, mini-sugar loaves, and in between, fields of meticulously contour-plowed land. It's the kind of view that made white settlers fall in love with this country, the kind of view that re-infects us, generation after generation, with a fervent attachment to it.

Of course, as the eldest son of the von Pezold clan, Heinrich explains, one day, when his parents die, he will have to leave to take up the family schloss in Austria.

After a short, violent downpour in the middle of the night, the morning dawns fresh and clear. Christof, their little boy, who calls his mother "medem" (madam), after hearing his nanny call her that all the time, runs barefoot around the dewy lawn, pursued by the three-legged Tommy. Above him, next to the Zimbabwe flag, flutters the von Pezold one: a double-headed eagle, a beehive, and a wheat sheaf.

"You should see my mother's family flag," says Heinrich. "It has a raven pecking out the eye of a Turk."

five

No Oil to Give

IT IS NOW TWO WEEKS since the elections, and still the results of the presidential contest have not been officially announced, though results for individual members of parliament are coming in.

The gateaux rack revolves slowly in its glass cabinet in the downstairs Gazebo coffee lounge at Harare's Crowne Plaza Monomatapa Hotel, while we wait for Theresa Makone, a Nottingham University–trained bio-chemist and the proprietor, among other businesses, of Cleopatra's, a beauty salon that my sister used to patronize. Georgina wants to congratulate her on winning an opposition seat in parliament, surmounting a government dirty tricks campaign. We have seen her being interviewed on TV, standing in a piece of urban wasteland that was the registered address for eight thousand ghost voters. She is still too scared to live at home, so she moves around constantly, staying with friends and at hotels. This is our third attempt to connect.

Outside, the swollen foliage of Harare Park threatens to burst into the window. Inside, Georgina inhales on a turquoise NicoPipe while we watch Tendai Biti, the MDC's number two, on CNN, giving a news conference in Johannesburg. All legal channels to get the presidential results released have been exhausted, he says. His party won't participate in either a recount or a runoff, which would be "more like a runover," he says. If Mugabe tries to hold on to power, he warns, it will amount to a constitutional coup d'état. The lines have been drawn.

Biti is hugely eloquent. Tough and urgent and determined without being bellicose or shrill. He says that Morgan Tsvangirai's life is now in danger if he returns to Zimbabwe. And he tells of the crackdown he fears is about to be launched by Mugabe, especially in rural areas. He ends with a chilling appeal. "In Rwanda the international community waited until there were a million dead Tutsis; in Somalia and Darfur they waited too until there were piles of corpses. Please don't wait until that happens to us."

Theresa Makone is a no-show.

THAT NIGHT, after Biti's warning, we watch ZTV, the state broadcaster. "Comrade Chinx," a war vet in a red beret and fatigues, is exhorting the viewers "to war."

People often complain that it's hard to fathom the inner workings of Mugabe's ruling party, ZANU-PF. But that's not really true. All you have to do is read the government newspapers, the *Herald* and *Sunday Mail,* and watch or listen to ZTV and ZBC, the state broadcasters, and you get it from the horse's mouth, the World According to Bob — a paranoid and distorted view. If you want to hear it raw and unmediated, then listen to the vernacular services. In chiShona, the venom being pumped out is reaching for the excesses broadcast by the Interahamwe's Radio (Mille Collines), which helped trigger the Rwandan genocide.

We are fighting Nazism again, continues Comrade Chinx, over footage from the civil war of guerrillas dancing, and lingering close-ups of weapons, especially the totemic AK-47. And he sings the liberation war anthem, "Vadzoka kuHondo."

"We are not *ex*-fighters," he insists, "we are current freedom fighters—*current*. I don't want anyone to call me an *ex*-freedom fighter." His words are intercut with footage of dead white farmers. The broadcast is chilling, little less than a death threat, and certainly an implicit incitement to kill. Then, in another sign of the bizarre competing realities that coexist here, there follows a cheery jingle, and the station cuts to a promo for a forthcoming program: *Let's Go Gardening,* in which an elderly white matron rollicks among some ferns, admonishing us not to over-water them.

THE FOLLOWING bright, crisp morning, driving south down an almost deserted 4th Street, one of the city's major thoroughfares, I find myself behind a pick-up truck bobbing with the blue helmets of riot policemen. Suddenly it veers over to the curb and the policemen vault out and, without any explanation, begin beating a knot of pedestrians, including two women with babies on their backs. They beat grimly, but with determination, using long staves, and boots and fists.

Eerily, though my window is open, there is no sound from the people, neither from the policemen nor their victims, just the thwack of the staves, the thuds of kicks and punches. And then above it, I finally hear the sound of the babies thinly wailing.

In the back of the police truck slump two black youths, their wrists manacled behind them, their faces swollen and bloodied. Without realizing it, I have slowed to a stop alongside, and one of the policemen looks up briefly. "Move! Move!" he shouts. "You are causing an obstruction," and irritably, he waves me past, his stave already raised for the next blow.

EARLY AFTERNOON finds us at Doon Estate, a cluster of artisanal shops on the city's eastern fringe, just off the Mutare road. The shops sell ethnic clothes, sculpture, pottery, basket-ware, furniture fashioned from reclaimed teak railway sleepers, and paper handmade from elephant dung. And, unlikely as it sounds in starving Zimbabwe, there is a Belgian chocolatier.

We have come to Kerry's vegetarian café to join the weekly Friday lunchtime get-together of Zimbabwe's independent journalists. But today there is only one, Iden Wetherell, editor of the weekly *Independent,* one of the country's last surviving indy papers. The last daily one, the *Daily News,* had its offices bombed back in 2000, just days after Mugabe's Information Minister, Jonathan Moyo, known by local journalists as Mugabe's Goebbels, had warned that the *Daily News* should be "silenced." No one was ever arrested for it—if you discount the troupe of Chinese mime artists here for the Harare International Festival of the Arts. Dressed in white fatigues laced with tubes of battery powered lights, which pulsed on and off, they were rehearsing a mime routine on a traffic island across the street from the *Daily News,* and were bundled into police trucks and taken for questioning. The next year the *Daily News* printing presses were bombed.

Iden Wetherell looks depressed. He sits alone at his outdoor table, a lean man with gray mustache and brush cut, wearing a blue long-sleeved cotton shirt and a pained expression, contemplating his fried halloumi and lemonade.

"I find myself friendless," he says, proffering a chair. "There's barely a journalist left in the country, because the atmosphere's so dangerous for them. Our newsroom is completely depleted.

"I've been very cautious about predicting change, as you know, but now I really think it's coming. The mold has been shattered. It's wonderful watching them squirm at the prospect." He picks up a folded copy of the *Herald* from the table. "I mean look at this, what their propagandist-in-chief, Caesar Zvayi, is writing: how MDC voters are not politically mature, so their votes don't really count!

"And now they try to wriggle out of an election that their own government-approved international observers have given a clean bill of health and signed off on."

Wetherell also rails against the chief government spokesman, the Deputy Minister of Information, Bright Matonga, known to local journalists as Notso. In reply to opposition protests at the unconscionable delay in releasing the presidential election results, Matonga has delivered this considered riposte: he really doesn't understand why the MDC is "getting its knickers in a twist."

Notso Bright is famous for an incident in which his white English wife, Anne Matonga, née Pout, from Essex, whom he'd brought back with him from university in 2001, led a jambanja, the following year, of a farm, owned by Vince and Monica Schulz's family for four generations. As they were arrested she shrieked in a regional English accent at the Schulzes: "Get off our land: we are taking back what you stole from our forefathers."

Interviewed later by Wetherell's *Independent,* while she tended the Schulzes' roses, guarded by Mugabe's youth militia, Mrs. Matonga praised President Mugabe for his "patience with the racist white farmers," and said that the Schulzes "had only themselves to blame."

There are rumors now (later confirmed) that she has been abandoned on the Schulzes' farm, as Bright Matonga, in a shrewd career move, transfers his affections to a new woman, Sharon Mugabe, reputed to be related to the President. It is her PR agency that has been running the "Fist of Empowerment" ad campaign.

IN THE HOPES OF persuading Mugabe to release the election results and avoid the coming crisis, Thabo Mbeki jets into Zimbabwe the next day, Saturday, 12 April. Mbeki is in an odd position. The region has officially mandated him to solve the Zimbabwe crisis, yet since it did so he has been toppled as leader of the ruling ANC party by Jacob Zuma, who is now effectively President-in-waiting. Now, as Andrew Pocock, the British ambassador, observes, "Mbeki has the position without the power, and Zuma has the power without the position." Inevitably, Mbeki's own political humiliation has diminished him. At sixty-five, he is white haired and white bearded, tentative. Next to him, Mugabe at eighty-four looks the more vigorous man, not a gray hair in sight.

As Mbeki steps off the plane and onto the red carpet, Mugabe reaches for his hand, but Thabo is coy in front of the cameras, slipping his hand away. At the end of the flying visit, however, at a photo op in front of an antique stuffed lion, inside State House, Mugabe slides his arm through Mbeki's, and the South African is content to leave it there as they pose arm-in-arm for the cameras, while Mbeki announces—to our cries of disbelief—"There is no crisis in Zimbabwe." For this bizarre denial, he instantly earns the indelible *Mad Magazine* moniker, Thabo "What crisis?" Mbeki.

When the cameras turn to Mugabe to comment on British Prime Minister Gordon Brown's criticism of Zimbabwe's protracted election-result delay, Mugabe dismisses Brown as "a little tiny dot on this planet."

IT HAS NOW been fifteen days since the presidential elections, and *still* the result has been withheld. In the meantime, Nepal and Italy have both been to the polls, and already know their outcomes.

To pressure Mugabe into releasing the vote count, the opposition announces a "stay-away," asking their members to boycott their work places. But how do you tell there's a strike when only 6 percent of workers are employed? Anyway, most senior members of the MDC are out of the country in fear of their lives, so nothing happens. The trucks of riot police trundle through the streets, the men singing martial anthems and banging their rifle butts against the metal floors. The jet fighters scream back and forth low over the city. Check points cordon the approach roads.

And still we wait.

FINALLY, Georgina and I connect with Theresa Makone, at Meikles Hotel. She is dressed in a long ethnic-print caftan, an Ethiopian silver and amber necklace, and nails painted mulberry. She's anxious and agitated. She hasn't heard from her husband, Ian, who is MDC secretary for elections, for several days. He's in Mashonaland East, she says, collating evidence of violence against MDC activists: brutal beatings and house-burnings. I ask if I can join him. She throws up her hands in horror. "Every day I fully expect to hear he has been killed. That is dangerous work, especially for you as a white person, you would never survive."

Theresa has one of her husband's cell phones, which keeps pinging with incoming text messages. She hands me the phone. "Look," she says.

Hi Ian, We have eight people from Mudzi badly injured, reads one. Another reports: *One death and numerous beatings in Hurungwe.*

She doesn't want to talk openly as she believes the room is bugged. The fact that part of my ceiling light-fitting inexplicably fell to the floor a few days ago only supports this notion.

"You know this place is crawling with CIO agents," she warns. "They sit in the lobby café all day drinking tea and eating cakes."

"Do they get very fat, eating all those cakes?" asks Georgina. Pale-complexioned and zaftig, like a young Anjelica Huston, she is ever curious about weight-related issues.

"No, no," says Theresa. "Because they have the Disease," by which she means AIDS. "Otherwise they would be *voluminous.*"

Theresa has just come back from rural Mutare South, meeting her constituency members. "They are very frustrated," she says. "They don't know what to do. For the first time these rural people didn't vote for Robert Mugabe, and now they are facing the consequences. I have a situation there where three hundred rural families—ex-farm-workers—are in the middle of being evicted from their land for supporting the MDC.

"We want the results in their original form, why do they want this recount?" She answers her own question: "To finish rigging the result.

"It's hard, very hard. We don't know what to do. We have the potential to make this country ungovernable—but in the end, too much blood would be shed, too many lives lost. Is it worth it?

"We feel marginalized, internationally, as though the world doesn't really care about our struggle for democracy. Because we have no oil to give anyone, if we had oil in the ground, they would all be here.

"The tragedy is that we could easily have gone through a peaceful transition to the democratic state we all cherish. But the army is on standby, just waiting for an excuse."

six

The Tears of a Clown

As we wait for Mugabe to massage the election results, we decide to drive east to the Chimanimani Festival, headlined by Zimbabwe's premier musician, Oliver Mtukudzi. We will leave on the morning of Independence Day. Even as the presidential election results are withheld, there are to be state-organized celebrations across the country. These are, in effect, praise parties for Mugabe.

Diana, a friend and art-gallery owner, has agreed to change some money for us with her black-market dealer, a local supermarket proprietor. Now at her dining-room table she tries to count out the money from a shopping bag filled with bricks of notes, in denominations of ten million dollars each — three billion in all.

Back in the hotel, Georgina sits on the floor, busy with her own culinary provisions, dividing out the LighterLife sachets of diet powder she has brought from London into their different flavors. LighterLife packs, she tells me, are only available as part of a full course, which involves counseling.

"I like the chocolate flavors," she explains, "particularly mixed with instant coffee in the morning, and Thai chicken, which is spicy and burns my mouth so I don't really want to eat anything else."

She moves to another pile. "This is the second division: vegetable, which is okay, and mushroom. But once I've gone through these, it's vanilla and banana, which are totally disgusting, oh, and caramel, ew."

In the background the TV is tuned to the BBC World. Across the bottom of the screen runs the news ticker: *Zimbabwe now a crisis measured in hunger.*

She looks up briefly from her diet powders, registers the headline, and immediately fixes me with a look. "I know, I *know*. D'you think I don't *get* the irony—that I'm trying to lose weight when half the people here don't have enough to eat."

"I didn't say anything!"

"Yes, but you *thought* it," she accuses, and punches me on the arm.

According to Georgina, by far the most important preparation we have to make for a long drive like this is to stock up on music. The revolution, she insists, needs a soundtrack. To provide it, we go to her friend Gavin's, who has just digitized his music and welcomes us to help ourselves to anything in his CD collection. His tastes, he cheerfully admits, "tend to the queeny." Confronted with rack upon rack of musicals, Georgina's eyes light up. And then, even better, ABBA, an entire smorgasbord of it. She scoops them into her big woven grass bag.

As we rattle out of the city, Georgina selects "Waterloo" as our Independence Day tribute. The lyrics which pump out of the buzzing speakers, she has decided, would be a fitting anthem of defeat for Mugabe.

"I'm confused. Are you singing this to Bob, or is he doing the singing?" I ask.

"They're supposed to be his words to us," says Georgina. "He's conceding defeat."

"But if he's cheating, then he feels like he wins, even when he loses, too."

She shrugs, suddenly glum, and gets out her NicoPipe. This one is black.

AT CHIMANIMANI, we are hosted by Doug and Tempe van der Riet, two of the last whites of my generation still living here. More boys from our local high school are in Western Australia now than in the whole of Manicaland province, Doug says.

That night, the van der Riets put us up in the old house of Dr. Mostert, the village doctor before my mother took over. His medical instruments are still here. His boxed sphygmomanometer, with its perished rubber cuff and air bulb, and its mercury column, still in the chest of drawers, and his stethoscope and auroscope, still in a black leather Gladstone, as though ready for him to go on a house call. In fact, he has been dead for years. The calendar on the wall is from 1988, and the book shelves are stocked with old Rhodesiana. I lie in bed listening to the plaintive, churring calls of the fiery-necked nightjars, and reading Dr. Mostert's *Jumbo Guide to Rhodesia 1972*.

THE NEXT DAY we sit on the terrace of the stone house the van der Riets have built overlooking the mountains. But the glittering quartzite ranges we climbed as kids are not what they once were, warns Doug. Today they are teeming with prospectors, who dig up the water-courses and pan the mud for gold.

"Some of the nuggets these guys are finding are huge," he says. "At the height of the gold rush, there were estimated to be over a million people panning for gold here along the mountains and valleys; you could smell them way before you saw them, because they wouldn't leave their holes even to relieve themselves, for fear that they would lose their digging site, so they crapped right there in their trenches, and carried right on digging."

In a recent cold snap, thirty thousand of them came down from the mountain, and dozens died of exposure in caves in the mountains. "You know those caves we used to camp in as kids," says Doug. "I don't camp in those caves anymore. There are skeletons in so many of them."

The van der Riets are almost entirely self-reliant now. "We have two dairy cows, fatten our own pigs, make our own bacon, sausages, provide our own milk, vegetables, salad, cream, yogurt. My dad makes the butter. Everything on the table we produced. Lettuce, onions, potatoes, carrots, peas, tomatoes. Chicken, guava, avocados, apricot, lemons, oranges, passion fruit — all organic — the soil is so fertile here. We sent away for this book called *Self-Sufficiency* by John and Sally Seymour, and learned how to butcher livestock. It's quite satisfying, this self-sufficiency. There's always a pig being fattened. Tempe home-schooled the kids for four years — if we didn't have to pay for the kids' education now — we wouldn't have to work — we could survive on what we grow. We made a cake of feta and a big wheel of Gouda, our own muesli, with roasted oats, honey, oil, sunflower seed, and we barter with each other in the community. We haven't really used actual cash at all for nearly six months."

When there are power cuts, which is often, they revert to cooking in a three-legged cast-iron *potjie,* over a fire, just like the old white pioneers used to in the 1890s. In a little over a century, white lifestyle here has come almost a complete circle.

But not everyone is as fortunate, Doug admits. Some of the people in the outlying districts with poorer soils, who are in the grip of a drought, are now so hungry that they only eat every other day. They eat red ants, they're so famished. And when he asked them, "Why don't you eat the fruit from the trees?" they replied, "Because the baboons are also hungry. They eat them first."

THE FESTIVAL is taking place on the central grassy meadow around which Chimanimani village is arranged. The memorial to the white pioneers, in the middle of the square, which we used to play tag around when I was a child, is long gone, smashed by war vets after independence. Once a year, on Pioneers' Day, there was a little service there, and we laid wreaths upon the dimpled granite plinth, in honor of our white forefathers. Well, they weren't actually my forefathers as such, since my parents came here later, after World

War II, but the pioneers were the first white settlers here, trekking up in ox wagons from South Africa in 1893.

Unlike Cecil John Rhodes's initial pioneers, the ones who came here, the Martin and Steyn and Meikle treks were looking for land to farm, not gold. They called this district Gazaland, not after the biblical one in Palestine, but after the abaGaza, a Zulu people who moved north during the Mfecane, the great scattering. In time, these people took the name of their king, Shoshangane, and became known as the Shangaans. They, in turn, dislodged previous residents, the Nxaba. And in 1832, as the Nxaba fled further north, they came across the Portuguese settlement at Macequece, a gold-trading post and mission station. The Nxaba attacked it, and during the fierce battle the Portuguese ran out of bullets. In desperation, they broke out their boxes of bullion, melted the nuggets over the fire, and poured them into molds to cast bullets of gold.

I had always been fascinated by that story when I was growing up. Imagine that, casting the bullets out of the gold that was your most precious possession? Literally using your riches to save your lives. And I used to think about the bodies of those Nxaba warriors felled in the bush, with gold bullets lodged in their flesh. And whenever I read in the press the phrase a silver bullet, or a golden bullet, to solve some problem, I thought of those Nxaba warriors, those Nxaba corpses, lying on the riverbank. And the fact that the golden bullets used by the Portuguese didn't turn out to be golden bullets in a problem-solving way, after all. The Portuguese ran out of gunpowder, and the Nxaba killed them all.

By SATURDAY NIGHT, the Chimani Festival is running hours behind schedule. It is already midnight and the crowd of forestry laborers and their families, with horse blanket capes around their shoulders and woolly balaclavas over their heads to keep out the mountain chill, are growing restive, impatient for the headline gig, Oliver Mtukudzi and the Black Spirits, Tuku to his many fans.

The MC finally bellows, "Are you ready for TUKU?"

"*Yebo!*" the crowd roars back, expecting Mtukudzi to appear.

"Well, he's *about* to come—but *first*, we have another act, Chris Lynam, who is a..." He consults his notes. "Who is a, a...well, some sort of clown."

The crowd groans with disappointment, as the single spotlight picks out a diminutive white man leaping onto the stage. He is dressed in a shiny white suit, a shocking pink shirt, neon braces, oversized black shoes. His long dark hair is teased up into a punk pompadour; his face is caked with white foundation, and heavy black eyeliner.

From inside his oversized pockets he pulls handfuls of white paper squares and throws them into the air.

"Snow," he announces.

The crowd regards him silently.

He throws more. "*Big* snow."

Behind me a mystified lumberjack murmurs, "Ah, but there is no snow in this country."

Lynam pulls his white jacket around himself and stands still, hands at his side.

"Bottle of milk."

In the same position, he jiggles a bit.

"Bottle of milk in transit."

The crowd is mute, but for some babies wailing.

"Eskimo talking," he says, popping handfuls of ice cubes into his mouth and spitting them out across the stage. Huddled in the darkness, the crowd is nonplussed.

Lynam juggles fire sticks. He swallows one of them, and there are murmurs of admiration. This they get, a fire-eater.

"There are three kinds of people in the world," continues Lynam, encouraged. "Those that can count and those that can't."

The crowd consult one another, and there is much shaking of woolly hatted heads.

Lynam kicks off his bulbous clown shoes, peels off several brightly colored socks, to reveal ballet pumps. He sheds his suit, and underneath it is a white tutu, in which he pirouettes and prances. Then, to the soundtrack of Ethel Merman's *There's No Business Like*

Show Business, he begins a striptease. Off come the tutu, the pumps, the leotard and tights, until only a pair of Victorian bloomers remains. Turning his back to his audience, Lynam is now ready for his finale. He places his legs apart and theatrically rips open the bloomers to reveal his G-stringed bottom to the crowd, the twin moons of his pale buttocks glowing in the spotlight.

"This," Lynam announces, now with his head upside down, looking at them from between his legs, "is my tribute to our President." He wedges a long tube into the cleft of his buttocks, clenches it in place, and reaches around to light the fuse. It is some sort of Roman candle, and immediately a pyrotechnic fountain of sparks spurts from his arse, high into the dark Chimani night. The forestry workers murmur some more. They are nervous now. There are CIO spies and Mugabe's militiamen and plain-clothes policemen among them.

From between his legs, Chris Lynam's mascaraed raccoon eyes regard their ranks of upturned faces, lit by the sparks showering from his own bottom, and repeats his tribute, as though it were an official toast at a diplomatic dinner. "To our President!" he shouts.

Georgina and I are hugging ourselves with mirth, crying with it.

THE NEXT DAY, Lynam drives us out to his farm. In mufti, he's compact and muscular, his boyishness belying his fifty-five years. For an hour or so we bounce along a dirt road, following the curve of the mountain range round to the east toward Mozambique, with a clown at the wheel.

"I woke up one morning when I was about twenty and just said to myself, 'I want to be a clown.'" He shrugs. "I got a place at Le Coq School in Paris, one of eighty places from three thousand applicants, but I couldn't afford the fees, so I taught myself by playing on the street and doing some acrobatic workshops in London. I think clowns are born, not raised." He calls his style of clowning "modern anarchic," or, on reflection, "maybe zany," and admits that it scares some people.

As we bump eastward, we cross over ruinous rivers. Gold-panners have gouged the banks, peeling them back from the narrow mountain streams, once so clear and cold and sweet, into a wide swathe of sludge. The waters now run red, as though the mountains themselves are bleeding from their wounds. The ground on either side of the rivers is pockmarked with craters dug by the gold-panners. They look like shell holes from a war.

The panners ride here on big flat-bed lumber trucks called "goneyets," after the hookers who service them. The hookers ask whether this truckful have "gone yet," or still have carnal needs to be serviced. You can only imagine what the HIV rate is.

Hayfield "B" farm has been a white-owned farm since 1922 when an Afrikaans dairy farmer called Muller settled on it. In 1980, buoyed by the optimism of Zimbabwe's independence, Lynam purchased it, together with three friends. He remembers when he first arrived, going to pay obeisance to Chief Ngorima, the tribal head of the communal lands in the valley below.

Initially he went back and forth from London, where his clowning work was, but then he came out here permanently in the late '90s. His interest in it was essentially conservation—Hayfield B is the site of the last lowland rainforest in Zimbabwe. Lynam, who had his wife and two small children with him, built a house and set about ripping out the invasive species, mostly eucalyptus trees, that threatened the fifteen-hundred-acre indigenous forest. "I had just a bicycle for the first six months of setting up the serious rainforest restoration, often riding the fifty miles from Chimani with hardware, bags of cement, milk, soap on the back."

During that time, he also founded the Chimanimani International Arts Festival, "to entice my mates to come out and see this extraordinary spot."

Above the rainforest, he planted a thousand macadamia trees, two thousand pineapple bushes, lychees and oranges. But today, as we round the last sweeping bend, we see that the macadamia trees are on fire; most have already burned down, their charred trunks smoldering.

"Maybe your presidential tribute wasn't appreciated," I wonder.

"All is not well," warns Chitsi, the manager, emerging from the undergrowth when he sees it's Lynam at the wheel. He says that a group of war vets have been on the farm since the elections. "They say it now belongs to them. I can't stay here with these people, while they are in this mood," Chitsi declares in disgust. "They say they are not supposed to lose elections."

Lynam has built not so much a farmhouse here as a soaring, four-story habitable log sculpture, with a view over the eastern end of the Chimanimani range and down the valley, where the Haroni River flows into the Rusitu and across the Mozambique flood plain, out to the Indian Ocean. From up here, on a very clear day, he says, once or twice a year, you can actually catch a glimpse of the sea—a shimmering mirage some sixty miles distant as the eagle flies.

After a while, a posse of unsmiling war vets approach. They are led by a man who wears a camouflage forage cap, and a T-shirt with Mugabe's clenched fist image stretched over his large belly, and the slogan: *Vote Mugabe*. His name, he says, is Willie Mafuta, which means fat.

Mafuta announces that the farm now belongs to them. "I don't hate the skin," he explains, and he runs his finger slowly along Georgina's bare arm. "But we have a small issue on which we don't agree—is this land here part of the communal area, or the farm?"

"It's farm," insists Lynam. "All pegged out by a government surveyor. Chitsi, are the maps here?"

"No," says Chitsi, "they are all stolen."

"We bought this land," says Lynam. "We didn't steal it from anyone."

"Well, now the government is taking land from white people," states Mafuta. "Are you Zimbabwean or not? We are ZANU-PF supporters here—which side do *you* support? We have some whites, like Joseph Sacco, who is ZANU-PF, but he is the same color like you. He is a *true* Zimbabwean, he participates in the party. We don't hate *all* whites. But you, you hate Robert Mugabe—the one who brought freedom to this country. You don't care about liberation in this country." And he repeats his question, this time more belligerently. "Which side are you on?"

"I didn't fight in the war," says Lynam. "I left the country during the war, to avoid fighting."

"*I* fought in the war," interjects another man, pushing past Mafuta, and puffing out his chest. "I am Ruben Zuza and I was in a detachment called 'we sacrifice ourselves.'"

Caiphas Mupuro, another vet, brings out his official war veteran ID card. It describes him as "Liberation War Hero," number 66450, Republic of Zimbabwe. His photo is set against the backdrop of Heroes' Acre.

"Look," he says. "It may seem heavy, but I am not being harsh, because I have even lived with whites. David Hughes from Harvard lived with us for two years."

He puts away his liberation hero ID, and when he continues, his voice has a threatening edge. "You just take your things, and you go. That's the fact."

We walk over to the house to gather up Lynam's belongings. But the place has already been pretty thoroughly looted: pots and pans, bedding, and clothes taken, basins and plumbing ripped out.

"This house was going to be so beautiful," Lynam says wistfully, as we walk slowly through the devastation. "I was going to add one more floor. Even now, I kind of wish I'd finished it. The roof tiles are salvaged from the old Union Avenue Post Office in Harare, you know."

He walks past a dusty manual on rearing silk worms and picks up a metal music stand. "This was part of a sketch, trying to put it together, and it keeps collapsing." He points to the main wooden joist. "This roof tree, we pulled up with Doug's Land Rover. Ah, we've had some fun here."

Lynam walks past the old cast-iron Fire King Deluxe stove and looks out at the mountains again. "We get four meters' rain a year, man—it's so lush. There was going to be a veranda here.

"In the morning the sun rises over the flood plain down there, and in the evening the mountains turn purple as the sun sets," he says, looking across at Dragon's Tooth, the jagged peak that looms above us. "I wish I'd had time to climb that face."

He points down at the land just below us, where vervet monkeys are swinging between the trees. "That hill down there, that's on my farm, I'm going to get it back, I tell you."

As we prepare to leave, the breeze freshens off the mountain. The war vets stand waiting in a grim-faced line. Right up until the end, even through the Land Rover window, Lynam implores them to respect the ecology of the place, to plant on the flat areas and not on the hillsides, and *please,* to look after the rainforest. "It's a sacred trust," he says.

But while Lynam was salvaging the few, randomly overlooked belongings from his house, I had walked out onto the end of the spur and peered over into the valley below to see that the squatters have already begun to clear-cut the last lowland rainforest in Zimbabwe.

But I don't have the heart to tell him yet.

seven

Down the Rabbit Hole

BACK IN CHIMANIMANI village the next day, we drive up the now rain-rutted road toward the elementary school I once attended, to a stone and timber house owned by Shane and Birgit Kidd. Shane is a freelance saw-miller; he cuts other people's timber under contract. He met Birgit in Finland when he was on a forestry course there, and brought her back with him to Zimbabwe. Shane is as slight and taut and tough as a stick of biltong. Birgit is sparrow-small, with a lustrous silver helmet of hair. Together, this unlikely couple have ended up as accidental activists.

Of course, it all started with Roy Bennett, whose coffee farm, Charleswood, you can see pressed right up against the foot of the glittering mountain range. No one gets under Mugabe's skin quite like Roy Bennett, a Shona-speaking former policeman, who joined the MDC when it formed in 1999. He quickly became a champion of the local black community, who nicknamed him Pachedu, "one of us," and overwhelmingly voted him in as their member of parliament. Mugabe's fury was soon felt, not just by Bennett, but by the whole of Chimanimani district. Bennett was thrown off his farm, which was occupied by Mugabe's war vets. They ripped out the coffee and burned down his lodge. Now Roy Bennett is in exile in South Africa.

The Kidds (who supported Bennett) were sucked into the center of political resistance to Mugabe's dictatorship through something as incidental as their ownership of the village bottle store, on the main square. I still remember it from my childhood, when it was owned by old Mrs. Ness. My mother, after finishing her medical rounds of the tribal trust lands, would go on a weekly liquor run there to pick up a bottle of Bols brandy for herself, and one of Gold Blend whiskey for my father.

When the Kidds decided to rent the store's back room to the MDC to use as the Chimani office, Mugabe's goons threw them out and took it over themselves. On one outside wall, the war vets drew an oddly simian picture of Mugabe, with no neck, entitled *His Excellency Since 1980*. On another they wrote: *Chimanimani District War Veterans, War Collaborators and ZANU PF Office*. Under this, they drew an AK, spitting bullets, like it would in a cartoon. Shane posed for a photo in front of it, so that it looks like the bullets are coming straight at his head. Then he painted over it.

This modest, frontier-style building became a symbol of the political identity of Chimani. And what followed was an extended tussle over this office, as it changed hands in ever more violent circumstances. In the process the Kidds, who insisted they had the right to rent their store to whomever they liked, and they liked the MDC, became the nucleus of opposition to Mugabe in this mountain enclave.

SHANE IS BRISTLING with anger at the recent elections. He shows me his three-page analysis of how the voting was rigged here, through a combination of outright fraud, deliberate miscounting, and the disenfranchising of opposition voters by polling-station officials working for Mugabe. The fraud is sometimes ridiculously obvious: in some wards, the results were just swapped. In others, they simply subtracted a digit from the MDC vote, to reduce it by a factor of ten. As he walks me through the figures, he can clearly show that the MDC would have won healthily here, notwithstanding the intimidation. Yet Chimanimani will be posted as a ZANU parliamentary gain.

Shane also lends me his journal. That night, in old Dr. Mostert's musty mausoleum, I begin to read it. The journal is a compilation of emails to friends overseas and his diaries, a telescoped account of an almost continuous range war, with the Kidds at the center— harassed, threatened, assaulted, abducted, arrested, imprisoned— recounted with humor and grit and humility. And scorn, both for their tormentors and for those locals who are intimidated, who collaborate or acquiesce. And in between, he rails at how bad this all is for his golf handicap.

Shane's nemesis through much of his account is one Joseph Mwale, local head of Mugabe's spying agency, the CIO, also sometimes sinisterly known as "the President's Office," under whose direct authority it falls. Of all the people who shattered the calm of this mountain enclave, none bears greater blame than Mwale. He is a tin-pot tyrant, trying to make his name as Mugabe's enforcer. Mwale's first brush with infamy was the gruesome murder of two of Morgan Tsvangirai's election agents, Talent Mabika and Tichaona Chiminya, while they were out campaigning on his behalf in his home district of Buhera, in southern Manicaland, back in 2000.

The eyewitness accounts of what Mwale did to these two are not for the faint-hearted. Just after leaving the police station where they had tried to report the brutal assault of one of their colleagues, their vehicle was blocked by a twin-cab truck with "ZANU-PF Manicaland Province" logos on its doors, driven by Joseph Mwale. He and his men leaped out, smashed the windscreen and windows of the MDC pick-up, beat the two campaigners, and poured paraffin over them. Then, according to several eyewitnesses (from both sides), Mwale lit a newspaper, threw it onto the paraffin-soaked election workers, and drove off. They staggered out of the vehicle, according to Sanderson Makombe, their colleague, who had escaped, and now came sprinting back. "They were running across the fields burning like balls of flame, you know. So when we got there, Chiminya was already dead but Talent, she was still speaking." The police were nearby but had merely watched, without intervening.

Makombe and his friends tried "to lift our colleagues, you know, with our own bare hands, they were still burning. Talent was still screaming, she was not dead yet, she had been badly burned. Her whole body was black with smoke and soot...And their skins were peeling from their bodies...but we just had to do it, to lift them."

This, then, was the reputation that preceded Mwale, when he arrived in Chimanimani and launched his signature reign of terror here.

It was not long before Shane Kidd clashed with Mwale and was thrown into jail. One of the documents Shane shows me is his prison diary, written clandestinely in an exercise book that Birgit managed to smuggle in. Shane records in it the midnight routine, when the policemen, at Mwale's command, spray freezing water through the prison bars, dousing the prisoners and their thin blankets, and leaving the cell floor ankle-deep in water. Some nights, he writes, the policemen supplement this by throwing buckets of piss over them.

Shane writes that when Birgit brings lawyers from Mutare, they are chased away by a gun-wielding Mwale. He is assaulted again, with rubber truncheons, and two weeks later, "I still have some lovely bruises on my back and arse." They are given thirty seconds to eat their meal, *sadza* (maize-meal porridge) crawling with weevils. They are mixed in with general prisoners, including mental patients who bay and howl, and leap about, day and night. And, "After seeing our heads shaved, Birgit arrives with her head shaved in solidarity, and this cheers everyone up."

"I defy you," he writes, "to sit on an open squat latrine with no toilet paper, in front of twenty-two other people and maintain a shred of human dignity." He holds it in for eight days, a personal record, he notes, before he succumbs.

When the guards confiscate the playing cards the prisoners have made from the cardboard cores of scarce toilet rolls, the prisoners entertain themselves by recounting the distorted plots of novels they have read. "The guards are absolutely paranoid of any form of literature or newspaper getting into the cells, even the adverts are censored," he writes. "But on a small piece of newspaper that one of my cellmates was tearing up for cigarette papers, they have overlooked a small item about a riot in an Algerian jail, where the prisoners burned their mattresses protesting about something or other. The collective opinion of the cell was, wow, mattresses! The lucky buggers!"

Here they sleep on concrete floors, sharing the threadbare blankets.

And there is the degrading tedium of jail too. One entry reads simply, "Took a dump, had a shower, went on another hunting safari for lice."

"One real pillar of strength through the last weeks has been Birgit—her constant visits with food, cigarettes and information about the outside world and what people are doing to help us, has boosted everyone's morale...She puts up with endless bullshit and intimidation and still carries on, she also picks up the guys' wives and relatives from all over the country and brings them through to visit.

"The guys are magnificent in their fortitude. I think that CIO is going to regret throwing them in jail. We are molding our own hardcore right here in jail. They've been here and know that they can survive, they are now genuine political prisoners, this is turning into a badge of honor and they are no longer frightened."

He writes that when he gets out of jail he is determined to "really get in people's faces...The one thing I am confident of now is my ability to handle prison, I no longer fear that, and I'm sure that I have the ability to make trouble wherever I go."

"Free at last," he writes finally. He's lost twenty-eight pounds in two weeks, a fifth of his body weight.

But the range war continues. The sign writer Kidd hires to draw a new MDC logo on the office is arrested halfway through the job.

THERE ARE MOMENTS of farce amidst Shane Kidd's journal too. He writes that one local resident, who has spent every spare moment building a boat so that he and his wife can start a new life in the Mediterranean, "eventually got his boat on the water in Beira, fifteen years in the making. It's a steel hull, thirty-four-foot long, and eight tons, only problem is that it's actually closer to twenty tons, top-heavy and went down in the water to its railings and wallowed like a drunken duck. The harbor master told him to take it out of the water..."

Kidd is asked by the black residents of Ngangu township to stand as their councillor in upcoming elections. "The problem is that it's a huge commitment and in this day and age means more confrontation with police, CIO and more prison time." But barely pausing to reflect on this, he goes straight on to write, "I have reluctantly agreed to do it. The elections are in August so at least when I go back to jail the worst of winter is over."

Kidd writes that "Talent [an MDC colleague] and I have decided to go to a witch doctor and put a spell on Mwale, hopefully we can do it sometime next week. I don't believe in it, but what I believe in doesn't count."

"I went to Chipinge to see Yannick Lagadec," he writes. "Yannick's just been convicted of insulting Mugabe (it's a crime to demean the president, akin to blasphemy) and is due for sentencing next week. The judge has told him he can expect prison, and his wife is in a flat panic, worried about rape and AIDS. It appears that I'm considered an informed source on prison conditions so they asked me over for a chat."

He's being imprisoned so frequently now that he's taken to calling it "falling down the rabbit hole," after *Alice in Wonderland*.

"The funny thing is," Kidd writes, when he finds himself languishing in the cells again, having first been assaulted, "that the more they arrest me, the more respect I get from the lower-ranking officers, they were only too willing to be of assistance and talk to me."

He's out a day later, but after two weeks' liberty, I find this entry.

"Dot dot, dash dash, dot dot. Good evening, Zimbabwe and all ships at sea, this is Shane Kidd (apologies to Walter Winchell) with the latest up-date on law-and-order in Chimanimani. Yes, you guessed it. I fell down the rabbit hole again." He's dumped in a cell at Chimani with the same prisoner, accused of rape, who was here two weeks ago, and they settle down on the concrete floor together, sharing a blanket. Meanwhile the police lie to Birgit about where he is, so she drives between distant police stations "playing hunt the prisoner."

Late the next night they cuff his hands behind his back, blindfold him, and push him into a police truck. As they drive along, "they start threatening me and telling me how I'm being taken to a secret location to be killed." The blindfold slips down, so they tie a jacket over his head and force him down on the floor. "We then settle down for an hour and a half journey," he writes grimly, "with the occasional death threat thrown in to lighten the atmosphere."

"[S]o it's another weekend in jail," writes Kidd. "This is really playing hell with my golf handicap. The high point is the cell search on Saturday morning. After everyone is searched individually, we are all put in the dining hall while the cells are searched. I'm called out of the hall and shown a package. One of the prisoners has taken some of my hair from the haircut on Thursday morning and wrapped it up in toilet paper to use for *mushonga*, African spiritual medicine. I found it hilarious, but the guards took it quite seriously. Hey, what do they want me to do, stop my hair growing?"

When Birgit is eventually permitted to bail him out, he records, "I've now spent thirty-three days in jail in the last three months. I've opened up a bet book to raise funds for the club, at Z$500 a ticket. You get to guess how many more days I will spend in jail before 30th December."

In the meantime, the magistrate in Chipinge, Walter Chik-wanha, who allowed him to be bailed, is dragged from his court-room by Mugabe loyalists and severely beaten. Lawyers defending MDC activists have had their houses and vehicles attacked. And Shane is disqualified from standing as a local councillor, because he doesn't have a Zimbabwean birth certificate, even though he is a Zimbabwe citizen and resident, and holds a Zimbabwean passport, and indeed, served as a councillor once before.

He writes: "The food situation in the village is getting a lot worse and people have started dying of hunger in the western part of the district (poor agricultural area, bad soils and rain shadow)." But if you are not a party member, you can't get food aid.

Soon Kidd is "down the rabbit hole" again. By chance he drives onto Roy Bennett's farm just as Mugabe's security men, police, CIO, and soldiers are there in force, arresting all Bennett's senior staff, and random people like Doug van der Riet, and some visitors from the UK, who just happen to be nearby. The way Doug remembers it, he sees Shane's bright orange VW Golf drive up, and Shane leans out of his window and says to Mwale, "My, my, what have we here, Joseph?"

Mwale tells him to get in the back too. Of course, Shane refuses.

"Just do it," urges Doug, because he knows what'll happen next if Shane doesn't get in. So does Shane, but he won't comply, just the same. In his diary, Shane puts it this way. "Mwale approaches, tot-ing an FN rifle, and I greet him by his first name, 'Hello, Joseph.' This gets him going, he *hates* being called Joseph. He turns the rifle around and hits me in the face with the rifle butt, and tells me of the dire consequences if I continue to call him Joseph. 'You know you are dead already,' he tells me."

Kidd is locked up again. During interrogation, Mwale tells him that the only way he will stay in Zimbabwe is buried in the ground. Chimani, says Mwale, is *his* district and he'll do as he likes here... "Mwale seems to think he's some sort of a general and is undoubtedly setting himself up to become the local warlord when things ultimately fall apart."

By the time Kidd is released, it is night. "Walking away from the police station in the dark I was greeting other pedestrians. One of them, whom I've never met before, said, 'Is that you, Mr. Kidd, what are you doing here?'" Shane explains that he's just been released from the police cells. "He comes up to me and says, 'Mr. Kidd, we people in Chimani are proud of you. Can I shake your hand?'" And they shake hands there on the road, in the dark where no one can see them, the injured white man, and the black villager, and then Shane makes his way back up the hill, through the sleeping village, to the indefatigable Birgit.

THE NEXT DAY the village almost burns down, reports Kidd. A grass fire started by the war vets on Frank Elias's old farm is whipped by high winds and rages out of control. It licks up Pork Pie Mountain, site of the eland sanctuary, which is soon covered with towering flames, "and fireballs the size of houses." From there, it sweeps down into the village itself, where the residents desperately battle to beat it back.

In Kidd's next entry, he reports the assault and torture of Mike Magaza, Roy Bennett's bodyguard. Bennett's wife, Heather, "could hear his screams of agony from the charge office and at one point saw him running out of the CIO offices with a bleeding head, only to be dragged back in by Joseph Mwale, where the torture continued."

In the prison, they discover "eight other MDC members from the surrounding area who have been in the cells for four days without food. All have been assaulted. Some have open head wounds and at least one has broken ribs."

Behind the accounts of the fires and the arrests and frequent jail time, the assaults and the torture, Kidd worries about his mother, who's in an old-age home in Bulawayo.

"I visited Mum on Friday," he writes. "She's getting smaller and smaller every time I see her. There is a book by a South American author called *One Hundred Years of Solitude*. In it, the grandmother gets smaller and smaller each year until eventually the great-great-grandchildren use her as a doll in their games and put her to bed in a shoebox. It reminds me a lot of Mum. She used to be four foot nine, now she's about four foot and getting shorter by the day."

eight

Birgit's Bad Hair Day

I AWAKE IN THE MORNING to the screech of butcher birds dueling in the monkey-puzzle tree outside Dr. Mostert's windows. From our camping supplies, Georgina and I assemble a makeshift breakfast of instant coffee and boiled eggs, and then I take up Shane's journals again.

He is hiking in the mountains when their house is surrounded by a mob, several hundred strong, from "The Party of Thugs," ZANU-PF, and soldiers in plain clothes. They throw rocks, which smash the windows and the roof tiles. Birgit is alone upstairs, trying "to make a few calls to the outside world for help. She has got it down to a fine art now, of just texting the word *HELP* to a group of embassies and lawyers and MDC officials." The mob breaks down the gate and swarms inside. Birgit takes a deep breath and comes halfway down the stairs to address them, as calmly as she can.

"Why are you breaking into my house like this?" she asks.

"We want to know why did you give your offices to the MDC?"

"One day you will know it and understand," says Birgit.

They demand to search the house to see if Shane is hiding in there, and they come behind her breaking things and raiding the pantry and looting the refrigerator.

Then, writes Shane:

> Man 1 *"gets into Birgit's face and starts shouting, 'I can kill you. I will kill you. Your ancestors have stolen our land . . . Go back to Britain where you belong.'"*
>
> *At this stage Man 2, who obviously has some local knowledge, tells Man 1, "Mrs. Kidd, actually, she is from Finland."*
>
> *"I am the 1st Finn to come to Zimbabwe, I have no ancestors here," Birgit interjects helpfully.*
>
> *Man 1: "Where is this country called Finland, is it next to Austria?"*
>
> *Birgit: "Try a little further north between Sweden and Russia."*
>
> *Man 1: "Ah, so you have been to Russia. What did you see there?"*
>
> *Birgit: "Plenty of Russians."*
>
> *Man 2: "This is your house, where are your guns."*
>
> *Birgit: "I have lived my life without guns and still I am without them."*

The mob forces her to carry a ZANU-PF flag, and marches her down the road, while they follow, jeering. A neighbor rushes to the police station to report that Birgit has been abducted, but is told it is "a political issue," and no concern of the police. While the neighbor is there, the phone keeps ringing as embassies and NGOs ask where Birgit Kidd is, and what's happening. The policeman tells them all, "I know nothing."

Birgit is marched to her bottle store, used as the MDC office. The Kidds had painted on the white wall: *MDC. Nothing illegal. Registered Political Party.* But the office has been trashed and everything inside it set on fire.

"Man 2," writes Shane, "hands Birgit a broom and tells her to clean the mess." So she does, and all the while, they jeer and chant at her, telling her that they are going to kill her and that she will soon return to Britain in a coffin. A truck arrives and a MDC local official, David Mudengwe, is pushed out of it, accompanied by CIO officers. In front of the crowd, they abruptly attack him, head-butting him in the face and kicking him with martial-arts high kicks, while the mob cheers.

"Birgit tried to intervene and help David," writes Shane, "but she was pulled back and held. They then stripped off his shirt and there was an MDC T-shirt under that so they attacked him again, giving him another beating, and stripped the T-shirt off his body. David was in agony, his face and body swollen from the repeated beating.

"One of the soldiers dressed in civilian clothes (Birgit has seen him around the village before in uniform) approached her and said, 'Let's see if you have an MDC T-shirt on under your blouse.' At this she finally loses her composure, and raising her voice, says, queru-lously, 'Don't you dare!' and surprisingly, he backs off."

Birgit has been told that a ZTV crew from Mutare has been summoned, and when it arrives, David Mudengwe is quickly chased away, and Birgit is paraded before the camera alone.

"When Birgit returned home," writes Shane, "she found Celia the ridgeback dying, one of the rent-a-mob had given her poisoned meat.

"This latest attempt to wreck the MDC office was simply the last in a long line of attempts and like all previous attempts it will fail as well. We will reopen the MDC office again."

Two weeks later Shane is summoned to the police station once more. Inside the charge office, four policemen repeatedly punch him. Another approaches him with a chair, its legs pointing forward, "like an animal trainer circus routine," writes Shane. The police charge him with assault and throw him into the cells. Later Joseph Mwale comes in with six soldiers. He grabs Shane from behind in a headlock, while the soldiers take turns slapping and punching his face.

His spell in the cells does not have the intended effect, however.

"Whilst in the cells," Shane writes, "I've decided to do more work with MDC in the village, take a higher profile and try and strengthen the office."

The first thing he does when he gets out of jail is to go to the MDC office with Birgit. He paints over the ZANU sign there and replaces it with his own:

MDC OFFICE—NO MORE FEAR

On another wall, as a joke he writes:

GET YOUR FREE GO-TO-JAIL CARD HERE! IF YOU GO TO JAIL 3 TIMES, YOU GET A FREE MDC WHISTLE.

A crowd has gathered to watch him repaint it. The police chief comes, says, "I can do nothing for you," and quickly leaves. Shane is up a ladder, painting the wall, when one of the CIO trucks draws up and security agents, war vets, and Mugabe loyalists pour out of it. They wrench the ladder from under Shane and begin assaulting him and Birgit.

"I have six people attacking me and Birgit has three people attacking her," Shane writes. "Let's be honest, I'm no Rambo and went down fairly rapidly, but I did get a few good punches and kicks in. I then concentrated on protecting my head with my arms to the best of my ability, while kicking out with those wonderful steel-capped boots. At this stage things were getting a bit blurry.

"Birgit meanwhile was contending with her own problems... Lazarus and two others then attacked her with rocks. She received multiple blows to the head and shoulders but managed to stay on her feet... Birgit tried to find refuge in the garage kiosk with Lazarus and co following behind and continuing to attack her. By this stage Birgit was bleeding profusely from her head wound and was blinded by blood, her left shoulder had also been dislocated and that arm was hanging uselessly by her side.

"Meanwhile I was still doing my impression of road kill..."

Birgit is rescued by a passer-by and rushed to hospital. Shane is badly hurt too, but still, minutes after the assault ends, he returns to the MDC office, which the war vets are repainting with pro-Mugabe slogans, and he berates them.

"I know it's a pointless exercise," he writes in his diary, "but the only reason that I'm doing it is to show them that they can beat me, but they can't make me fear them."

Then he walks up to the government district administrator's office, "where I'm about as welcome as a plague carrier, and start giving him a hard time, about who the hell he thinks he is, telling the war vets that Birgit doesn't own the bottle store anymore. To tell you the truth, my heart isn't really in it, the adrenalin is wearing off and the shock is starting to set in, and I'm feeling decidedly woozy."

He phones a friend to collect him, and while he waits, "I amuse myself by spreading blood around his office. The body is way past walking mode, and was telling the ego to sod off, it wasn't the ego that had just been stomped on and the body had the casting vote and the ribs are unanimously behind it.

"The net result," writes Shane, is that "Birgit had sixteen stitches in the head and a dislocated shoulder. I was a lot luckier, no stitches just badly bruised ribs and upper body and some cuts and lacerations. One bright moment; some reporter from VOA [Voice of America radio] was on the phone to Birgit and asked her what she was going to do for protection in future. Birgit replied that she would wear a hard hat. The rest of the week has been taken up with hospital, lawyers and doctors. See attached photo of Birgit having a bad hair day."

In the photo Birgit is in profile, her silver bob and face caked with blood. This is her good side. On her other side, the Chiping doctor is stitching an angry gash.

In the police report filed by the Kidds, they name the assailants. Lazarus Shahwe, one of Mwale's men, leads the attack on Birgit, "with rocks, fists and boots." He finds a six-foot gum plank, "which he then used to beat Birgit on the head three times," splitting it open. Yet nine months later, it is to the Kidds and the MDC that

Lazarus runs, seeking sanctuary from Mugabe's men, having now fallen foul of them himself.

SHANE HAS CALLED one of his journal entries *Days of Our Lives*, because "our lives are turning into a rather dreadful soap." He wrestles with the news, brought to him by someone who has overheard Mugabe's men plotting, that "apparently we are to be kidnapped and then 'disappeared!'" and tries to figure out why he's sticking his head so far above the parapet, when most others are crouching well beneath it.

"Doug asked me today why we do what we do. I rather glibly replied, 'We each have to draw our own line and make our own stand.' But that's not really the answer.

"I'll be buggered if I'll be told what I can and can't do in my own country. But there is more to it than that. While we were at the MDC office in Mutare, this morning, three Chipinge women came in, one of them was an MDC councillor in Chipinge, all three have just had their homes burned and destroyed. The councilwoman was one of those who attended all my trials in Chipinge a couple of years ago as a show of support."

When she hears that the Kidds have reclaimed the MDC office in Chimani, says Shane, "it brought a smile to her face, and a little hope."

THERE IS A disturbing epilogue to Joseph Mwale, which I hope is only a provisional one. He was rewarded for his hard-core tactics by being promoted and transferred to Harare, as part of Mugabe's close security team. And to this day, he has not been prosecuted for the murders of Talent Mabika and Tichaona Chiminya, and the many, many assaults he personally carried out and ordered.

A few months later, at Princeton, I met an anthropologist, David Hughes, who had done doctoral field work in Zimbabwe. His name was familiar, and then I remembered what I'd been told by Caiphas Mupuro, who had taken over Chris Lynam's farm. This was the American who had stayed down in the Rusitu valley. Hughes confirmed it—he was actually at Berkeley, not Harvard—and told me that it had become too dangerous for him to continue his research there, that people he talked to were being beaten by Mwale's CIO agents. Hughes had finally met Mwale at Heroes' Day celebrations in Chipinge where, because he was a visiting American, he was hauled up onto the stage as a VIP.

As Mwale got drunker, he summoned Hughes and began complaining that the CIO had been treated unfairly. "The army and the police, they also kill people. More people than we do, but they don't have such a bad name. You know why?" he asked.

"Why?" Hughes obliged.

"Because *they* have public relations officers. That's what *we* need in the President's Office. We need public relations officers. Then we wouldn't have such a bad reputation."

Mwale's solution to the CIO's murderous reputation was not to kill fewer people, but to spin it better in PR terms! It gives you an insight into the depth of their dysfunction, agreed Hughes. In the meantime, he had settled upon a new subject for his own anthropological study, the last of an endangered species: the white farmer.

nine

Boys to Men

AFTER A FEW DAYS IN Chimanimani, we set off south to Silverstream, where Georgina and I both grew up. It is now three weeks since the election. We cross the Silverstream River just above the rapids which tumble into plunge pools where we used to swim as kids, and where Violet our nanny once nearly drowned and our elder sister, Jain, saved her. Silverstream feeds into the Crystal Creek and on into the Rusitu, where it flows through the valley below Lynam's jambanja'd farm, and out onto the low, steamy Mozambique flood plain.

At the top of the village, above the factory, which processes wattle bark into tannin to cure leather, is our old house, a simple colonial bungalow, with a corrugated tin roof. Outside, I recognize the landscape of my memories, the rolling green lawns of Kikuyu grass, and the malachite kingfishers, which still patronize the pond. The cork oak, flame tree, Northumberland pine, silver oak, syringa tree, jacaranda, the belhambra with its long dangling bracts of white flowers at this time of year, and the coral tree, all sentinels of our childhood.

George and Tanya Webster now live here. Where my father used to have his old slip-covered armchair, next to the big brick fireplace, in the sitting room, where I used to fall asleep with the dogs, Tanya Webster, a large cheerful woman with curly black hair and glasses, now sits, knitting blankets, while kittens swat at her wool. A copy of *The Purpose Driven Life* sits on her side table. Her husband, George, heavyset, genial, with short, steel-gray hair and mustache, dressed in a black T-shirt and shorts, shows us around.

Our house is the same but different. Ancestral English bric-abrac has been replaced by African tchotchkes. A trio of plump wooden hippos, a copper wall clock in the shape of Africa, a standard lamp made from a varnished tree branch, a family of ceramic guinea fowl, black with white spots, arranged in descending size.

The old cast-iron wood stove has been replaced by an electric one; an en-suite bathroom has been added; the veranda, where I used to lie on the red-cement parapet in my flannel pajamas, watching the thunderstorms roll down from Spitzkop, is now enclosed.

George Webster's great grandfather came up to Gazaland with the original pioneer column, in July 1893, from Haywards Heath in the UK, via Groot Marico in South Africa.

"My mum was from Bradford, she met my dad in World War II, in the RAF, and came out after the war," he says. "My dad told her, 'There are a hundred workers on this farm who speak only Shona, and you speak only English. Either we have to teach a hundred guys to speak English, or you must learn Shona.'" Soon she spoke it fluently, as does George, which is just as well as he's the only white man left in Silverstream. He stays on, mostly so he can help his eighty-eight-year-old father, who is still clinging onto "the Meadows," their family dairy farm down the Chipinge road.

Like his father before him, George Webster went into the air force. "In those days, during the Rhodesian war," he recalls, "we used to fly a Canberra jet on a daily recon mission all the way up to the Kenya border, to take aerial photos. It used to fly so high—nearly seventy thousand feet—that from up there you could see both sides of Africa, and it was so cold you had to scrape ice off the cockpit instruments. One took a hit once, but it made it home."

In late 1980, after independence, he resigned from the air force, along with seventy other technicians, after an ex-guerrilla who had invented his qualifications was brought in over them.

Webster has only been out of Africa once — for six weeks to visit his son Colin in London. He spent the time helping to set up a biltong drier, as his son had done a deal with Sainsbury's in Wandsworth to take all their unsold fillet at half price, when it reached its sell-by date, and turn it into biltong.

The corridor down the middle of the house is lined with photos of fishing trips off the Mozambique coast, school rugby teams, British soldiers. All but one of the kids are gone: a daughter is in Calgary; a son is in the Royal Engineers, seeing service in Iraq, Afghanistan, and Northern Ireland; another lugs furniture in London, and makes biltong; and the last one, Liam, is about to join him. It seems there is no future for them here.

Webster tells me that five busloads of soldiers in civilian clothes have been deployed into nearby areas where Mugabe lost the vote. And an old Afrikaans farmer, Schalk du Plessis, was just wrenched from his truck by war vets who cuffed his hands behind his back and tied his neck to a tree with fence wire.

As du Plessis sat there against the tree, with the wire around his neck, he saw that his guard was wearing a baseball cap bearing the slogan *Jesus Loves You*. "So," says Webster, a committed Christian himself, who distributes Gideon Bibles in the tribal areas, "old Schalk challenged him. 'How can you do this to me and yet you profess to be Christian?' he asked." And the war vet got embarrassed and untied him.

We pause to watch the satellite news on Sky TV — Tendai Biti, one of the MDC's leaders, is saying that ten of their supporters have now been killed, five hundred injured and four hundred arrested or abducted by Mugabe loyalists in post-election violence. A Chinese freighter packed with weapons for Mugabe — AK rifles with three million bullets, mortars and rocket launchers — has sailed away from Durban, after the South African trade unions there refused to unload it. The Websters cheer.

That night I walk down the wide planked corridor to my old corner bedroom, to sleep there again for the first time in thirty years. The windows still have the same grenade screens that were welded onto them after our neighbor Piet Oberholzer was murdered, and the branches still scratch against them, like they did all those years ago, scaring the boy that I used to be.

I sleep profoundly, dreaming of my childhood. Of m'Apostolic trance dances, and leopard hunts, cattle herding on horseback, and shy pangolins in forest clearings, nibbling food from my palm, *ngangas,* whom we still called witch doctors then, rocking on the mud floors as they chanted, traditional beer brewing. And deep into the night, on wind-borne surges from the compound, I hear the throb of drums, just like I always used to hear.

In the morning I am awoken by the mournful train whistle announcing the shift change at the factory. And the cockerel crows serve as a snooze alarm. Over tea, Tanya wonders where the staff are. "They haven't turned up this morning," she says, an undercurrent of fear evident in her voice. "I hope nothing terrible's happened to them…" She tries the phone but it is dead.

George takes us down to the factory, where he does my father's old job. "Your father was like a god to us when we were growing up," he says. "I never thought *I'd* end up running this place."

The Wattle Company, as the plaque on the office wall recalls, was established as Forrestal Land, Timber and Railways Co., in 1945, by Baron Emile Beaumont d'Erlanger, who, as the head of the Channel Tunnel Company, dreamed of tunneling between England and France in the early twentieth century. Now owned by black Zimbabweans, this Silverstream factory is a working monument to radical improvisation — most of the machinery here is more than fifty years old.

An old Mercedes five-tonner I can still remember remains in service. It was a real beast to handle, called — they all have names hand-painted on their snouts — *Boys to Men*, because if you learned to drive it, you had made that leap. Behind it is *Big Brother*, a tractor.

The four huge roaring Hadean boilers are still fed constantly, red flames making short work of the logs being tossed into their gaping black cast-iron maws by rows of sweating, shirtless men. "We used to have one stoker to each boiler, now we need two on each," says Webster. "The average man is smaller and weaker than his father, due to malnutrition, AIDS, malaria. Silverstream is now one of the worst areas for malaria in the whole country — there's this mutant strain coming up from Mozambique."

In my youth, Silverstream was blessedly malaria-free. Areas like this, and most of the colonial capitals, were built above the malaria line, but climate change has nudged up average temperatures, to put them into the mosquito zone.

The factory is running out of bark to process into tannin. Since late January, Webster says, their foreign currency earnings have been withheld by the Reserve Bank head, Gideon Gono, to fund Mugabe's election campaign. Now the factory is short of spares, diesel. The whole fleet of trucks is grounded.

The Wattle Company should have a complement of twenty-two hundred workers to keep the plantations and the factory going. But, in a country with 94 percent unemployment, it can only raise eighteen hundred. "We have gold on one side and diamonds on the other, so our guys don't want to work," complains Webster. "They can earn more in a day there than they can here in a week.

"At one point there were nearly a million people digging for diamonds. We had workers who would go there to dig for the weekend — the police were charging Z$10m to dig for twenty minutes. Some got great finds — I had one guy come up to me at Chiadzwa with a cake tin full of diamonds!"

Before we leave, Tanya takes us on a farewell tour of the garden. Across from the old Northumberland pine an imposing palm tree now rustles, new since our time. In this little corner of the country, at least, the Websters, as Kipling once put it, in his poem to British imperialism, still hold "dominion over palm and pine." Then Tanya explains that they dug up the palm from outside a farm homestead in Lemon Kop that was being jambanja'd by war vets.

Georgina and I get down on our knees on the lawn, beneath the coral tree. It is considered a magical tree. Zulu people plant a coral tree on the grave of a chief. The bark is used to make a poultice to heal wounds. We are collecting the small, shiny scarlet seeds that the coral tree has shed. We call them "lucky beans." As kids, we used to push a needle through their black eyes and thread them on a string to make bracelets. Tanya brings out an old jam jar and we fill it with lucky beans.

BACK ON THE ROAD the next day, we descend into the Savé Valley. The first big baobab, which has prominent veins like those on well-muscled forearms, also has a message whitewashed on its gray bark: Vote MDC 2002. That was the last time power eluded the opposition, and its legal challenges from then are still snarled up in Zimbabwe's craven courts. At the side of the road, women sell maize meal decanted into tiny bags, and cream-of-tartar fruits, in their furry green maraca husks. Small boys hold up roasted mice, kebab'd on sharp sticks. Years ago, we thought it amusing to send out photos of this as a holiday greeting card, with the caption Happy Crisp Mouse.

A vast python, thigh-thick at its mid-section, stretches gorily dead across the entire width of the road, ludicrously unlucky, as there is almost no traffic. Public transportation is paralyzed by high fuel prices, and lack of spares.

We pass through the shimmering silver arch of Birchenough Bridge, and on into Bikita. On several occasions, Georgina notices people being pushed in wheelbarrows, off to the side, along footpaths, away from the road, and we comment on the transport shortage.

It's only later, to our shame, that we realize that these are the first of the torture victims of Mugabe's interrogation bases, too badly hurt to walk, being pushed home in wheelbarrows by their desperate family members.

Georgina's friend Rita Harvey has asked us to look in on her elderly mother, Jeanette, who lives in the Pioneer Cottages, sheltered accommodation for the elderly in Masvingo town, after being thrown off their farm.

"Go past the burnt-down OK Bazaars, and right at the robots," says Jeanette on the phone. She is sparrow spry, bright eyed, alert, notwithstanding her hearing aid. Her forty-year-old special-needs son, Forbes, sleeps on the enclosed porch of their tiny cottage, surrounded by his collection of miniature liquor bottles.

"We spent fifty years building that farm up and they took it from us just like that. They've destroyed the windmills. I don't understand, if they want to farm, why destroy the windmills? Now there's no water.

"For his last four years, my husband, Keith, was bed-ridden and not completely lucid. He kept saying, 'I want to go home.' And in the end, he did. He's buried under a flat-topped acacia tree on the farm. He picked the gravesite himself."

She shows us photos of her family. "Of my eight grandkids, not a single one is still in this country." For a moment I think she might cry, but she quickly composes herself.

"I find it difficult to drive now. Mostly we walk, there's nothing much to carry back from the shops now—the shops are empty. I don't know what's going to happen.

"The Zimbabwe Pensioners Support Network people come three or four times a year with a seven-ton lorry. They bring us sugar, cooking oil, jam, rice, and flour. Mrs. Odendaal says she'd starve without it. Someone came and knocked at my door the other day with two loaves of bread, and said, 'This is from a church in Pretoria.' Another brought soap and toothpaste wrapped in a towel, with a few sweeties thrown in. And at Christmastime, we each got a little box— a small bottle of whiskey and one of wine and some razors. We don't know how to say thank you—the trouble they go to—spending their own money, finding out what we need. Forbes likes the biscuits."

"Yes." Forbes nods, grinning.

"We are very fortunate, I understand that. It's so hard for Forbes, though. On the farm, he had a role, he could help with the cattle. He can't read, and I can't hear. So, when we watch TV we have to help each other!"

She stands in her tiny garden, next to her carefully tended guava tree and bauhinia, to see us off. But as we leave, she turns fearful again. "We've been warned that they're going to start invading houses next," she says, "to get 'hoarders.'"

WE DRIVE ON to Harare in silence. Georgina sucks on a silver NicoPipe. At the side of the road youths wave long sticks with plastic bottles on the ends. These are black-market fuel-dealers; the dealers in gold, diamonds, foreign currency, phone cards, all have their own particular choreography. We pass a car transporter heading north to the capital, packed with high-end Mercedes—luxury rides for the fat cats, while most are ragged and desperate. We encounter four roadblocks in quick succession, but the policemen's hard brown eyes sweep over us and find nothing of interest; they're looking for baksheesh from those who've been shopping in South Africa.

As we drive through Chivhu, which Jeanette had still called Enkeldoorn, "Lone Thorn"—its old Afrikaans name—Georgina starts to recite one of the series of silly limericks I'd composed when the state place-name-change commission had been expunging colonial vestiges:

"A farmer from Enkeldoorn said,
"'Rather than change, I'd be dead.'
"When told it's now Chivhu
"Said, 'I don't believe you.'
"And then put a gun to his head."

Then she turns the music back up and goes to sleep.

WE HAVE BEEN driving fast because it is the anniversary of the death of our sister, Jain—killed in the Rhodesian bush war twenty-eight years ago today, weeks before her wedding. As soon as we reach Harare, we head straight through the city to the northern suburb of Borrowdale, to Christchurch, where Jain's ashes are entombed next to Dad's.

Together we sweep the grass tailings off the two gravestones on the crematorium lawn. As we do so, a marmalade cat strolls over and nudges our legs to be petted, and then curls up, purring, on Dad's gravestone as it observes us through lazy green eyes.

"It belongs to the old pastor, Father Bertram," says Rodgers Sokiri, the church gardener. "The one who buried your father. He left to live in South Africa."

We phone my mother from the graveside and tell her what we're doing.

"What's it like there?" she asks. "Describe it for me, Peter."

So I tell her that there is a marmalade cat purring on Dad's gravestone, and cockerels are crowing and black-eyed bulbuls are chirping and hopping from branch to branch of the jacaranda trees. That the flamboyant trees are in flower over a bank bursting with white roses. And that amidst them there is a single, startling crimson one, beneath which the cat now settles and begins to wash itself assiduously. That lush banana fronds sway over the boundary wall in the late-afternoon breeze. I tell her that rather than flowers, we have brought lucky beans from the coral tree in our old garden in Silverstream, and that we are pouring them into the runnels of the letters carved into Jain's gravestone, so that they are now picked out in lines of scarlet.

"How is it in London?" I ask.

"Raining," she says, and I can hear her quietly weeping on the end of the phone, all those miles away.

ten

My Blood Is Too Heavy

I N OUR WEEK-LONG ABSENCE, Harare's private hospitals have started to fill with victims of Mugabe's crackdown against the opposition, which his generals are calling Operation Mavhotera-papi?—"Who Did You Vote For?"

Denias Dombo lies broken on a bed in Dandaro clinic, his dark head propped up against the bright white pillows, trying to eat a slice of bread. His left leg is in plaster from hip to heel, just the cal-loused khaki sole peeping out the end of the sheet. Both arms are in plaster casts too, right up to the veined ridges of his farmer's biceps.

He winces as he turns to pick up his teacup because several of his ribs are broken. "Can you lift my leg back up," he asks. "My blood is too heavy." On his bedside table is a copy of Robert Louis Stevenson's *Kidnapped*.

"I'm halfway through it," he says, following my gaze. "I passed tenth grade, you know."

Dombo trained and worked as a mechanic, until one day nearly twenty years ago when a colleague accidentally switched on the engine he was adjusting, and the spinning fan blades severed two of his fingers—he holds up his plastered left arm to show the digits ending at gnarled nubs just up from the knuckle. After that, he returned to his ancestral home at Mudzi, on the lip of the Zambezi valley, where until last week he farmed groundnuts and maize, and lived in a tidy brushed-earth kraal with three thatched houses and a granary up on wooden stilts, and his seven cattle which slept in a thorn-tree-enclosed pen each night. Around now he should be harvesting his groundnuts, instead of lying shattered in a Harare hospital.

But earlier this year Denias Dombo made a terrible mistake. He believed it when he was told that Zimbabwe was to hold free and fair elections. "It was my job," he says, "as the district organizing secretary for the MDC to apply to the police for clearance to hold party meetings." So everyone knew his party affiliation. As it turned out Mudzi did not go well for the MDC. They lost all three parliamentary constituencies to Mugabe's ruling ZANU-PF. You might think this would be a cause of celebration for the victors. But that's when the trouble started.

One Thursday, in mid-April, Denias Dombo set off from his kraal to investigate a report that a local member of the MDC had been beaten by political rivals from ZANU-PF. Before he was out of earshot, though, he heard a vehicle growling to a halt outside his home, and he turned back to investigate. As he approached he saw "bright flames—my brick and thatch house already on fire" and the two men who had set it alight, scampering back to their pick-up truck.

He recognized both men. One was the newly elected ZANU-PF MP for the area, and the other was a prominent ZANU-PF member and neighbor. The vehicle in which they sped off had ZANU-PF party signs on its doors, and in the back sat a group of youths in party T-shirts, with pictures of Robert Mugabe's face across their chests.

Dombo yelled after them, "I see you, I know who you are and you are the ones who have burned down my house."

Everything inside was destroyed. "We Africans are used to

putting all our valuables in one place, in what we call the sleeping room," explains Dombo, "and all our most precious things were there, our beds, a wardrobe, a kitchen unit, all of the family's clothes, our blankets."

So Dombo collected the MDC district vice-chairman and his own brother and together they walked fifteen miles, through the night, to the nearest police station, at Kotwa, to report the crime. He made his statement to the police and then walked the fifteen miles home.

Later that afternoon the police arrived, took a cursory look at his burnt house, and departed. Twenty minutes later, about thirty youths in ZANU-PF T-shirts swarmed into the kraal, armed with sticks and iron bars. They were yelling and throwing rocks. Dombo and his family tried to barricade themselves in the kitchen. But their attackers broke down the flimsy door and began stoning the family huddled inside.

That's when Denias Dombo came to a decision.

"I decided, better for me to come out, or they will kill my family."

So he told his wife, Patricia, who was carrying their four-month-old son, Israel, told his fourteen-year-old daughter, Martha, and her nine-year-old sister, Dorcas: "I'm going to go out and when they run after me, you must all run away as fast as you can, and hide." Then Dombo took a deep breath and ran out toward his attackers, and, just as he had anticipated, they converged upon him, with their rocks and iron bars and their heavy sticks, until, he says, "my blood was rushing out everywhere." He tried to protect his head with his arms while they beat him. "I heard the bones in my arms crack and I cried out: 'Oh, Jesus, I'm dying here—what have I done wrong?'" And as they beat him, on and on, his assailants made him shout, "*Pamberi na* [up with] Robert Mugabe," "*Pamberi ne*ZANU-PF," "*Pasi na* [down with] Tsvangirai."

"And I did," he admits. "I shouted all those slogans because I was in deep trouble." But still the beating continued. Until the ring-leader, one Jeavus Chiutsa, finally looked at his watch and said, "Let's leave him here, we'll come back and finish him off tonight."

So they walked across to the road, and stood and watched while Denias Dombo tried to stand up, teetered, and fell down, tried to stand up once more and fell again. And then he looked down and realized that his leg was broken; he could see the jagged shard of his left shin bone "waving out," as he puts it. And one arm hung limp and shattered too. "And they saw I was going nowhere," he says. "So they blew their whistles, and *toyi-toyi*-ed [war-danced] away down the road, back to Vhombozi school," which had served as a polling station and had now been co-opted as a ZANU-PF torture base. There, he heard later, they celebrated. "They killed a goat and roasted it over a fire and sang, 'We have done it — we have killed their leader.'"

Unable to escape, Dombo lay down by the embers of his burnt house. "The pain was so great," he says, "there was blood everywhere, coming out of my nose and out of my mouth, coming down from my head and into my eyes so that I couldn't see clearly. I was in such terrible pain and I thought I was dying, and I decided, better to kill myself than just wait for them to return and finish me off."

So Dombo picked up a length of thick wire, and wiping the blood from his eyes, twisted one end into a tight noose around his neck and summoned his remaining strength to reach up and attach the other end to a hook in the brick wall of his charred house. He took a deep breath and threw himself down. He felt the wire tighten around his throat, felt the sunlight dim, felt himself grow faint, felt the hurting fade, and the life inside him ebbing away. Then he fell heavily to the ground. The wire had broken.

Dombo can't go on; a great jagged sob wells up from his chest — it is the first time he has really recounted the detail of what happened, and faced the enormity of it all. At his bedside Georgina is crying too, and she reaches over to grasp his hand, and we stay like that for a few minutes, as an air-force fighter roars overhead, and Dombo struggles to regain control. Slowly his sobs subside and he takes up his story once more, in a tremulous voice that is barely more than a hoarse whisper.

After the wire broke and he fell to the ground, Dombo lay there trembling with pain, the wire noose still twisted around his neck, until he heard a piping voice calling to him.

"*Baba, Baba, simukai, ndapota*," which in the local Shona language means, "Father, please wake up." It was Dorcas, his nine-year-old daughter, kneeling at his side. When she saw him lying there, covered in blood, his bones broken and wire twisted around his neck, she began to weep.

"It's okay, it's okay, I'm not yet dead," he told her softly, patting her arm. "But you must go and get help quickly or I might still die."

He asked her to fetch another neighbor, a fellow opposition supporter, Wellington Mafiyoni.

Soon Mafiyoni arrived and gingerly loaded Dombo's shattered body into a wheelbarrow. He trundled Dombo five hundred yards out into the bush and laid him down on the ground, pulling some branches over him as camouflage.

"Be brave," he urged, "and try not to cry so they won't hear where I hid you."

Then he set off to walk the fifteen miles to the police station to get help.

"It was cold, and I was still bleeding and the pain was severe," says Dombo.

And as he lay there that evening on the cold, hard ground, with the jagged end of his broken shin bone sticking out of his flesh, the mob returned. Dombo listened as they searched for him and he heard them decide that he must already be dead. And he heard them setting about his prize possessions, his seven cattle, with axes.

"They cut the tendons on their back legs," he sobs now. "I could hear my cows crying to me. But I could do nothing."

As they killed the cattle and looted the house, he could hear them singing a victory anthem. It went like this, he says, singing in a hoarse whisper in his hospital room: "Mugabe *torafoshoro nepick* to bury Denias Dombo." "Mugabe take your shovel and pick to bury Denias Dombo."

Later he heard a vehicle stop outside his house, and heard the mob following it down the road, singing and chanting their victory songs.

Dawn came, and then the day heated up, and the flies buzzed around Dombo's open wounds, and he fell in and out of consciousness. And when he was conscious he thought he would surely die of "thirst and hunger and pain." And then, sometime in the afternoon, his colleagues, alerted by Wellington, arrived at his hiding place. They constructed a makeshift stretcher by tying their jerseys between two long branches, and they carried him to the road where the ambulance arrived with a police escort, as the driver was too afraid to come alone.

The ambulance took him to Kotwa clinic, but there was no medicine there; all they were able to give him for his grievous wounds were two aspirin, and he was transferred to Parirenyatwa, the big government hospital in Harare, where there was nothing either, and finally, through a medical charity, he got treatment here, at Dandaro.

"I need another operation to set my bones properly," he says, "but my doctor told me that I am still too weak, my blood pressure is still too low for that."

His broken ribs still hurt, and they stop him from sleeping, and he can't move his leg. And as he lies here, sleepless, he dreams of his children.

"I don't think I'll ever see them again," he says.

Then he holds up his broken arms.

"For me, this is a death sentence—I can't provide for my children any longer."

He starts to lose it again, and through his tears, he rails. "I have lost everything. All I had accumulated has turned to ashes."

His plow and his cultivator were stolen. His groundnut crop, which he should be harvesting now, is either rotting in the field or stolen too.

He doesn't know where his family is, his wife and daughters and his baby son, or how they will survive with their kraal burned down and their grain plundered, their cattle slaughtered and eaten by Mugabe's marauding mobs.

"The MDC were going to try to send a message to my family but

I heard that the MDC offices were raided and many there were arrested, so I don't think they managed."

Dombo reaches painfully into his bedside table to retrieve a small Bible—the New Testament, Psalms and Proverbs. He thumbs through it to find a tattered, much-folded piece of lined paper with the phone number of someone he hopes might know where they were. He presses it into my hand and asks me to try to locate his family.

"Please, sir, I am begging you."

And then, apologizing as he does so, he turns his face to the wall and begins to weep again.

DOMBO'S WARD MATE, Tendai Pawandiwa, thirty-two, wears a red baseball cap and flicks listlessly through the pages of a four-year-old issue of *People* magazine. "Who Is Brooke's True Love?" "Will Young and Eminem—What's the Low-Down?" lure the headlines.

On his cabinet is a bouquet of roses, still cellophane-wrapped, and wilting without water. "Who gave them to you?" I inquire.

He lowers his magazine and shrugs.

"I don't know."

Pawandiwa comes from Mtoko. He was ordered by the local ZANU-PF chairman, Tafirenyika Shada, to attend a party meeting, where he was accused of being a troublemaker for supporting the MDC. Later that same day, a group of ZANU youth, wielding sticks, attacked his kraal. Pawandiwa and his wife and his sister fled into the bush but he was pursued by the mob, and they finally caught up with him near a river.

"They grabbed me and pushed me into the river, telling me that they were going to baptize me in the name of ZANU-PF. Then they pushed my head under the water and tried to drown me."

Finally, he managed to wrestle free and then he walked fifteen miles to the main road. His body also bears the stigmata of elections, Zimbabwe-style, lacerations on his back and legs.

Now, as he sits here, he worries most about his three-year-old daughter, who was left behind with her very elderly grandfather.

* * *

IN ANOTHER WARD, Tonde Chakanedza, thirty-eight, lies on his bed in a green-striped T-shirt, donated by a local clothing store. He is swathed in bandages, on his arms, legs, and buttocks, and peels one up to show the oozing lacerations beneath. Also from Mudzi, he was beaten by a group of over fifty Green Bombers, as Mugabe's youth league are called here, from the green fatigues they wear.

Next to him, in an identical donated T-shirt, lies Norest Mucho-choma, thirty-one, with a small goatee beard. He was taken from his village last week by a group of men, one of whom claimed to be a policeman, who said he was under arrest.

"What for?" asked Norest, but the cop told him, "We'll tell you when we get to the police station."

Instead, they took him to the local school, which had served as a polling station. "This," said the rogue cop, "is the scene of the crime. This is where you voted for the wrong party."

They made him lie on his stomach and began beating him with sticks, "as big as this." He points to the bedpost. "There were two hundred and ten votes for the MDC in this ward," they told him, "and we will find all of you."

They were about twenty of them being beaten at the school by ZANU youths, led by war veterans, and he insists I write down the perpetrators' names: David Kanjere, and Clemace Murambidze, and Clifford Makuatsine.

"And when one got tired from beating us, another took over. They also jumped on us with their heavy boots, and kept asking us for the names of other MDC supporters, but I refused to tell them. They said we had to burn MDC T-shirts and party cards and that they would baptize us from MDC to ZANU, from Tsvangirai to Mugabe. 'By the time of the re-run,' they said, 'you must change to ZANU-PF or you will die.'"

By the end of the beating, Norest Muchochoma was vomiting and urinating blood, then he lost consciousness. Finally, some time the next morning they were permitted to leave and he crawled the two miles home. Later he made a full report to the police, even though his assailants warned him not to, and then other party members brought him to hospital.

Before the elections, says Muchochoma, his kraal head had instructed the villagers to pretend to be illiterate, "so the police could 'help' us to vote, but we refused to tell them we don't know how to write," he says. "We do know how to write and we wanted to vote freely."

"If there is a re-run how will you vote?"

"We will vote for the MDC. ZANU made sure of that by beating us."

TICHANZII GANDANGA lies in an upstairs ward. His head is bruised and bloody; he peels off the bedspread to reveal two massively swollen legs. He was at his office in Harare city center at 6:30 one evening a week ago when four men in civilian clothes burst in, saying they were police officers. They tried to handcuff him and when he resisted, one pulled out a pistol and threatened to shoot him. Then they shoved him down the stairs and into the back seat of a metallic-gray Isuzu twin-cab, with dark-tinted windows. One sat on his legs while another put him in a headlock. They pulled a black bag over his head so he could no longer see. Gandanga believes that the men were members of Mugabe's spying agency, the CIO, and the sequence of the interrogation that followed is instructive. After every unsatisfactory answer—and they were all unsatisfactory—Gandanga was hit with the butt of a pistol.

Q: We know you are the MDC director of elections for Harare Province.

A: Yes, it's a matter of public knowledge.

Q: We know you have sent sixty-four people to South Africa for training as guerrillas because we have rigged the elections and now you want to start a war.

A: I know nothing about that.

Q: And you are also going for training.

A: No. I know nothing about that.

Q: Describe what you do as director of elections?

A: Logistics, campaigning, anything to do with the elections.

Q: Where is Morgan Tsvangirai?

A: As you have read in the papers, he is now in South Africa.

Q: No. We know he's in Botswana. Where exactly is he?

A: I'm not sure.

Q: Your blood will spill for all of the MDC.

All the while, the vehicle was moving and the stereo was turned up loud, playing a religious song, "Nyika Inorema" — "Life Is Hard on Earth."

"You are terrified, helpless," says Gandanga. "But somehow you adjust to the situation."

After an hour of questioning, they took the blindfold off him, and pushed him out of the car. He noticed another SUV behind them. They began to lash him with whips made of tire rubber, and they kicked him in the face. Nine men came out of the car behind and joined in. Then they ripped all his clothes off until he was naked. They un-cuffed him, forced him to lie face down while someone stood on his neck, and they beat him again with tree branches. This continued for about thirty minutes until his flayed back was numb. Finally, he faked unconsciousness and they stopped beating him. They dragged him naked into the road and beat him again on his buttocks and back. He remained motionless. They pulled him across the road and then he heard the vehicle start up and get closer and closer, until it ran over his legs, then it backed up, running over them again. His body was so numb, he hardly felt any pain as his legs were squashed, just the thump, thump, as the tires rolled over them.

"Then, through the corner of my eye, I saw it coming a second time to run me over and I just closed my eyes and prayed the wheels wouldn't run over my head this time, and crush me. They went over my legs again, and the vehicle drove away. I managed then to roll off the road and I looked down at my legs and thought, 'Will these legs ever work again?' I managed to wriggle my toes slightly."

Gathering his strength, he dragged himself away from the road to a tree, and broke off a branch and using this as a crutch staggered back to the roadside and tried to flag down passing traffic. Three vehicles went by. But it was dark and what the drivers saw was a naked, bloody man, propped up by a tree branch, frantically waving them down, so no one stopped. After an hour, a truck pulled to a stop up ahead and Gandanga slowly dragged himself to the vehicle and managed to pull himself up to the closed window.

Unsure of the good Samaritan's political affiliation, he told him that he had been abducted by thieves, robbed, and dumped in the bush. The driver's mate hauled him up into the back of the truck. Now the pain was terrible and Gandanga became almost hysterical with it as he lay trembling. The driver took pity on him and gave him his jacket, and he wrapped it around his bloody nakedness. After a while, the driver stopped, and allowed him up into the warmth of the cab. When Gandanga started to feel woozy, he asked the driver to write down the phone numbers of his wife and close colleagues, in case he lost consciousness.

"Do you know where you are?" asked the driver.

Gandanga had no idea. It turned out he was on the Wedza road, about sixty miles from where he had been abducted in Harare. It was an old white farming area, now jambanja'd, and the good Samaritan turned out to be a resettled farmer, and a Mugabe supporter. When they ran low on fuel they pulled in for the night at the homestead of another new farmer, who gave Gandanga his carved walking stick. But later they became suspicious about his politics — "They said thieves don't usually run over their victims' legs," explains Gandanga. "But the local headman said: 'It doesn't matter about his political affiliation. We still have to help him.'" The next day they took him to Marondera, into cell-phone range, and Gandanga called his wife's brother, who came to collect him.

Now he is worried. "When they realize that I survived, they may try to get me again. They know my address, they've visited me there before. I will have to relocate to a safe house.

"My wife and my four-year-old son, Shepherd, came to visit me in hospital." He points to his swollen feet. "Shepherd said, 'Daddy, where are your shoes?'

"We are in a deep political crisis," says Gandanga. "The police won't deal with perpetrators of political violence—reporting it to them, it's a waste of time. We have people with their fingers cut off, their feet burned—and nothing happens. We need to think outside the box as a political party—the state is at war with its own citizens—we are not armed, and they are. We know very well that we won the elections. ZANU is scared. This is a strategy to reverse our victory—forcibly—in front of our eyes. It's clear from the questions in my interrogation that they want to incapacitate the MDC—to eliminate its key people. So many of us are threatened, hurt, displaced. Our main leaders are outside the country. Our structures are damaged. We need to make strong decisions. Here power is being taken by force, so what's next? We need to contemplate our options. Even if we win a re-run, they will never announce it. And it's daydreaming to think that the re-run will be fair. Already people are being terrorized."

eleven

Chronicles of Narnia

I SPEND THE AFTERNOON transcribing the testimony of Dandaro's wounded, backing it up on flash drives, and emailing it out of the country, my anger and fear growing as I review their gruesome experiences. I try to imagine what it must feel like to be tortured. I have read that time slows. It becomes elastic. "For in a minute there are many days," but Shakespeare wrote that about a different agony, the agony of yearning. I try to call my family in New York, wanting to hear the reassuring voices of my young sons, Thomas and Hugo. So many of those in Dandaro don't even know where their children are. As usual, I can't get an international line. It only adds to the claustrophobia of it all.

That evening, Georgina and I go to a party given by the Hon. William Brandon. His father was an English law lord. Brandon Jr. is a first secretary at the British embassy here, though everyone seems to assume that he's Our Man in Harare. But not for much longer — barely three months into a three-year posting, he's about to leave.

We have been doing our best to assist him work his way through the last of his good South African wine. Toward the end of one hard-drinking evening, recently, Brandon suddenly roused himself from the torpor of his fireside armchair to announce that he'd had an interpretational epiphany.

"I've got it!" he said. "It's C. S. Lewis. We're living in Narnia, and Morgan Tsvangirai is Aslan!" And he fell back into the creased leather depth of his armchair, while we considered this.

Some see Aslan, the talking lion, king of the beasts, as a Christ figure—after all, he is resurrected, and returns to free Narnia. Aslan is also the son of the Emperor over the Sea, a distant but powerful authority over Narnia—as such, an unsettling echo of Mugabe's taunts that Tsvangirai is a mere puppet for British neo-imperial interests. Though C. S. Lewis was at pains to say that Aslan, notwithstanding his generally peaceable disposition, was "not a tame lion."

In Brandon's version of the allegory, Mugabe would have to be Jadis, the White Witch, who freezes Narnia into a hundred-year winter. Only seventy to go, then? It's a dispiriting prospect.

Brandon recharged our glasses.

"*In vino, veritas?*" I toasted bitterly.

"What?" said Georgina.

"In claret, clarity?" I ventured.

"It's pinotage," said Brandon, drily, and wandered off down the gloomy corridor of the empty house, perhaps to pen an encrypted chronicle of his own to Vauxhall Bridge Road, lionizing the opposition leader and extending ice-queen Mugabe's winter of our discontent.

TONIGHT IS his farewell party.

Polly, his wife, and their daughters (eleven-year-old twins and a nine-year-old), and their eighteen-month-old son have already gone. Brandon is packing up the house before he too will return to the UK.

Their premature departure was triggered at 3 a.m. one night, not long after their arrival, when his wife awoke to find four large men standing over them, stripped to the waist, their shirts tied around their mouths and noses to mask their identities. The men were armed with sharpened crowbars and pipe wrenches with which they had peeled back the iron burglar-bars. They ripped his wife's rings off, and she was terrified she would be raped (one of the burglars sported a prominent erection) or, worse, that their daughters would be. So they cooperated. The men allowed Brandon to pull on his pajamas, and then force-marched him to unlock the safe.

"We are doing this because we cannot feed our wives and families," one of them said.

But they were disciplined and confident, and of military bearing. And they had managed to evade the house security, the electric fences, and the guards, and they seemed to know the layout of the house.

They took U.S.$2,000 from the safe and jewelery worth much more, leaving Brandon and his wife bound on the bed, but the kids undisturbed. After they had gone Brandon turned to his wife and, with admirable sang-froid, declared, "Well, I think that went rather *well,* considering." And she concurred. They had got off lightly. But after that she could no longer sleep at night, and the kids were terrified.

AT TONIGHT'S PARTY, I find myself talking to a rather corpulent black man in a clerical collar. Because my head is bursting with the torture stories, and because I assume that as a churchman he should be particularly appalled by man's inhumanity, I let the stories tumble out of me. But it becomes apparent that he's growing distinctly uncomfortable with this conversation; he's glancing around for rescue. Georgina has been outside, still trying to make calls requested by the people we've met in Dandaro, telling their relatives where they are. When she approaches, I introduce her.

"Yes, I can see you are related," he observes. "You have the same nose—the same frying pan, as they say."

As he says this, she discreetly tugs my sleeve.

"You know who he is, right?"

"Well, obviously a priest, but I didn't quite catch his name," I admit. "Something vaguely Cuban, I think. Fidel?"

"Father Fidelis," she says. "You know, Fidelis *Mukonori?*"

The realization seeps into me. The man I have been hectoring about Mugabe's torture camps is the head of the Jesuit Order in Zimbabwe; but more importantly, he's Robert Mugabe's personal chaplain and spiritual adviser.

"Well, one hears these allegations of abuses, generally," he is saying now, taking advantage of my shocked pause, and waving his hand in airy dismissal. "But one is not sure if they're true, really, of the details, or just exaggerations. Anyway, I've been away for the last three months, in Rome, helping to elect a new Jesuit Superior-General. He's the head of the Jesuits worldwide, you know, heir to St. Ignatius."

Warming to this new and much safer topic, Mukonori tells me that the Jesuit chief is called the "black pope," not because of his skin though, he quickly qualifies, but because of the color of his cassock. Laughter rumbles up from his belly. The General Congregation of Jesuits, two hundred and seventeen of them from all over the world, including himself, gathered in Borgo Santo Spirito, the order's headquarters in Rome, for several days of prayer and what they call in Latin *murmuratio,* the murmurings. During these discussions canvassing is forbidden; in fact anyone who shows even a flicker of desire for the top job, "the crime of ambition," must be ruled out. Then the vote is held by secret ballot.

While he talks, I am trying to weigh up the risk of further exposing my presence in Zimbabwe against the potential reward of getting Mugabe's spiritual trainer undeniable, first-hand exposure to the bloodied victims of his President's policies.

Once elected, the delegates all drop to their knees and kiss the new general's hand, Fidelis continues. He holds office for life, and can only be removed by the General Congregation, convened by the general's five "assistants." Apparently, this has only happened once, in 1664, when Goswin Nickel SJ, a German General, was removed because he sank into senility.

"Come with me tomorrow and I'll walk you through the wards," I find myself saying, cutting across his continuing explanation of the arcane traditions of Jesuit leadership. "You can talk directly to those who have been tortured. You'll get all the details first hand." Mukonori starts to dissemble—he is busy tomorrow, and the following days, with many pressing commitments. But I kept insisting, and finally he agrees, more to get rid of me than anything else.

THE NEXT DAY we go to the races with Heinrich and Amanda, and their son Christof. Borrowdale Racecourse has limped on, through all of Zimbabwe's crazy decline, though with a vastly reduced field. And the sea of faces that once lined the stands and queued at the Tote to wager is now reduced to small knots of people, few of them betting—what's the point when the currency of your winnings is almost worthless. From here you get a view of the city skyline which could foster the illusion that it's still a dynamic, confident place, a view of course that melts like a mirage as you actually enter it. Neighboring the racetrack is Pockets Hill, home of the Zimbabwe Broadcasting Corporation (ZBC), marked by a looming aerial that pumps out Mugabe's toxic views to the city's townships and out across most of the country, radiating a message of hate and revenge.

Upstairs in the Members' Enclosure of the racecourse, the hard-core remnants of the equine fraternity gather in a room lined with photographs of old racing triumphs. They surge to the balcony to watch the latest race gallop by. Dandaro is barely a quarter of a mile from here. Dandaro where Dombo lies, with his broken legs and arms, and Gandanga with his blood-bloated legs that were run over repeatedly by a CIO truck, and Norest, the angry welts of the whip still ridging his back and legs, Tendai, lying on his front as the deep lacerations on his buttocks suppurate into the gauze dressing. That is what's so bizarre about this place. That even as the violence goes on, there is somehow an illusion of normality, a tuning-out of the awfulness that surrounds us, just as surely as the airwaves above us thrum with ZBC's malign message. Yet here people are placing bets on horses, and drinking bad sparkling wine. That, I suppose, is the genius of the human condition, its ability to adapt, even to the most extreme situations.

AT THE TIME THAT Father Fidelis has notionally promised to come to see for himself, Georgina and I return to Dandaro. The duty nurse hustles us in—there have been CIO agents around earlier, she says nervously, and we do our rounds, delivering the scrounged items that have been requested, a pair of shorts here, flip-flops there, air time for a cell phone. Dombo has asked for more books—he's consumed *Kidnapped,* and is ready now, I think, for some C. S. Lewis. Fidelis's appointed time comes and goes, and from the business card he's given me I start to call him on his various numbers, but his cell is switched off and his land line goes unanswered. I am unsurprised.

Dombo and I are discussing C. S. Lewis when there is a gentle knock at his door, and a shocked nurse shows in Fidelis, his large presence filling up the little ward. I can't believe he's here. I clasp his hands. "Thank you for coming, thank you so much."

I introduce him to Dombo, who recounts his story, and we move him round the wards of the torture victims. Dandaro is full of them. At the end Fidelis's smooth, plump face has sagged, and his twinkling eyes have dulled. Now Fidelis knows there's no denying what has been happening here, that this is real, the savagery of it all. And he knows that I know that he knows.

There really is no middle ground here any longer—especially for a man of the cloth. Moral choices must be made.

"Can you do something?" I ask. "Can you talk to the President?"

"I'll definitely get the message up the line," he promises.

Even as he promises, I'm aware of the absurdity of it all, my request and his promise. It's the President who has unleashed this wave of terror—of *course* he knows it's going on, even if he leaves the details to underlings and never gets his own hands soiled.

"How will this all end?" I ask.

Fidelis suddenly softens. He sighs and smoothes his large palm over his face.

"The old man is tired," he says. "He wants to go, but there are others around him who will not let him step down. There are peace initiatives going on as we speak. I think it will be fine."

He shakes my hand and turns away. And as his footfall clacks down the parquet corridor and the hospital doors swing shut behind him, I know in my bones that it won't be. It won't be fine at all.

twelve

What Fear Smells Like

THE OFFICES OF THE Counseling Services Unit (CSU) occupy two floors of a low brown face-brick building on a dusty side road uncomfortably close to ZANU's crowing tower block. Its unmarked door is covered by a heavy metal security cage, but it is still terribly exposed. CSU is the main clearing house for the injured and traumatized, for the victims of Mugabe's political violence and torture. If they can make their way into Harare, this is where they'll end up.

Beneath a sagging CSU banner, a roiling storm cloud with an improbable ray of sunshine piercing it, and the motto "Rehabilitation, Empowerment, Growth," the waiting room is teeming. No sooner have its occupants been taken to clinics, hospitals, or shelters than new ones limp in, many still in shock, seriously injured. The country's state hospitals have all collapsed. They have no drugs, little working equipment, sporadic power. And their doctors are on strike. Hyperinflation has eroded their average salary to just U.S.$10 a month. In any case, most of the people huddled in CSU's waiting room are too afraid to go to any government-run institution after their treatment by Mugabe's men.

The scene here reminds me of the huge canvas that my mother once showed me in London, hanging on the wall by the great staircase of the hospital at which she trained, St. Bartholomew's. It is called *The Pool of Bethesda,* after the biblical scene, and its painter, William Hogarth, modeled it on real patients, a vast scene of the suffering, the groaning sick, the lame and wounded, all pleading for help.

In this CSU Bethesda, some are in casts, some swathed in bandages, some with eye patches, slings, crutches. The place smells of wood smoke and sweat, dust and urine, and blood. This is what fear smells like.

Donnard Gambezi, fifty-one, from Mudzi, sits on an old sofa with his wife. He has on his best straw hat, bright blue work jacket, padded white athletic socks and slippers, these last two from the charity box, as he fled without shoes. His grizzled jaw rests heavily in his hand, his eyes the angry red of the unslept. He is an MDC polling agent for the Bangauya Ward, whose job it was to make sure there were no voting irregularities there. He found irregularities, all right: sixty Mugabe supporters stormed his house. "They said, 'We want your X for ZANU-PF but you have put it for MDC, so now we've come to beat you and destroy you and your family.'" And they did just that. "They beat me in shifts with batons and sticks, took me to their base and beat me some more until I couldn't walk or even sit." When he was finally released, he says, "I walked for three days to get to Harare, sleeping in the bush at night."

The man next to him (who is too afraid to be named) is an MDC official from Mt Darwin. There they were attacked by six hundred Mugabe supporters, taken to Mukumbura base.

Another man groaning on the floor says, "The veterans came with AK-47s, they tied me with wire, here." He points at his crotch.

"*Mboro* [penis]?" I ask.

"Uh uh." He shakes his head.

"*Machende* [testicles]?"

"Yes." He nods, and tells me they tied his balls with wire, and yanked the wire to pull him around, until he fainted from the pain.

After he and his group finally escaped, they tried to cross the border into Mozambique, "but the Mozambique soldiers said, 'We don't want you,' and they threw us back. So we walked, all the way to Harare, during the nights. Others of us are still hiding in the bush even now."

Thomas Kanodzimbira, thirty, sits on the floor, cross-legged. He still has a shunt needle in his arm from a drip. "They wanted eight of us, who had started the MDC in Dande. They said they would take our wives, so we are worried," he tells me. "They hit us with sticks, *matombo,* stones, sjamboks, barbed wire. Even the ZANU-PF councillors and local MP were doing it to us. They said, 'You are the ones who are causing our President to be defeated.'... They took all of our grain, our goats, our plows, so our families have nothing to eat."

No one was spared the violence. Not the women, not the children, not the elderly. Kanodzimbira is particularly incensed at the treatment of his father, who is well into his eighties, and should be venerated in the Shona tradition that pays enormous respect to the elderly. "My father worked for the Salvation Army for sixty years," he says, "yet they came and beat him too, even though he is not political. They said to him, 'You are the one that borned these MDC people.'" He shakes his head angrily.

The young woman next to him, too scared to give her name, says that when they came for her, she and her family ran into the bush and hid there for three days and nights, without food, and on their return, they found that their houses were burned down and their cattle had been stolen.

The stories flow raw and unmediated. Another polling agent, Takawira Chamauya, twenty-eight, from Masvingo Central, where the MDC won, now has a broken arm and leg. "A group of twenty-five war vets led by Eliah Mugabazi, armed with sticks and bayonets, said to us, 'You have sold your "X" to the opposition and now you will pay for it.'

"First, they destroyed the thatching of all our houses, so when it rains our families have no shelter. They beat us there and then took us to Chedenje Dam, where they have a base. There were many of us MDC prisoners, taken there to be 're-educated,' they said. One of us, Zvidzai Mapurisa, just a young guy, a member of MDC youth, they beat him, pushed his head into the water, beat him again, pushed him back into the water, on and on and on like that for hours, until finally, he died. They were happy then, Mugabe's people, they danced around and sang that they had killed an MDC member. We reported it to the Muchakata police post but they did nothing, just took the body away."

Like many others, they are waiting for operations to set their limbs, and then they will have little option but to return home. Even though they are scared, they have nowhere else to go.

"What if there is a re-run?" I ask.

"We're no longer interested in doing that job for now," Takawira says vehemently, "because there is no protection — from the MDC leadership or from the police."

OWEN MACHISA, thirty-four, is here with his wife, Fungai, and their young kids, Bright, who's seven, and Felix, four, who have fallen asleep on their laps. Owen is MDC secretary of Hurungwe West. He had been working as a tree-feller in South Africa but he came back especially to participate in the elections, because, he says, he believed in democracy.

He doesn't anymore.

"First the soldiers came and threatened us, saying all MDC people would be attacked." So as a precaution, Owen and his family retreated into the bush. Sure enough, Mugabe's supporters came and torched their homestead, a small cluster of huts. Owen and his family waited in the bush, but after a few hours he concluded that the attack was over, and that it was safe to return. He and Fungai salvaged what they could and started clearing up the charred chaos. Owen was relieved to find that his most precious possession, his chainsaw, had been overlooked and was still intact. At nightfall, they settled down to a restless sleep in their roofless hut.

But at 10 p.m. Mugabe's men suddenly attacked again and the Machisas ran for their lives for the second time in a day. This time, the mob found Owen's chainsaw, swaddled in its blanket, and they poured the petrol from its tank over the huts and set fire to them once more. This time, boosted by the petrol, the fires burned fiercely, the flames leaping high into the darkness of the Hurungwe night, a malign beacon of revenge, flickering on the terrified faces of Owen and Fungai, Bright and Felix, as they watched from their hiding place in the bush.

Soon all that was left were circular charred rims on the ground, to mark the place that had been the Machisas' homestead. "Our home and all our belongings were destroyed," says Owen. "And my chainsaw, they...they stole it." He finally chokes up. "You know I am a tree-feller, that's how I made a living. Now I am *nothing*."

The chainsaw is the tool he needs to provide for his family; it represents to him the possibility of starting again. Now that it is gone, he can see no future. He becomes nearly hysterical, incoherent. "Better my wife goes back home with the children, even if only to die there—they have no money, no food, no clothes."

Fungai doesn't seem to register this dire forecast. She stares down at the scruffy carpet by her feet. Her eyes are blank. She is clearly still in shock.

Owen hugs the kids closer to him. "Better for these ones if I die myself," he howls, as the two little boys, awake now, look up at him, anxious and upset themselves, at his distress. "They are now outcast, they are labeled MDC children."

Watching Machisa dissolve is Anna Kadurira, a beautiful eighteen-year-old girl, with the smooth complexion of a burnished acorn. She is dressed in a pink sleeveless blouse and white plaster cast, and like Fungai, she also has that thousand-mile stare. I point at her cast and before I can ask, she murmurs in a low, flat voice that when they beat her buttocks with logs, "it was so painful, I put my arm back there to protect myself, and my arm, it got broken."

She pauses and looks at me for the first time, before continuing.

"While they were beating me they kept shouting, 'You want to sell the country to the white people.'"

As we speak, many are painstakingly filling out Victim Report forms, helped by CSU staff. And new groups keep appearing, knots of red-eyed, traumatized people who have traveled miles and miles over many days, dragging black plastic bin bags containing what meager remnants they have managed to salvage, a little maize meal, blankets, plastic bottles of cooking oil, chipped enamel plates, cheap Chinese umbrellas, all that remains of their broken lives.

THE SECURITY CAGE rattles again and two disheveled little boys, Trymore and Francis Zondo, five and seven years old, with dusty bare feet, pad in out of the dark, trailing their grandmother, Esther Dewe. Trymore holds a bloody rag over the bridge of his nose. Francis, his older brother, in a blue jacket too big for him, has a grubby, red-stained bandage loosely bound around his head. It keeps falling down over his eyes, to reveal an angry gash beneath.

They were asleep at midnight when their house was attacked by a gang of Mugabe's militia. The boys' faces were cut by shards of glass that burst down on them as their bedroom windows shattered. "Then they threw burning grass through the broken windows to smoke us out," says Esther, and she shrugs hopelessly.

The two little boys share an office chair, huddling together under the flickering glare of the neon strip light, bewildered and homeless and exhausted, watching their *gogo* do her best to answer the questions from a CSU staff member, who is filling out their victim reports. Finally, the exhausted boys doze off, right there on the office desk, their heads resting upon their thin forearms.

IF YOU LOOK at the patterns of the violence, says Dr. Frances Lovemore, CSU's medical director, in her office on the second floor, it's mostly in Mugabe's strongholds, to get rid of people who, they say, betrayed them.

She looks up at a wall map, which has pins in it, color-coded for the kind of abuse. There is a thicket in the northeast, and another one west of Harare, but there are pins across the entire country now, as the pace of the attacks accelerates.

"Ugh, there's that rat again." She lifts her feet onto the table as a large brown rodent scurries across the carpet and behind the desk. In the last few days CSU has seen seven hundred victims, which she believes is less than a tenth of the total in this catchment. The others are too scared to travel, and don't want to leave their land in case they lose it forever.

"Of those we see, we try to get them to lawyers, to prepare legal and medical affidavits, but we're overstretched. We can prove systematic torture during this post-election period. Justice is essential, so there need to be reparations and redress."

Frances uses a phrase I've started to hear: "smart genocide," a grotesque science that Mugabe is apparently honing. There's no need to directly kill hundreds of thousands, if you can select and kill the right few thousand. Is this really a "refining" of genocide? As Stanislaw Lec, a Polish-Jewish poet, once wondered, "Is it progress if a cannibal uses a knife and fork?"

Some call what is happening here "politicide." As genocide is an attempt to wipe out an ethnic group, so politicide is the practice of wiping out an entire political movement (and Mugabe had done this before, of course, when he shattered ZAPU, by siccing his troops on their office bearers, during Gukurahundi).

And now the murders here are accompanied by torture and rape on an industrial scale, committed on a catch-and-release basis. When those who survive, terribly injured, limp home, or are carried or pushed in wheelbarrows, or on the backs of pickup trucks, they act like human billboards, advertising the appalling consequences of opposition to the tyranny, bearing their gruesome political stigmata. And in their home communities, their return causes ripples of anxiety to spread. The people have given this time of violence and suffering its own name, which I hear for the first time tonight. They are calling it *chidudu*. It means, simply, "The Fear."

I ask Frances how she's coping herself, and this gives her pause. She's been too busy to consider it before. Angry, she says. She's really angry at what is being done to these people. Then she briskly changes the subject. But just before I leave, the tone of her voice softens. "It's strange you know, I haven't cried," she says. "Not once, through this whole thing."

She has a look I recognize. Georgie du Plessis, the CSU nurse, has it too, a closed-off look, the one that says you can't afford to get too emotionally involved, because there is too much to do. I recognize it because my mother had that look for twenty-five years.

thirteen

Dreamland

A S W E W A I T F O R the official results of the presidential elections, and Mugabe's men rain down violence on the land, Harare's International Festival of the Arts, HIFA, begins on 29 April. For Manuel Bagorro, a fellow alumnus of St. George's, and the founding director (with some help from Georgina), each festival is an excruciating navigation between the siren of free expression and the rock of Mugabe's censors, who will close him down if they deem the festival subversive.

If he keeps it too safe, Manuel risks playing window-dresser to the dictator. Some Zimbabweans, like my architect friends the Beatties, boycott the entire festival, believing it helps give a spurious sheen of cultural tolerance to a violent and deeply repressive regime. If Manuel stages shows too critical of Mugabe, he will endanger the whole festival, but he has nudged the limits in the past.

His last festival here was entitled *Showtime;* he intended the double entendre to mean it was time to show what was happening in Zimbabwe. And the South African director, Brett Bailey, devised an opening production that included actors being beaten by the band's backing singers, the "Sequel Police," the number "Talkin' Bout a Revolution" by Tracy Chapman, and a parody of "Ol' MacDonald Had a Farm," in which a white farmer who had recently been evicted and jambanja'd shuffled across the stage, playing the role of the white farmer who had recently been evicted and jambanja'd. At the National Gallery next door, where some of the performances are held, the gallery director, Heeton Bhagat, turned the permanent collection to face the wall, and displayed instead a huge installation of Victoria Falls made entirely of worthless Zimbabwe dollar bills pouring over the brink.

The whole enterprise reminds me of my days reporting in Eastern Europe before the Berlin Wall came down, as dissidents probed repressive communist regimes, searching for critical space. Just as it was in Eastern Europe, artistic attack here has to be allegorical and implied.

Bagorro is required to submit scripts in advance, where they are reviewed by Mugabe's CIO, the organization that employs Joseph Mwale. And CIO agents mingle with the crowds here to monitor the event. Maria Wilson, the Executive Director of HIFA, had a running feud last festival with the CIO field officer in charge of spying on the event. He was boorish, drank too much, threw his weight around, and annoyed people, she said, and told him so. At the end of the week, he came to bid her farewell. "Bye, darling," he said, and, "mwah, mwah," air-kissed her on both cheeks. "You see," he said proudly, "I've learned to fit in." A week of thespian company had turned him into a theater lovey—a rare instance of reverse Stockholm syndrome.

This year's festival is called *The Art of Determination,* and its logo is designed around a large X, symbolizing the vote, which is still being "counted." I find it hard to attend. The principal venues are in Harare's main park, just a couple of miles from Dandaro clinic with its wards of wounded. But Manuel urges me at least to see the opening show, *Dreamland*—which will be performed only once. Written again by Brett Bailey, it is choreographed by a fellow South African, Sbonakaliso Ndaba.

Throughout the performance of *Dreamland,* fragments from

Zimbabweans' dreams are projected on a huge screen behind the stage. These have been collected by the drama therapist Paula King-will, in a series of dream workshops she held among Zimbabweans of all walks of life. They reflect the terrain of terror and anxiety inhabited by this nation, even as they sleep:

> "There was a maze in the living room. Tanks and bombs and those vine things that when you touch them your hands start bleeding until you can see your bones in your hands."
> Nyaradzo, 10 years old, schoolboy

> "I dreamed that there was war. I raised my son in my arms to cover him and protect him from all these cockroaches. People being torn to death, dying and being shot at."
> "Twister," 30 years old, poet

> "I dreamed that a girl drowned at the swimming competition. The coach said, 'Forget about her,' and the swimming pool filled with blood."
> Priska, 13 years old, orphan

> "I was pushing a wheelbarrow with a dead body in it. I was being followed by soldiers. I started to dig a hole. It was so deep I couldn't see the bottom. The ground started to crumble into the hole. Suddenly a branch appeared. I grabbed it."
> Rutendo, 24 years old, insurance broker

> "My house was being blown by fire and then there was nothing. I was crying, 'Oh! We are buried! We have nothing! Where will we stay?' Later I became a bird and I saw there was blue water all around."
> Deborah, 42 years old, torture survivor

DREAMLAND is performed on the outdoor stage in Harare Gardens, surrounded by bamboo groves and ilala palms. The tiered bleachers are full to their eight thousand capacity, and more people sit on the lawns.

It opens with a hundred performers, all in striped, old-fashioned prison pajamas, who enter the stage and are knocked into sleep by a tremendous crack of sound. Behind them, the screen dissolves into a huge X—the mark of the vote. A larger-than-life, grotesque figure, the tyrant king, with a bloated, blood-red mask, glistening wetly in the klieg lights, and a white vinyl military uniform (previously worn by Idi Amin in Bailey's play *Big Dada*) drags his cello to the end of a lonely ramp that juts out into the audience.

"*A long time ago, in a beautiful land far from here,*" intones the narrator, and we all know he means Zimbabwe, "*there lived a king who had bewitched his people.*

"*This king loved music. He played from morning till late at night.*"

The king begins to scrape at his swollen cello.

"*There was a time when everybody had music, and the land was full of song.*"

The choirs, in their prison-striped pajamas, begin in turn to burst into song. The first starts "Blame It on the Boogie." Another sings "Senzeni Na?" ["What Have We Done (Wrong)?"], the haunting liberation lament. A third launches into "Nkosi Sikelela" ["God Bless Africa"], the renowned anti-apartheid anthem. But as each choir starts to sing, it is quickly beaten down by baton-wielding, Darth Vader–helmeted "hyenas" in military fatigues, until the terrified choir members vomit votes into ballot boxes, and each in turn falls into a trance.

In the advance script, the version sent to the censors at the President's Office, Bailey had called the nefarious enforcers "hyenas," but we all know they represent Mugabe's riot police.

"*And many of those with the best voices simply went away,*" continues the narrator, against a backdrop of migrating birds, to represent Zimbabwe's swelling diaspora. "*The king swallowed the songs of all his people. And the only sound to be heard in that beautiful land was the drone of the king's voice.*"

The king boogies in a stiff-limbed, octogenarian's shuffle, as he sings "I Never Can Say Goodbye," while on the screen behind there flashes up Heeten Bhagat's neon-tinged video of bulldozers demolishing townships during Mugabe's bogus slum clearance, Operation Murambatsvina, "Clear Out the Dirt."

> *"But in that time, there were songs that the King could not*
> *reach.*
> *These were the people's most precious songs:*
> *The songs they sang in their dreams...*
> *In the dry valleys of Dreamland, the silent choirs sang their*
> *songs:*
> *The battered men in forgotten jails.*
> *The broken women on foreign soils.*
> *Families resting in unmarked graves.*
> *The hungry, the lost, the landless.*
> *And their songs rose like thunderclouds over the*
> *land."*

A choir of young children, between five and ten years old (clasping their bedtime teddy bears), begins to sing "Somewhere Over the Rainbow" in pure, piping voices. Mugabe's sinister hyena men come up behind them and, one by one, pull rough red bags over their heads, and haul the kids offstage, until there is only one little girl left. She starts the last line but never reaches the end. She too is abruptly bagged and dragged offstage.

All around me, in the packed open-air arena, the Zimbabwean audience weep for their country. I see Frances Lovemore, her face wet with tears. It is the first time, in all her dealings with the wounded and the dispossessed, that she has allowed herself this luxury, the first time that she has let herself cry.

The show ends with a German counter-tenor, Daniel Lager, singing "Pie Jesu" (Andrew Lloyd-Webber's motet, based on the last two lines of the medieval poem *Dies Irae*, Day of Wrath—Judgment Day, used in the old Catholic requiem mass) against a screen filled with blood-soaked hands, and scenes of violence from Rwanda and the Congo.

And then, in an effort to provide a rousing finale, Zimbabwean performers appear: the dance troupe Tumbuka; Thomas Mapfumo singing his old Chimurenga song "Mhondoro," invoking the ancestral spirits to save the nation; and Comrade Fatso, a slam poet, urging Zimbabweans to "rise up." But with so many freshly bloodied themselves from trying to do just that, tonight, I'm afraid. We are all afraid.

fourteen

You Can Never Go Home Again

GEORGINA WANTS to go home. Well, she wants to visit the places she still thinks of as home, starting with her little stone cottage, a converted stable, on Summerfield Close, in northern Harare. The house is at the bottom end of her ex-parents-in-laws' property, but they have left the country too now, and put the whole place up for sale. *Sungura* music blares from the big house on the hill; goatskins are pegged out on the lawn to cure; maize cobs dry on the veranda. The cage inhabited by a golden pheasant that Georgina called Terry Waite, because it had been in captivity so long, is now occupied by a brace of fluffy white rabbits being bred for the pot. The swimming pool is almost empty, vines growing down into it. The trampoline frame is vacant, its drooping springs rusty. Through the dirty windows of the big house, we see the gold-plated wall sconces and dusty chandeliers, and the carpet faded in the shape of the absent grand piano.

We walk across the overgrown lawn, littered with pine cones. The wooden slats of the fence around the cottage are broken, the palm tree has collapsed against the side of the house, and the thatch has shredded, patched now by black plastic weighted down with rocks. In the new extension that Georgina had built, the kelp-green paint is peeling off the corrugated-tin roof, and voracious bamboo shoots are growing into it.

Georgina goes over to the tall teak drum that serves as the door bell. She beats it, to see if anyone is around. But the brittle drumskin is ruptured and it gives out only a thin, weak thump.

While we wait, Georgina runs her hands over the intricately carved Zanzibari front door. "We found it in the capital, Stone Town. I went there for Christmas with Jeremy," she says, and suddenly she grins. "We wanted to visit the birthplace of Freddie Mercury. Our hotel was dry, and it had a Christmas tree operated by motion sensors that sang 'Jingle Bells' every time you walked past."

No one comes to the feeble beat of the drum so we walk round the side of the cottage and duck into the home-made greenhouse. Its torn plastic sheeting luffs against the creosoted log frame. The delicate orchids are dead now, but the elephant ears have run amok, filling out the whole space, pressing against the ripped plastic walls as though to liberate themselves from the constraints of the conservatory. Getting down on our hands and knees, we start to brush away the dust and leaves from the bright Gaudíesque mosaic floor that Georgina created from shards of tile, interspersed with family mementos: an old watch of Dad's and his old tortoiseshell comb; bits of broken floral crockery; frames from Jain's sunglasses; miniature perfume bottles; shells from Mozambique; old keys to forgotten locks; bits of broken jewelery (some of which Georgina notices have been dug out of the floor); a magnetic medallion of St. Christopher, patron saint of travelers, that my mother used to put on the dashboard of her Mini as she drove on her rounds in the tribal reserves; Georgina's first toothbrush; the bell from her first bike; a horseshoe from her chestnut pony, Top Ace; family handprints; and paw prints from Spot and Boy, Georgina's Dalmatians. And the date, 19/05/1998. It is like a family album in the floor, a sentimental map of her identity.

Georgina runs her finger over Boy's paw print. "He died in

Edmond's arms, after we had gone," she says. Taking the hem of her skirt, she starts to polish part of a broken mirror sealed into the mosaic. "I hoped to mitigate the effects of seven years' bad luck by giving the mirror a purpose," she says. "Don't think it worked…"

Lloyd, the gardener from the big house up on the hill, finds us there and unlocks the cottage. Inside, it is almost empty. In her absence, Georgina's in-laws have auctioned off her furniture, and all that remains now is what didn't sell. A Cape Dutch daybed, and Mum's old kitchen sideboard, which the auctioneer has labeled "This dresser was made in 1847 — came up with the Moodie Trek," a lie.

We peer through the window into Georgina's office, which is now occupied by an unofficial tenant. "Her name is Pestilence," says Lloyd. Pestilence is meticulously neat. A little iron bed, a tiny TV on a box. A faded Toulouse Lautrec print on the wall.

"I'm glad it's being used," says Georgina. She wants to go to the shed where her remaining belongings have been stored, so Lloyd pushes his way past the giant banana fronds, through the waist-high grass. It grows up through the abandoned wrought-iron garden furniture.

"Are there *nyokas* [snakes] here?" Georgina asks nervously, eying the overgrown desolation.

"Ah, no," laughs Lloyd. "Now that the big dogs are no longer here, cats are not afraid so they come and kill the rats and then snakes have nothing to eat. Snakes and cats are enemies, you see." Lloyd seems understandably relieved the tan Ridgebacks have gone. They were the ones that the madam used to sic on him so they didn't lose their fear of blacks.

The shed door is locked but it has been substantially eaten away by white ants. Lloyd gives it a gentle shove and it disintegrates in a shower of sawdust. Inside there is tack for Top Ace, Georgina's old riding boots, her acting awards and drama-college photos, dark-room equipment, and her daughter Xanthe's *Mary Poppins*–style baby carriage — an original Silver Cross. She starts to tear up and we go outside.

"Well, the placenta tree's still standing," says Georgina, looking up at the head-high red mahogany she planted on Xanthe's afterbirth.

"We had built our little dream house, and I was desperate to put down roots here. I thought I was married for life, and I wanted Xanthe to look at her tree at twenty-one. I thought I was here forever. And I wanted to give her roots too." She laughs.

"Rather too literally, perhaps."

Turning to Lloyd, she explains the mahogany's significance.

"I will take good care of it, medem," he promises, and gives the tree a reverent little pat.

Edmond, who was the housekeeper and generally managed the place, isn't here today. "He is gone to church," says Lloyd.

So we get back into the car and drive slowly away in silence.

THE SUN HAS gone now, dropping behind Heroes' Acre, and the unlit city quickly sinks into crepuscular gloom. On Ridgeway North, Georgina gives a shout to stop the car. She has spotted Edmond walking back from church. He is easy to recognize, even in the gloaming, because he and his wife, Precious, are both dressed in Mum's hand-me-down white doctor's coats, which they use in lieu of the white robes worn by the vaPostori, one of the African Initiated Churches. Edmond carries their new baby, whom they have named Memory.

"Because life was better before," he says.

Precious and Memory have just returned from their tribal home out in Mt Darwin. "Ah, it was terrible there," she says, keeping her voice low, even though we are alone in the dark at the side of the road. "At each roadblock our bus was stopped and we were forced to get down and shout slogans for Mugabe before we could pass. And there are torture camps there too. Our chief was asked to provide names of all those who were MDC supporters in his area, but he said he didn't know. So groups from outside came in, burning houses, cutting cattle's legs, destroying grain stores and dragging people to the torture camps. People were having their wrists and knuckles crushed there."

* * *

THAT NIGHT I CAN'T SLEEP. In the morning we are to return to St. Aubins Walk, our family home for twenty-five years. It's the last place I saw my father alive. Even as I was hugging him, and we were promising each other that we'd meet soon, I remember thinking, I'm never going to see you again.

I find it hard to go back too, in the knowledge that we let the house—my mother's only asset—go for next to nothing. When she sold it, the money, principally in Zimbabwe dollars, went into an escrow account while my father's estate was wound up. And there it sat for nearly a year, apparently because a clerk of court wanted a U.S.$10 bribe to release it. By the time I realized what was happening and went out to Zimbabwe, it had been so massively eroded by hyperinflation that it was worth almost nothing, less than the cost of an economy-class flight from London. Now I lie awake, listening to the nightjars trill, and alternating between sadness and frustration at it all.

I am looking forward to seeing Gomo again, my parents' housekeeper. The last time I was here, I worked with him and Richard, the young gardener, for four days straight, emptying the house of two generations of our stuff, dividing it between things to go to London, to my mother and sister, and things to come to me in New York. Anything that didn't make the cut, which was the bulk of it, I gave to Gomo and Richard. On a big bonfire in the garden, we burned papers, decades of my father's meticulous bills, and receipts, and admin, dealing with amounts that now seem archaic, before it metastasized uncontrollably into its multiple zeros.

IN THE MORNING, Richard lets us in at the gate. After we greet he tells me that the new owners are away and the house is locked. I ask him where Gomo is. He looks at me strangely.

"Ah, he is gone, Mr. Peter." Richard casts his eyes down at the lawn. "He is . . . dead, since last year."

I can't believe it. Gomo died and no one told me. My father had relied on him increasingly as he had declined himself. Softly spoken and gentle, smiling and reliable. His wife had died some years before.

"He became sick," says Richard. "His girlfriend, she was sick too, and she died first." He lowers his voice. "I think she made him sick with the AIDS. He told me, 'I am going home now because there is no one to look after me here.' He reached home in Mt Darwin on Monday. And by Friday, he was dead.

"Even me, I get very lonely now, because I remember the way we all used to live, doing this and that, staying all together here, looking after the medem. It's now dark days."

Richard has returned yesterday from his home in Mudzi, visiting his three young children, and he is still shaken by the experience. "Each family must give a bucket of mealie meal and Z$50m for the soldiers who are coming there. The chief collects the moneys to buy goats for the soldiers to eat. They say they are providing security to prevent massacres, yet *they* are ones hunting us."

He reaches into his pocket and brings out a frayed and tattered letter, unfolding it for me to read. It is an attempted *laisser passer* from his local *sabhuku*, his headman:

> Richard stays in my village. He is going to Kotwa to see his
> brother, who is sick. After that he will proceed to Harare.
> Please don't disturb or harass him or beat him. I am the
> headman, the ZANU-PF secretary of my village.
> Please comrades,
> Pamberi neUnity!
> Pamberi understanding!
> Pasi neMDC!
> How are you comrades?
> I am well.
> Yours, secretary for ZANU-PF
> Headman.

"He is not really ZANU-PF in his heart," says Richard, "but he is afraid of being killed. Most of the headmen and the chiefs do it like that."

I hand the letter back.

"If I don't have this letter," he says, "I will be pulled off the bus, and they will make me disappear for good and I'll never be seen. Those without letters were pulled off the bus, and taken away, to be beaten. They say we are MDC spies. They won't let us bring our families to town. They just burn our kraals and tell us not to come back again."

Fastidiously, Richard folds the headman's letter and replaces it in its envelope, and buttons it securely into his breast pocket, as if it is his own little Schindler's list.

fifteen

Wounds of the Heart

OUR OTHER HOME was in Mhangura in the northwest of the country, on the edge of the Zambezi escarpment. To get there we set out on the old Great North Road. It originates in Cape Town, continues the length of South Africa and up through Zimbabwe. At Harare, it veers west and goes up over the Great Dyke mountain range (a uniquely stratified chrome-rich igneous ridge, over three hundred miles long, visible from space). It winds through the once-productive farming areas of Banket and Chinhoyi, and down through Lions' Den, and Karoi—which means "little witch," so called because it was the site of witch trials by immersion (if you sank you were innocent)—to the Zambezi River at Chirundu, where it crosses into Zambia, with a left fork to Lake Kariba.

A thicket of cardboard placards along the roadside outside Harare bear scrawled messages competing to sell us bait to fish there. *Anaconda worms for sale; Lekker Fishing Worms; Worms Depot, Quality Worms; Red worms of note.* The ones offering Puff Adder Worms and Malawi Worms, Georgina says, are actually selling marijuana.

The district to the left of the road between the towns of Banket and Chinhoyi is Zvimba, Robert Mugabe's heartland. This, in Shona custom, is his *kumusha*—his spiritual home, where his ancestors are buried, where his clan totem, *garwe*, the crocodile, resides. Here, he had his new Chinese friends build him a rural mansion, near his state-of-the-art pig farm. Here, he is building a grandiose shrine to himself. The size of a football field, it will house such mementos as his clothes, copies of his speeches, photos, and letters, and a sixteen-foot crocodile, trapped in Lake Kariba—stuffed and mounted—and presented as a birthday gift last year, by one of his craven cabinet ministers, Webster Shamu, the Minister of Policy Implementation, who said it represented the President's "majestic authority."

The Catholic bishop of this province is Dieter Scholz, a stern, ash-haired German Jesuit who came to this country forty-five years ago. Much of that time he spent at the isolated Marymount mission in Rushinga, on the cusp of the Zambezi valley. It was there he learned to love the dialect of Korekore Shona they call Budya, a haunting, ideophonic tongue, garnished with onomatopoeia. "It's pure poetry," he eulogizes. "But now only the old people speak that deep Shona. The rest speak Shonglish—peppered with English words."

During the civil war, recalls Scholz, "Rushinga was a real hot spot. The whites beat local people, but so did Zanla, and when Zanla killed 'sell-outs,' they refused to let the bodies be buried.

"The roads were land-mined so Father Gregor Stephanz learned to fly. I was his navigator. We rented a Cesna 182 Skywagon from the Mashonaland Flying Club to get in and out."

When Scholz began to work for the Catholic Justice and Peace Commission, monitoring human-rights abuses by the Rhodesian government forces, "they used to tap my phone, but it wasn't very professional. Sometimes when I picked up the receiver, I would hear the recording of my past conversations played back to me, and once when they intercepted our mail, by mistake they put a copy of their intercept in the envelope forwarded to me."

Scholz worked out of Silveira House, the Jesuit headquarters in Harare, named after Dom Gonçalo da Silveira, an early Portuguese Jesuit who ventured into the Zimbabwe hinterland in 1560, establishing the first Christian mission here. Silveira managed to convert the reigning Mwene Mutapa, after the king had become enraptured with his glistening icon of the Virgin Mary, and insisted on hanging it on the wall of the royal hut. Sadly, the following year, the Mwene Mutapa spectacularly backslid, goaded by jealous Swahili gold-traders. He ordered Silveira murdered as a sorcerer. Though he was tipped off, Silveira refused to flee, preferring to meet his fate, and his body was tossed into the Musengezi River that flows through Rushinga, and down into the Zambezi. Scholz's relationship with the current big man describes a similar trajectory.

For Robert Mugabe, says Scholz, "Silveira House was like a home during the war...We employed his two sisters, Brigit and Sabina, to give them an income, to give them work, and above all to give them protection. Robert Mugabe hasn't forgotten that."

Once he took power, "Mugabe went to the cathedral every Sunday. He would kneel throughout, except for the homily, when he sat. And he always took communion."

And when Scholz was consecrated Bishop of Chinhoyi in 2006, Mugabe attended, whisked in by helicopter. He even brought a present.

"After two and a half hours, Mugabe needed to go to the toilet," he recalls of the ceremony. "So he got up from his own little stage and went to his bomb-protected limo, and all his bodyguards trooped around him. And I asked myself, how free is this man? He sits there behind his tinted windows. He has never trusted the people. It didn't have to be this way. I think he is tortured as much as his people, by the life he has to live."

Scholz remembers asking him then, "What would you like to do when you retire?" Somewhat wistfully, Mugabe replied, "Read, write my memoirs, farm..."

But in Easter 2007, when the Catholics finally published *God Hears the Cry of the Oppressed,* a pastoral letter critical of Mugabe's violently repressive rule, relations quickly soured. From then, says Scholz, "our priests were persecuted, threatened, constantly intimidated." Some of them—he has thirty in his Chinhoyi province, twenty-two of them black Zimbabweans—had to flee their parishes. "Lawlessness prevails. If I go to the police, I will be arrested for 'disturbing the peace,'" says Scholz.

"That is another mystery in his life, which I am unable to fathom—how is Mugabe able to reconcile in his conscience his faith and his politics and his actions.

"In a sense, I would say that Robert Mugabe is a prisoner of his own past and he is a prisoner of his own political generation. I see in his character many similarities with Ian Smith—[particularly,] obduracy...

"ZANU has never really changed from a guerrilla movement into a political party. In all elections since the mid-'90s, even when they won, they still assaulted those who voted against them. Mugabe never managed that transition. He's a civilian front for the generals, especially Perence Shiri and Constantine Chiwenga. He's always relied too much on people who bear arms, he has an obsession with security. The generals are running things now. We are living under a military dictatorship."

And once again, Scholz is being monitored by spies.

"CIO agents come and listen to my sermons, to see what I'm saying. Normally I try to explain the gospel. For example, the multiplication of the loaves and fishes lent itself to a sermon on the greed and selfishness of our leaders. But no parishioners will speak out freely unless they are on their own with me. It's the Fear. They all live in fear."

Now, in the rural areas of his province, Kariba, Hurungwe, Rushinga, Dande, "things are really bad. My priests report that people are being brutally beaten. It's like the People's Courts during the war, people are accused of being 'sell-outs,' stripped naked, beaten with planks, forced to shout ZANU-PF slogans, some are beaten until they are dead."

In the months after the elections, says Scholz later (on gloriaTV, a Catholic broadcaster, motto: *the more Catholic the better*), "there was an attempt to physically eliminate the opposition to the ruling party, the MDC, to eliminate that opposition through physical beatings, torture and killings.

"Such cruelty," he muses, "it's a mystery. Anybody who has had difficulty in believing that there is not only evil in the world, but the Evil One who sends out his other evil spirits, as St. Ignatius says in the Spiritual Exercises, the First Week...Ignatius speaks in the images and language of his time, about Lucifer sitting in the great plain of Babylon, on a throne of fire and smoke, calling together all the demons of the world and then sending them out with his instructions to commit evil.

"During those three months...I understood that the images and language in which St. Ignatius spoke in the sixteenth century, they are more real than I had thought. We've seen evil running through the whole country, from north to south and east to west."

How does he keep his faith? He sighs deeply before answering.

"When I'm angry in the evening, I go to the chapel and I pray for my equilibrium to be restored, to let my anger pass. A third-year seminarian, who is to be ordained deacon, comes to me, and says, 'My father was murdered yesterday, sixty-three years old, because they suspected him of being a member of the opposition, which he was not. The militia came and beat him to death in front of his wife.' How can one *not* be angry? And when I phoned the police to report it, they said they could not open a docket because they didn't have a photocopier!

"This is what I mean when I say that the truth will have to come out, the perpetrators will have to be named, they will have to be confronted with their actions and then we can begin with the process of reconciliation, perhaps even of an amnesty.

"There cannot be reconciliation without truth, the truth has to come out, it has to be acknowledged. I think forgiveness has to be asked for, and [only] then, it will be given.

"The wounds of the heart heal much more slowly than the wounds of the body," says Scholz. "I see that now.

"Pray for Zimbabwe," he pleads in farewell. "Pray for peace, pray for the courage of the leaders who lost the elections, to let go."

After lunch around a lazy susan, we set off again, intending to take the spur road at Lions' Den, north to Mhangura, a copper-mining town, where our family once lived. Scholz warns us that there is now a torture base there too.

GEORGINA is reading aloud from our borrowed copy of Dr. Mostert's *Jumbo Guide to Rhodesia 1972*. It tells us that Mhangura is "a thriving township in its own right," with a population of 7,730 including 640 "Europeans." We do a slow, sad lap of the town, past the Ingot Inn, the old single quarters, the town school where Jain once taught. All of it is now decrepit, and the rows of houses are dilapidated. We pass people chopping down the avenues of trees, to use as firewood, as there is no electricity. Soon the town will be entirely deforested.

We pull into the Catholic church, which is just across the road from the police station. But the local priest is nervous to have us there. He confirms that there is a torture base here, to which people are sent from other areas, because Mhangura is so isolated. "Be careful," he warns, as he shuts the door firmly behind us.

We pull in at the Mhangura Mine Club, where we whiled away much of our school holidays. The swimming pool is defunct. In the deep end, the collected rainwater is black and choked with rubbish. Over it still looms the high diving board.

"It used to seem so scary," says Georgina. "Now it looks quite small."

The thatch umbrellas that provided shade over the garden tables have rotted and fallen onto the lawn, and now all that remains are their rusting metal ribs, like the hoops under Victorian skirts.

Georgina is dying to go to the loo, but the stinking toilets in the pool changing rooms are without water. Porcelain basins and cisterns lie shattered on the floor, amidst metal ballcocks and dismembered taps.

As we walk over to look at the overgrown bowling green, two ragged kids amble up, one with a bird's nest in his hands.

"What happened to the pool?" I ask them.

"Ah, it is buggered," says the taller boy. "There is no mains water supply for the town, these days, just a borehole."

"Are there any white people still living here?" I wonder.

"Uh uh," he says. "They ran away, long time back, when the mine closed down."

"What's inside your nest?" inquires Georgina.

He shows it to her. Three hyperventilating baby birds peer from their down-lined sanctuary.

"Did the nest fall down?" she asks.

"No." The boy grins. "We climbed up and pulled it off the tree."

"But now they will die," says Georgina.

The boy shrugs, and they run off, giggling.

"Bastards," she says mildly.

OUR OLD HOUSE is at the top of the hill, by the now defunct reservoir, looking down on the town. The gate lies open. In the driveway stands a very battered pick-up truck, with bald tires, broken lights, no wiper blades. It lists heavily to one side, where its suspension has clearly collapsed.

We knock on the door and call out, but the place seems deserted. The garden is crispy and parched and khaki, and littered with junk. The doorframes are damaged and many of the windows have broken panes, some of them roughly patched with cardboard inserts.

The garage door yawns open; inside are a few bags of fertilizer and other farm supplies.

"Remember your sixteenth birthday?" asks Georgina.

My father had presented me with a gift-wrapped manual for the Suzuki 125 motorbike. When I opened it, he beckoned me to this garage and lifted the door. Across the floor was the motorbike, disassembled into its component parts. "You put it together, it's yours." Dad grinned.

Of course, I threw it together too fast and there were pieces left over at the end. I had to break it down, and start over. But after that,

I knew that motorbike so intimately, literally inside out, that I could always repair it. Which had been his intention all along.

Just as we are about to leave, a woman emerges from the old staff quarters and tells us to wait. Then a man in worn blue fatigues and bare feet comes out to greet us, rubbing his hooded eyes with the backs of his hands, clearly just awoken.

We introduce ourselves and explain that we used to live there, and that we just wanted to see it again, to remind ourselves of our childhood.

"I only work here," he says. "The owner is away. But you can look from the outside."

We walk around the back, and peer into the veranda. The insect screen is in shreds, and great whorls of cobweb drape the many tears.

"It is just as I remember," lies Georgina.

Ahead of us, he is now unlocking the door, and invites us into the gloomy, unlit interior. The ceiling panels are stained from old leaks, and many of them sag. The baths store muddy brown water, and *chigubus,* big plastic containers, line the floor next to them.

"When the mine closed in 2000," he explains, "they had no money. All they offered us was our houses. And soon our pensions became worthless."

"Our father, George Godwin, used to be the chief engineer on the mine," I say.

"Really?" He smiles. "Mr. Godwin," and finally he can contain himself no longer. "That was my job too," he says proudly. "I was also the chief engineer. I was his successor. My name is Paul Shumba. I have my engineering degree from Coventry in England." And he puts out his hand to introduce himself.

Once his job disappeared, Shumba jambanja'd a farm in the nearby Doma area. "You remember the old Erasmus farm?" he says. "That's the one I farm on now. I commute from here. But it's very tough, this farming business. I am finding it hard to make a living. I have to rent this house to tenants, and myself, I live in the *kaya* behind, the workers' quarters."

We continue through the gloomy house together, and in the

sitting room, we come to a wooden room-divider I recognize. "My father made this," I say. Shumba smoothes his hand over its dusty shelves. "It is very well made," he admits, admiring the way its mortises and tenons fit snugly. "Built to last."

And then he looks around at the rest of the house, as though seeing it now through our eyes. "I am sorry about this place," he says, suddenly ashamed. "It is not in good condition."

As we leave, he shakes my hand again. "Next time you come and visit," he promises, "I will try to make it more presentable."

He stands there barefoot, in his torn blue fatigues, on the parched, junk-strewn lawn, as the gathering darkness envelops him, chief engineer Shumba, M.Sc. Eng. (Coventry).

sixteen

Defense Injuries

THE AVENUES CLINIC is where my father died, up there in
that corner ward, with a view westward out over the tops of the
jacaranda trees to Heroes' Acre, while the Salvation Army brass
band played "Abide with Me" in the car park below. It's a private
hospital, so it's still functioning, while state hospitals have ground
to a halt. It has framed pictures of wild animals in the stairwells,
and a receptionist actually answering a phone, and even a news-
agents, off the lobby.

At 6 a.m. sharp, Nurse Georgie du Plessis from CSU starts her
morning rounds, her hardback exercise book stuffed with details of
the patients she needs to check. I follow behind, wearing the generic
clothes of a consultant, with Georgie as my *laisser passer*. No journalists are allowed, on pain of arrest and worse. But it turns out, as I
suspected, that many of these nurses here knew my mother; she
helped train and tend them at the staff health department of Parirenyatwa Hospital. "How is she?" they ask. "How is Dr. Godwin? How

is it in England? Tell her to come home. We need her here. We are so busy with all this trouble."

They ask after Georgina too. "We want to see her on the TV again."

"She was with me here," I tell the nurses, "but she has just gone back to look after my mother." In fact, Georgina has just called to say that the woman we hired to look after Mum, in her absence, turned out to be a proselytizing Jehovah's Witness.

ON HER ROUNDS, Georgie is a picture of bustling efficiency, going from patient to patient, examining X-ray charts and operating schedules.

With the MDC leadership still out of the country, Mugabe's brutal campaign to smash the party continues unabated, and the Avenues Clinic has been transformed into one large repository of torture victims. Every bed is full.

White man's flesh marks easily; it is a pale canvas on which the path of pain is easily painted. But it takes a lot more to mark a black man. Somehow, the palette of black wounds seem more violent, tearing down through dark skin, into the yellow curd of subcutaneous fat, the red gristle of muscle fibers, down to the shocking whiteness of bones.

Here in ward 2N, bed 1, is Shepherd Geti, thirty-three, who has septic lacerations on his buttocks. They have been so badly beaten that much of the tissue there is destroyed. He was arrested by three guys claiming to be policemen but refusing to produce ID cards. They took him to the local school, Donswe (in Masawa ward), where "they sang their songs and beat their drums, and thrashed me and my friend with thick sticks, then told us if we went to hospital they would kill us." But after his wounds became infected and he went into a high fever he came anyway. His wife is still at home and he is so afraid that Mugabe's men will return for her this time.

Here in bed 2N-13 is Edison Marisau, from the Mbire district of Guruve, where he is a village chairman for the MDC. He has second-degree burns. ZANU-PF members came (on 20 April) and burned his house down, with him hiding inside it. He managed to get out, though all his belongings went up in flames. When he went to the police they said, "We can do nothing as we are no longer working as the police, we only work for Mugabe's party." In the next-door village twelve houses were burned down and two men killed there.

Here, in bed 2N-7, is David Mhende, a thirty-five-year-old with a terrible head injury caused by one of Mugabe's men wielding an axe. "It just missed my eye," he says gratefully. And here in bed 2N-9 is a twenty-nine-year-old man from Masvingo, with a broken leg and broken hands. He is asleep. Georgie consults her notes. He is a victim of political violence too, beaten by Mugabe's post-election posses.

In ward 1S, we catch up with Mr. Coric, a Yugoslav orthopaedic surgeon who has never been so busy. What he is seeing mostly now is what he calls "defense injuries." It's a chilling phrase — one the doctors use to describe the shattering damage caused to your arms when you hold them up over your head, in an effort to protect yourself from the blows. The blows of the boot, the blows of the log, the blows of the whip, the blows of the rock, the machete, the axe.

Now Mr. Coric has run out of the metal plates and pins he uses to set shattered arms and legs, so he can no longer operate, other than to clean up the shards of bone. He doesn't know what else to do. "I can't just discharge someone with fractured tibias," he says, head in hands.

In ward 1S-2 are C. Mutekele and Happiness Mutata. Georgie goes to their bed ends and takes a quick look at their charts, comparing them against her book. Happiness has a fractured right leg and fractured right arm, and no plates or pins, so neither bone is set yet. If they start to mend then Coric will have to break them again and re-set them. They are PEV victims too. The pace of the terror is so fast now, we are distilling it down to acronyms. PEV. Post-Election Violence.

In 1S-10A, beneath a "nil by mouth" sign, lies Reason Kapfuya, an MDC member from Mrewa-UMP (Uzumba Maramba Pfungwe). He is a big man with his head partly shaved to expose a violet-tinctured wound tacked together by black nylon sutures. Both his arms are broken too, and one leg.

"Who did this to you?" I ask.

He looks at me as though I am an imbecile. "ZANU-PF," he says. "Mugabe's people."

Next to him is Hilary Cheinuru, an MDC polling agent from Gutu West. He was ordered to go to a ZANU-PF meeting, but begged off, saying he was unwell with malaria. He was badly beaten with logs and knobkerries. "But I'm not finished," he says. "I'm going to be very serious and work harder than before. By giving us this threat, they are giving us power. We've faced the danger, so now we are used to it."

Also in ward 1S is Reason Mashambanaka from Mrewa, with part of his hair also shaved, to reveal a gashed skull. His whole family was attacked while they were asleep. He is fifty-three. "They beat my seventy-two-year-old mother, all over her body with sticks, and even my children though the littlest one is only three years of age."

Jonathan Malikita, thirty-nine, in Bed 15D of ward 1S, is the chief election agent and campaign manager for Maramba in Mashonaland East. It used to be a ZANU-PF stronghold, which the MDC was trying to infiltrate for the first time. He was a schoolteacher but in 2002 he began working for the MDC full time. "After the elections," he says, "they began terrorizing us. At midnight there was a shower of rocks, which broke the roof of my house. There was glass everywhere from broken windows, then they set the house alight. I ran naked from it and fled to the house of Florence Machinga, the MP for Wuzumba, seeking shelter. But they followed me there and burned her house down too. They attacked me there, there were more than a hundred of them." He insists that I write down their leaders: Modesta Mushambi, a ZANU councillor; Kenneth Dzema; Cephas Chikomo, the ZANU District Chairman; Itai Kandemire, a war vet. "They were trying to chop my head off with their axes and I put up my arms to protect myself. My arm was chopped in three places."

"It was a truly terrible fracture," agrees Georgie, shaking her head as she reviews his chart, "with bones sticking out at right angles."

"And then they left me there because they thought I was dead," continues Jonathan. "I heard them say it, 'He's dead now, we've finished him, MDC has gone.' If they hear I am still alive…" He trails off.

And what about a run-off?

"If I go back there, they will finish me off for sure. It will be terrible. There will be a massacre."

His wife, Esther, and their youngest child, Denzel, eighteen months old, are over in the pediatric ward.

In Bed 1S-1 is Grace Gambeza from Mudzi. She is twenty-nine. She has septic hematoma on her back and buttocks and fractured arms. DW, says the chart—defense wounds. She also has a tiny baby that is still breast-feeding. The nurse brings her in, a bundle wrapped in a white hospital sheet, and tries to hold her to Grace's breast to feed. With two broken arms, Grace cannot hold her baby to her own breast. It is one of the saddest things I've ever seen. Grace weeping silently, her broken, un-set arms lying uselessly at her sides, as the nurse holds the crying baby to her breast and tries to get it to feed. Georgie looks up from her patient log, shakes her head, blinks rapidly and takes off her glasses, pretending to clean them. Then, not trusting herself to talk, she turns on her heel and marches off to the next patient.

Bed after bed, in ward after ward, on floor after floor, is filled with Mugabe's victims. A hospital full of those he has injured, tortured, and burned out of their homes.

As I shuttle between the torture victims, moving from bedside to bedside, long after Georgie has left, and on my return, to bedsides here and in other clinics, copiously noting down the details of their experiences, I feel helpless, frustrated and angry. I'm not sure what I can do to help. My role is unclear to me.

I seem to be part chaplain (like my grandfather before me, ministering to wounded sailors in World War I), part scribe, part journalist, part therapist. Part lawyer (as I once was) taking testimony.

And as these shattered people recount their full experiences in a complete narrative, many for the first time, they sometimes break down. It is as if, until now, these brave men and women have concentrated on staying alive, by taking each minute, each hour and day, at a time, and only now, as they join it all together for a stranger, into a complete narrative, do they see the enormity of the whole thing, of what they have been through. And their stoicism can sometimes suddenly dissolve, surprising even themselves, as they get a view of the trajectory of their own suffering. But it seems cathartic too.

I wish there were a better word than "victims" to describe what these people are. It seems so inert, so passive, and weak. And that is not what they are at all. There is dignity to their suffering. Even as they tell me how they have fled, how they have hidden, how they have been humiliated and mocked, there is little self-pity here. "Survivors," I suppose, defines them better. Again, and again, as I play stenographer to their suffering, I offer to conceal their names or geographical districts to prevent them being identified. But again, and again, they volunteer their names, and make sure I spell them correctly. They are proud of their roles in all of this, at the significance of their sacrifice. And they want it recorded.

I shrink from generalizing what "they" have gone through, because it can feed into that sense that this is some un-differentiated, amorphous mass of Third World peasantry. Some generic, fungible frieze of suffering. One that animates briefly as you intersect with it, rubber-necking at it, a drive-by misery that disappears as you motor away over the horizon.

And for the first time, in trying to work out why I am here, and whether it is constructive, doing what I am doing, I find myself settling on a phrase that I have always avoided, a description I had found pretentious, but that now seems oddly apt — *bearing witness*. I am bearing witness to what is happening here — to the sustained cruelty of it all. I have a responsibility to try to amplify this suffering, this sacrifice, so that it will not have happened in vain.

I feel too like a prompt at a play. After dozens of hours of this, I often know now, before they speak, what they will say next. I didn't write the words, nor can I change them. But I know what they'll be because I have heard them before, because there are so many who have been through this torture factory, and that's what it is—it is abuse on an industrial scale, with the torturers following a script handed to them from above. There's no spontaneity to this evil; it is ordained from the top. It is hierarchical, planned, and plotted. Mugabe's men have even given it a name. They call it Operation Ngatipedzenavo, "Let Us Finish Them Off." And just as Operation Gukurahundi, which I witnessed in Matabeleland all those years ago, was an operation to shatter the structure of an opposition party, so this one has the same aim. Two operations separated by nearly twenty-five years, but apparently, nothing has changed. Beneath Mugabe's spurious air of correctness, this is the bloody reality, these shattered limbs and broken lives. This, quite simply, is the base upon which the tyrant's power ultimately rests—and it is one of fear.

seventeen

Alone, Unarmed, Afraid

WITH NO FOREIGN JOURNALISTS allowed here, most of the opposition leadership having fled, and NGOs hamstrung by restrictions, there is a vacuum in which Mugabe can conduct his campaign of violence. It's a vacuum that the diplomatic community now tries to fill.

Leading the charge is the U.S. ambassador, James "Jim" McGee, an African-American career diplomat with four previous African postings, in Senegal, Côte d'Ivoire, Madagascar, and Swaziland. He is only five months into this highly antagonistic posting. Washington has named Zimbabwe one of its "outposts of tyranny," just below a "rogue state" in an "axis of evil" in the U.S. demonology, and imposed a travel ban and bank-account freezes on about two hundred senior members of Mugabe's regime. In the weapons of diplomatic disapproval, these so called "smart sanctions"—designed to punish the princes without hurting the paupers—seem to be the diplomatic equivalent of grounding. They have also provided

Mugabe with a ready-made excuse for all his self-inflicted economic ills. Mugabe blames everything on "Western sanctions."

McGee is the latest in a long line of U.S. ambassadors viscerally disliked by Mugabe. His predecessor, Christopher Dell, proudly displayed on his office wall a framed headline from Mugabe's town crier, the *Herald*. It read, *Mugabe to Dell: Go to Hell*. Into this already high-octane mix, Jim McGee deliberately detonated with all the diplomatic finesse of an IED. The *Herald* was given only momentary pause by his color before denouncing McGee as George Bush's *Uncle Tom*, the American president's *house negro*. It had already sharpened these racist barbs on Colin Powell and Condoleezza Rice, and would recast them in due course for Susan Rice. McGee didn't care one jot. He was looking to elevate the profile of the Zimbabwe crisis, and get it onto the UN Security Council agenda.

I MEET MCGEE at 6 a.m. inside the courtyard of the heavily guarded U.S. embassy in downtown Harare, for an improvised fact-finding mission to look into reports of widespread intimidation and violence. The trip is supposed to be surreptitious, so that we can get to areas without Mugabe's men having advance notice. But it has been leaked. The chief suspect is the dean of the diplomatic corps, a post that accrues automatically to the longest-serving ambassador, in this case the Congolese — described by a Western diplomat, in somewhat undiplomatic terms, as a "little shit." So McGee has decided to send a decoy convoy in a different direction, to throw our CIO tail off our scent. It includes, as the third car, the U.S. ambassador's official armored limo, flying the gold-fringed U.S. pennant, to indicate he is on board, and several more SUVs with diplomatic license plates. Playing the role of Jim McGee, who stands six foot four and is north of two hundred pounds, in the dummy convoy, is the best body double McGee could find, his gardener.

This morning the real McGee wears neatly pressed chinos and a dark-blue golf shirt with the emblem of his old air-force unit, 6994 Squadron, on its breast, and their nickname: *Electronic Goons*.

Motto: *Alone, Unarmed, Afraid.* In my experience, Jim McGee is seldom any of these things. He served nearly six years in Vietnam, doing "air intercepts," listening in on communications of the North Vietnamese military (he learned fluent Vietnamese) and triangulating their positions, on which to call down air strikes. He was awarded three Distinguished Flying Crosses, one for helping to rescue the crew of a downed American B-52 before the approaching Vietnamese forces could reach them, and the other two for surviving four hundred and seventy-one combat missions. After Vietnam he went back to college, and joined the Foreign Service in 1981.

We are accompanied in the real convoy by eleven vehicles, which contain five other ambassadors or chargés, from the EU, UK, Japan, Holland, and, rather courageously, Tanzania, and by half a dozen of McGee's staffers, several local journalists, and some black Zimbabwean Presbyterian pastors, who want to show the diplomats first-hand evidence of "Post-Election Violence" in their area, Rhimbick, near Mvurwi, about an hour northwest of the capital.

The previous week they have alerted their church colleagues in America to the dire situation there. One pastor emailed to say that some of his parishioners have fled, "and are living in mountains and forests as I write. They can't risk going back home; it's suicidal." Other parishioners had sought refuge in the church. "There are a couple of torture centers set up by ZANU-PF thugs," and the churchmen themselves had been targeted. One pastor (Andrew) "had to walk at night with his wife and two children to escape the promise of torture. He only managed to escape because they were watching for cars to come and pick him up, so thank God that he was advised to walk to safety. They had told him that he would be the first person to be killed in the area by the ZANU-PF leaders. The crime: all the practical service and help that the Church gives is believed to be from MDC, disguised as Church ministry." There is the bitter scent of betrayal in the air too. A turncoat Evangelist is said to be "moving around with these people identifying those that are to be tortured. If this is true, one would not be surprised, because the Easter story now makes sense. Please pray for the Church in Rhimbick, and pray for us..."

In our CD-plated convoy we are hardly inconspicuous, but theoretically, under the terms of the Vienna Convention, the diplomats have immunity from arrest, and the rest of us stand a better chance if we stick with them. Trying to get in to the battleground areas any other way is more or less impossible, with numerous roadblocks and roaming militia checks.

I ride with McGee in the second vehicle, to Mvurwi—once a mostly white-owned commercial-farming district, now only sporadically cultivated. Rhimbick Farm, where the pastors have said there is a torture base, is our first destination. We park in a long line on the roadside. Inconspicuous we are not. The elderly white sawmill manager there peeps round the door, and is astonished to see this sudden convergence of diplomats. He intimates that bad things have been happening here, and points up the hill. "That's their base," he whispers and disappears back inside, terrified to say more. We walk up to the commandeered old farmhouse. Each evening, the pastors say, a hundred or more ZANU youths congregate here. Our delegation swarms over it and we find a small group of militia members.

Ambushed like this and outnumbered, they don't seem that frightening. They deny any wrongdoing, saying they have just been "campaigning." But as the conversation continues, and several prisoners emerge to tell their stories, I walk ahead into the house itself—this is what the victims who've been through it describe as a torture base. It includes several "black rooms," without windows, where political opponents are thrown, in between beatings.

There is little furniture, just some rough wooden benches, and thick wooden sticks, which, the victims say, are used to beat up the many who have passed through here.

In the old sitting room, now filthy and soot-filled, there is a folding table, on which I spot a backpack. I unzip it and inside it find four hardbacked school exercise books. Each is entitled "Rhimbick Commanding Center." Some of the books are mostly administrative, listing personnel and pay. The commander here is "Comrade

Taurai Muyambodza," and his contingent consists of "War Vets, War Collaborators, Youth." One book is sub-headed, ominously, "Interrogation Book." In it, Comrade Muyambodza has systematically recorded their beatings and interrogations, in longhand. The book lists "Wanted" people, including Kelvin Chareka, whom they are looking for because "he is MDC." It records communication with a network of other such interrogation centers.

A letter falls from between the pages. It is from Umsengezi Command Center, sited at a nearby ex-farm, dated four days earlier, giving information about "wanted" people, including headman Mhandu. "We want to find him and interrogate him because he didn't stop his people from voting for the MDC," says the letter. Most damning is that the book makes quite unapologetic reference to the violence they have meted out during the questioning. "To be beaten or to confess, what do you want?" reads an account of a typical interrogation. Other pages list people "who are to be beaten."

Suddenly one of the militia members rushes in. "What are you doing? Stop that! Stop!" he yells, wild-eyed, and snatches the books away, shoves them in his backpack, and runs into the bush behind the house.

From the interrogation center, we go to the nearby village. Initially it appears deserted, but as word spreads that the ambassadors are here, and there is no danger, the villagers start to appear. Soon they are gathered in nervous huddles telling how they have been interrogated and beaten at Rhimbick, and showing us their wounds. They are understandably scared of what will happen to them after we have gone, so McGee's staff distributes business cards with the embassy's emergency number, and then the diplomats' road show reassembles and rolls out.

It is about twelve miles to Mvurwi hospital, and on the way we pass a large World Food Program depot. Bags, plump with grain, are stacked up high. This is how Zimbabwe eats. The same Western powers that Mugabe routinely demonizes in his banal biopsy of blame are the principal donors of food to his people. These towers of grain bags are all that stands between Zimbabwe and full-scale famine.

Our convoy coils into the dusty parking area of the small hospital, a government-run one, which is barely functioning. We overwhelm the nervous nursing staff, what few there are. The U.S. ambassador meets the matron in her office, where she tells him that they have been flooded with victims of the violence. Many are coming in two weeks after being injured, so their wounds, typically defense wounds, she says, are often horribly septic. And yet, most discharge themselves, prematurely, afraid that they will be targeted again if they stay in hospital.

While he keeps her busy, the rest of us mob the wards. Here too we find graduates of the Rhimbick interrogation center, including one former ZANU-PF councillor, Carpenter Mwanza, thirty-seven, who tells us he was tortured after being accused of transferring his support to Simba Makoni. "I was taken to a room there called the 'black room,' with no windows," he says. "And they beat me for five hours."

As we prepare to leave, a plain-clothes officer arrives. He is slim, in a dark leather jacket and wraparound sunglasses. He flashes his ID card at McGee, showing that he is from the Police Internal Security Intelligence Unit, PISI, and demands to see McGee's credentials.

"I am the American ambassador," says McGee, showing him his card.

The PISI officer is unimpressed. "Inspector Matamba has ordered us that you have to report to him at the police station," he says. "It is just behind the hospital. You will come with me. We walk there." It is a command. You can see it doesn't occur to him that McGee might refuse to comply. PISI is as feared, in its own right, as the CIO.

"No," says McGee simply. "We're leaving. Now. You have no jurisdiction over us, we are diplomats." He brushes past him and climbs back into his vehicle and orders the driver to go. Behind us, the convoy is already mounted up, ready to roll.

The officer is taken aback. You can see that this has never happened to him before. He beckons frantically, and more policemen arrive, these ones in uniform. They spill out of their gray Santana, breathless, armed with matt-black pump-action shotguns, and AK rifles, with their sickle-curved magazines. Quickly they heave shut the hospital gate, and secure it with a twist of barbed wire.

One of the staffers tries to take some shots of the scene and the PISI officer, furious at being photographed, darts toward him. "Cameras are not allowed," he screams and demands the camera. But the staffer hops into his CD vehicle, and disappears behind a tinted window. McGee interposes himself, and the officer walks away.

Getting back into his own vehicle, McGee eases down his window. "Let us out," he demands.

The policemen refuse, standing silently in a line in front of the closed gate.

We are at an impasse, and McGee is starting to lose it. His jaw tightens and he lets out a purposeful puff, like a rhino contemplating a charge. "Screw this," he says, and clambers down from the vehicle again. He marches up to the PISI officer, towering over him. The two of them face off—the bear and the mamba. Then the officer eases his left shoulder back, so that his leather jacket creaks open, to reveal the dark brown honeycomb of his pistol handle, protruding from his shoulder holster.

Jim McGee doesn't notice, or if he does, he doesn't care. "You," he says, jabbing his forefinger at him. "Let us out *now*. Or I will report you at the very highest level."

The PISI officer shakes his head vigorously. "No," he says firmly, standing his ground. "You have to come with me to the station. Those are the orders."

"This is bullshit!" says McGee, exasperated, and he turns away. I see what he has in mind and I draw breath to counsel caution, but Jim launches himself toward the gate. The policemen there finger their weapons, and the PISI officer comes running after him. "No, no," he shouts, the pitch of his voice rising now, "you are *not* permitted to leave!"

McGee barely breaks his stride. As he reaches the gate, the uniformed officer in front of it shouts, "Stop! Stop!"

McGee stops. And behind him, I sigh. It's all been bluff. Thank God. Then he draws himself up to his full height again, throws his shoulders back.

"Or *what?*" he says. "What you gonna do? *Shoot* me? Go ahead." And with that, he starts to walk toward them.

The policemen are beset with confusion, chattering between themselves, fingering their weapons, while the PISI officer barks into his two-way radio, trying to raise his superiors.

McGee keeps walking slowly, until he reaches the line, then he brushes straight through them, reaches down to untwist the wire from the latch, and starts hauling the gate. When it's open wide enough, he booms at the posse to move on out. One by one, the vehicles drive out past him, as he waves them through, standing between them and the row of armed policemen, who look on, agitated and nonplussed.

When they have all passed through, McGee hops up into his vehicle. "Let's go!" he tells the driver, and we accelerate on through the open gate ourselves. As we drive away in a gratifying shower of dust, he turns to me, breaks into a huge grin, and whoops. It's clear this is the most fun he's had in years.

HOWARD MISSION HOSPITAL, run by the Salvation Army in the heart of the Chiweshe tribal area, is our next stop. It has tidy grounds, with whitewashed stone borders around its flowerbeds, and a general air of orderliness. A sign outside acknowledges that it is a recipient of U.S. funds for its HIV work. "Ah, one of ours," says McGee approvingly.

The medical chief, Captain Dr. Paul Thistle, a Canadian obstetric surgeon, is conducting an emergency C-section in his operating theater when we arrive, and as before, we spill out into the hospital itself, while McGee waits for him.

Inside we find dozens more victims, many from the Chaona district. One of their number died at the place they were beaten, they tell us, a torture camp they call Gum Tree Base, near Chaona school. Another died here in this hospital, from his wounds. The rest are traumatized and terrified. They have been beaten on the soles of their feet, a method of torture called *falanga*, and on their buttocks. But don't think of this as a "normal" beating; think of deep, bone-deep, lacerations, of buttocks with no skin left on them, think of being flayed alive. Think of swollen, broken feet, of people unable to stand, unable to sit, unable to lie on their backs because of the blinding pain. Husbands and wives have been handcuffed and beaten alike. Their wrists still bear the cuts of the cuffs.

They were beaten, they say, because they failed to attend a "compulsory" ZANU rally, a re-education session. One of them, a young man of twenty-five, Shine Mzariri, is trying to discharge himself from hospital, despite a broken foot, and unhealed back and buttock wounds still leaking through layers of bandages. He thinks it'll be safer outside, but doesn't know where to go. "I am hesitating to go home," he says redundantly.

His bedmate Fideus Mapondera is sixty-one. You can feel his outrage. "I was just *plowing*," he says, "and they beat my wife Silvia as well." Then he turns his face to the wall to hide from me the fact that he's weeping. Weeping with shame that he couldn't protect her, couldn't protect himself.

Finally, Dr. Thistle emerges from surgery. He pulls off his mask and snaps off his gloves, and confirms the victims' accounts, their wounds, their cause, and the death toll. But you can sense his unease. Here he stands, running the only medical facility for a quarter of a million people. He and his staff do three thousand surgical procedures a year; they deliver two and a half thousand babies. A quarter of the women who give birth here are HIV-infected, and the hospital struggles to minimize mother-to-child transmission. Howard is the sole local provider of anti-retrovirals, clawing thousands of Chiweshe residents back from certain death in such a dramatic way that they call it the Lazarus effect. And Howard is at the forefront of the struggle to treat the effects of widespread malnutrition among the district's hungry children. And they do this with only three doctors, at present not even that. At present Thistle is the sole doctor here. You can see why he is torn. If he is too outspoken about this political violence, he will jeopardize all the good work this hospital does.

Because he knows, we all do, that Mugabe, when irked, is quite capable of expelling him, of cutting off food aid, or throttling a hospital, of letting his people die. It is as if he has taken an entire nation hostage, using them as human shields. He has killed so many already, with barely a blink. You can see Dr. Thistle struggling with this audit of agony. Humanitarian agencies here do it all the time, measuring the good they do and, in public at least, choking back their repugnance toward the tyrant who can stop it all in a heartbeat, if provoked to do so. Dr. Lovemore at the CSU does it, so that she can continue to pick up the pieces of broken humans and try to mend them.

This is how little his own kith and kin now mean to Mugabe. He holds them in such low regard that he will decimate them, even as he chunters querulously on, lecturing the world about historical wrongs, raging like an aggrieved adolescent, casting blame everywhere except where it most belongs, with himself.

Yet Zimbabweans have grown used to it. It is what they now expect, their new normal. The playwright Tom Stoppard observed that the worst thing about tyrannies is the way in which they render the crazy, commonplace. Through an awful alchemy, the grotesque becomes quotidian, as you forfeit your ability to be shocked.

ON THE HOME STRETCH back to Harare, just past the 007 Hideout Bar, we slow down at a police block, and when the officer tries to wave us down, McGee rolls down the window, and says, "We're diplomats, you have no right to stop us." He turns to his driver. "Drive, Misheck! Drive on through!" And the column behind us follows in his breach.

But a few miles further on, the police are ready for us. They have been reinforced by CIO agents, and they've drawn two vehicles across the road so we cannot pass. These are senior officers, unperturbed by his indignation, unimpressed with his diplomatic immunity. They demand to see McGee's papers. They make it clear that we are detained, and then they congregate around their cluster of vehicles to discuss with each other and headquarters what to do next.

"I've never been detained before," says McGee.

They hold us there on the road for an hour and a half, as ever more senior officers and security agents arrive from Harare, discussing the protocol of what to do with the diplomats, how far they can push this. In the CD vehicles behind us, the local journalists stay hidden behind smoked glass, safe for the time being in their little diplomatic islands. As for me, the security officials seem to assume I'm part of the diplomatic delegation.

Among the security officers are the two CIO chiefs from Bindura, the very men who've been directing the violence we have seen the results of today. We're all feeling raw, having just spent hours in the company of their victims. So when these two CIO officers walk over to Kevin Stirr, the U.S. embassy's democracy and governance officer, and ask what we've been doing, he replies, angrily, "We've been looking at the people you're beating up."

"We'll beat *you* thoroughly too," says one of the agents.

"Are you threatening me?" Stirr says, striding after them. "You're threatening me!" he says, shouting now. "I'm making a formal complaint."

The officers look a little alarmed, and quickly climb back into their olive-green Renault—751–859M. They start up, but Stirr wrenches the door open, reaches in, and tries to grab the keys. As they tussle, McGee arrives and Stirr explains.

The ambassador steps in front of their car, ordering the CIO agents to stop, as he wishes to record their threat to his staff member, so he can register a diplomatic protest. The CIO agent at the wheel has retrieved the keys now and starts up the engine. He puts it in gear and lurches forward, hitting McGee's thigh. The ambassador lets out a roar, but stands his ground. Inside the car the officers now looked panicked; this has suddenly escalated beyond anything they imagined.

McGee takes out his digital camera, and they hide their faces in their hands as he snaps away.

It is a small victory, but sweet nonetheless, to see the bullies themselves squirm for a change.

Finally, after an hour and a half, the police release us, on condition that McGee and the other ambassadors report to the Ministry of Foreign Affairs the following day. "Which I've no intention of doing," McGee says as we re-embark.

"What the police just did speaks volumes," he concludes, back in the car, and weary from his third altercation with them in a single day. "What they're running here is a military campaign." And though he has another two years to go of this posting, he ventures, "I don't think I'll last my full term."

eighteen

It's Hard to Play Cards with Two Broken Arms

A S THE PACE OF the violence increases in the following weeks, victims are streaming into Harare, but there is nowhere for them to go. CSU is only a way-station; Harvest House, the MDC headquarters, is constantly being raided by the police; and churches that have tried to open their doors to the refugees have also been harassed and closed and the refugees arrested or chased away. Now impromptu safe houses have popped up across the northern suburbs.

Mike Mason and his family run one of them out of their home in Borrowdale. Behind the house, the Masons have rigged up a large olive-green army-surplus tent, whose floor is strewn with mattresses and blankets. At present, it sleeps forty-five people.

Darkness gathers, and the refugees boil a large pot of water to make *sadza*. Among them are nine kids. They should be at school but instead they are huddled here, hidden away in this safe house, far from home, far from school. Trymore and Francis are here, the two little boys from CSU, the ones I saw when they first arrived, exhausted from yomping in through the bush. And their grandmother, the old *ambuya,* is here too, helping to stir the boiling *sadza* pot.

"We send trucks in to get the injured out," says Mason. "That's how we ended up doing this. But many can't get out. They're told not to go to clinics, not to report to police, not to leave the area — on pain of death. There was one guy in Gokwe, who loaded up a ten-ton truck with the injured, about thirty of them — and these were just the very worst. But they were stopped at a roadblock and were all assaulted and told to go back, so they never made it out. Many will sicken, their wounds, fractures, gashes, burns will get septic and infected without treatment and they will die.

"Now they're rounding up farm workers and appointing voting supervisors and making them responsible for ensuring their group votes the 'right way,' or otherwise, they say, they'll return and kill each supervisor."

From time to time Mike walks out into his garden, past his small plant nursery, to the very end of his lawn, and there he climbs up onto a metal chair strategically placed among his rose bushes to speak on his cell — it's the only place he can get a signal. He's standing on the chair now, in the dark, canvassing for mattresses, blankets, fuel. Sometimes as you approach his house you can see just his head with a cell phone at his ear, poking above the Durawall.

He moves restlessly back and forth from the phone chair in the rose beds to the computer in a bedroom that is used as an office, and out again to the large open veranda where tea and rusks are always being served. The metal garden gate trundles back and forth frequently with constant arrivals and departures: refugees going to medical appointments and returning for supper, other MDC Support people bringing donations of clothes, food, Bibles.

"Many of the refugees are just languishing in their hospital beds," says Sharon, his wife. "They say, 'We are bored and depressed.' So we try to get them biscuits, sweets, newspapers, books, playing cards."

"*Ja,* but it's hard to play cards with two broken arms," says Mike.

Ever since they lost their farm in Tengwe eight long years ago, "where," he says with a chuckle, "we were known for our parties, if not for our tobacco," the Masons have been helping to run MDC Support, helping to provide logistical backup.

"I just couldn't sit by and not get involved. This is far beyond 'Mugabe stole my farm and put me in jail,'" both of which happened to him.

In the back garden there are several metal shipping containers bearing the remnants he was able to get off his farm.

"It's not much," he admits.

Sharon describes the final attack on their homestead.

"They had guns that time. Before he scarpered, our security guard appeared briefly at the window and shouted, 'You're in trouble, and I'm gone!' I phoned my sister to say, 'Look after my kids if we die.'"

Mugabe's men had already beaten and chased their farm workers into the bush. When a convoy of armed white farmers arrived to try to rescue the Masons, the Mugabe militiamen fled into the bush too, where they found themselves hiding next to the farm laborers they had chased away. The farm foreman said to the militia leader, "What's the point of this, then—you chased us here, and now *you* are chased here, and we find ourselves hiding together, though we are hiding from you!"

And he got beaten for his trouble.

After he was thrown off his farm Mike worked for a tobacco company, "but when I refused to set foot on stolen farms, they made me redundant."

On his laptop in the bedroom, Mike shows me photos of some of the latest violence. "Look at this little kid, Sampson, he's three, and he was hit in the eye with a rock fired by a catapult. His skull is fractured and they think he'll lose the eye."

The little boy is standing solemnly, one eye hugely swollen shut and discolored. In the next shot, he is clutching a new toy, and grinning, notwithstanding his gruesome wounds.

"He's such a little trouper," says Sharon. "Despite what's happened to him, he nearly always has a smile."

Mike's last safe house was located and raided by the police, who searched it for five hours and accused him of hiding drugs. He's worried now that there is too much traffic in and out of this property and that it will soon attract police attention.

The gate trundles open once more, and in drives another ex-farmer, Rusty Markham.

"Howzit," he says, grinning. "*A luta continua!*"

It's the old guerrilla rallying-cry from the civil war, now co-opted for a new struggle. He's against a run-off, he says, after the mayhem he has been helping to cope with.

"There's no point in a run-off other than depopulating the countryside."

"Yeah," agrees Mike. "The membership has been dispersed and their IDs burned so they can't vote."

He brings news of the Rogers, a farming couple (whose son, Barney, plays cricket for Zimbabwe) who have just been very badly assaulted. Mugabe's "Green Bomber" militia invaded their farm and took workers hostage, using them as human shields as they chased the couple upstairs in their house. Mrs. Rogers has cancer and was due to go down to South Africa the following morning for a bone-marrow transplant. Instead, she found herself surrounded by armed militia.

"Her husband shot several times into the air and she used a Mace can, and then things really turned ugly," says Rusty.

They were seized, beaten, and then dragged around the garden by the hair. Both were very seriously injured.

In the fading light, out on the veranda, at another computer, two young black men are quietly working their way through a pile of handwritten statements from victims of political violence. Pecking at the keyboard is Daiton Japani, the MDC organizing secretary for Hurungwe, who has a large gash on his head.

While he was at the police station in Karoi, trying to file a complaint about election violence, Daiton was surrounded by Mugabe's militia. They threw rocks at him, and then began shooting at him, "right there at the police station," he says, shaking his head. He was only saved, he says, because one of the policemen managed to push away the barrel of the gun as a militiaman fired.

"I have been warned that they are looking for me," he says, "in order to kill me."

The other man is Tawanda Mubwanda. This is his first day out—he's been in hiding for the last four weeks. He is tall and bespectacled. His father, Tapiwa, the district director of elections for Hurungwe North, was the first person murdered in post-election retributions.

"There was a ZANU-PF meeting and one of their resolutions was to kill my father," explains Mubwanda. "About five hundred party youth came to his village on April 12th, just after dark. They beat him and stabbed him and he died on the spot. He was fifty-three, turning fifty-four this year, in July. Since then, I have been in hiding. Today is my first day out. I feel obliged to help, I'm trying to keep my mind occupied and working on a worthwhile cause. We collate reports from the rural areas—many there are not allowed out, even for medical treatment. So they write accounts of what has happened to them and smuggle the reports out to us."

He slides across the table a handwritten note. It is from Givemore Tsangu in Hurungwe.

I K.G. Tsangu, I was attacked by the ZANU-PF thugs on the 9th April 2008. They attacked me during the night. Cause of being an MDC activist.... On 22nd April they accused me of being helped by MDC party for treatement. On the same date they send more than two hundred youth thugs to finish me off. At their first attack I managed to fight back and they ran away. By so doing they sent more than before to kill me. Fortunately I was away in my maize field. They harassed my wife after she told them she was not aware of my post. One of my relatives wives told the thugs that I had gone to my maize field. They followed to the maize field and find not me...

They covered the maize field in search of me. My wife followed them in need of seeing me being slottered. I met her on the opposite

*road. She cried in front of me. She told me the whole story. I told
her to go home and I to follow the youths.*

*My wife refused me to do so since she heard them saying they
wanted to left me dead or vomiting blood. She told me to go and see
what they had done at home. They crush my 12inch TV, drill and
angel grinder heavy duty. Drill and grinder which I was using on
my welding job, they took them. The youth which did this were not
of my place. My wife did not know even one of the thugs. At present
they are still at the farm house (Komboni)*

*The leaders of the thugs, the War Veterans group which
include Madamombe Petter or Nyamadzawo first name and Jawet
promised all the once beaten MDC members to be killed if the
ZANU PF loose the reran presental election. I do understand that
they can fulfil what they are thinking…*

*The thugs at my area are all afraid of me. My problem is they
come in hundreds when they want me.*

*The people at the farm are not allow to share or talking to me
and family. No one is allowed to stand with and discuss anything
with me. People are forced to pay one goat and chicken for
admitting that you have done away on supporting MDC. If you did
that then fine is given to subchief.*

*Myself I refused to show them my party cards which they
demand and if you tell them that you don't have any of them they
put you on a thorogh beat[ing]*

My wife is new to this area of mind. We were in Harare.

*Yours threatened MDC member from the Part[y] Formation,
Hurungwe Kazangarare*

Thank for your attention.

I slide the statement back across the table. "Do you know what
happened to him?"

"We think they have killed Givemore since he smuggled out
this letter," Mubwanda says.

When I return the next evening, the power is off again. Sharon
is trying to get the generator started, but for now, we are all in the

dark. Mike looks exhausted. He is still standing on his chair, out in the garden, on the phone, trying to get one of his trucks into Chiweshe with coffins to bury the MDC members who have just been murdered there.

"It was the most brazen attack," he says, "at Muzarabani Business Center. They shot three guys at point-blank range, in front of over three hundred people! They said, 'This is what happens to you when you vote for MDC.'"

On my way out, behind the house sitting by himself, hunched over, rocking, I come across a new arrival. Timothy Makwenjere. One of his eyes is grotesquely swollen. I kneel down beside him and introduce myself. Makwenjere has spent the last few days on the run, and still has a haunted, hunted air. In a hushed monotone, he tells me that he's a mechanic at Muriel gold mine in Banket, and chairman of the MDC there. "On election day, we won nearly all the votes on the mine," he says. They were jubilant.

But the next day there was a knock on his door, and he opened it to find a group of Mugabe's militia, who set about him with metal bars. Then they smashed all his windows, and went down the whole row of houses doing the same to them.

As I turn my car to drive away, my headlights shine upon Timothy. He is still sitting outside the window, swollen head in hands, still rocking back and forth. His wife now squats silently on the ground beside him, her face dark and closed and scared.

THE NEXT MORNING, early, I drive over to the Avenues Clinic and slip back into the children's ward, to check on the little boy with the injured eye, the boy in Mike Mason's photo.

Sampson Chemerani is still asleep, his little knees drawn up onto his VW Beetle T-shirt, his face puffy in repose—one eye massively swollen, surrounded by a gory abrasion and a wound on his temple. He is the youngest of seven kids. They come from Shamva, where their village was burned down last Sunday because they were MDC supporters. The next night at 2 a.m., as they lay huddled in the open, among the charred remains of their huts, they were attacked again, this time by more than twenty ZANU-PF youth with sticks and rocks, and in the melee Sampson was struck in the eye.

His mother, Margaret, sits in her charity clothes, a headscarf, a bright floral dress, and a wide-lapelled gray jacket that is way too big and sags over her shoulders. She is a rural woman and politely claps her crossed palms together in greeting.

"Sampson doesn't really know what happened," she says, her voice low so as not to wake him. "He is too young to understand."

Each night Margaret patiently rocks Sampson to sleep, and once he finally drops off, she drags the thin foam mattress from under his hospital bed and lies just below him, because he has night terrors, she says. He sees Mugabe's chanting thugs bearing down upon him again, with their flaming torches, their clubs and rocks and whips. And he wakes up whimpering.

On the end of his bed hangs his medical record, charting his injuries. In an effort to cheer him up, the nurses have glued to its cover a picture torn from a magazine. It is a *Tyrannosaurus rex*, and it fiercely bares its glinting ranks of teeth. Underneath is a caption: "The truth about killer dinosaurs." I stand there looking at it and silently fuming. The truth of our own killer *Tyrannosaurus*—the "tyrant lizard"—is evident all around us. I pray that he too will be the last of his breed of tyrants, soon to become extinct.

nineteen

A Regime on the Rampage

AFTER SIX WEEKS of orbiting Africa since the election, trying to drum up political support, Morgan Tsvangirai finally flies back to his beleaguered home on 24 May. There have been a number of very detailed tip-offs of plots to kill him, which is one reason he has kept delaying his return. En route to the airport I pass through two police roadblocks, and see dozens of their sharpshooters standing in the tall grass on either side of the road. Whether they're here to protect him or do him harm seems moot.

At the airport, there are a few local journalists and a posse of Western diplomats waiting. Jim McGee joins us, a little late, he says, because he had to return to his vehicle to take off his pistol and unload it. "I always travel armed when I'm alone here," he says. "It's registered," he adds, "though I'm not quite sure what the laws about concealed weapons are here."

It's Saturday and he's in mufti: blue jeans, a peach sweater, and a gold neck chain, and he's alone, having given his staff the weekend off, because they've been working under such pressure for so long, he says.

We are still trying to pay for our coffee—at Z$600 million a cup—handing over banded bricks of banknotes, when Morgan sweeps through the arrivals hall below us, and climbs into a waiting Prado SUV. A pick-up truck of bodyguards squeals off behind him, so quickly that one is left behind, and has to sprint after it and vault in, breathless.

A ZTV crew train the barrel of their camera at McGee. "Why are you here?" shouts the reporter. The game, as McGee knows perfectly well, is to get him to admit that he's here to meet Tsvangirai, and so confirm the notion that the opposition leader is a stooge of Washington and the West.

"Me?" says McGee, with an "aw shucks" expression. "I've come to see off the Spanish ambassador," and he claps the surprised Spaniard on the shoulder.

"You're not here to meet Morgan Tsvangirai?" accuses the reporter.

McGee feigns surprise. "Morgan Tsvangirai's here? *Really?*"

TSVANGIRAI first makes hospital bedside rounds of torture victims, and then addresses the hundreds of displaced supporters who have crowded into his party headquarters, Harvest House, in central Harare, where they have sought sanctuary from the violence.

In the vast gloomy cavern of the open-plan offices, tier upon tier of supporters are carefully organized by size, small children and nursing mothers seated on the floor in front. Many are badly injured, some in wheelchairs, or on crutches. The lethal white gleam of plaster casts and bandages is everywhere, even on some of the children.

The walls here are lined with black plastic bin bags containing what little clothes they could flee with. The questions they ask him are mostly practical ones; they want blankets, clothes, food, sanctuary. One woman has her hand raised patiently throughout the Q&A session, and he eventually gets to her last. Trembling with grief, she tells him that when she fled Mugabe's assailants she became separated from her two-year-old child. "Please, *please,* help me find my baby," she sobs.

A few hours later, Tsvangirai gives a press conference at the Mirabelle Room in Meikles Hotel, furnished with brass sconces and mirrored ceiling. There are no foreign reporters here—they have all fled—but a full contingent of local ones.

"I return with a very sad heart," he says. "Democrats have been targeted by the dictatorship. This regime is on the rampage...Forty of our people have been killed, more than twenty-five thousand have been beaten, tortured. Not since Gukurahundi have we seen such violence. They are targeting our brightest and strongest activists, hunting them down."

And he makes a direct appeal to his rival. "Mugabe is a failed liberation hero. He can set his people free again. He can open the door to a new Zimbabwe."

MORGAN TSVANGIRAI lives in a cul-de-sac in the Harare suburb of Strathaven, in an unremarkable house, with pale pink walls and a red tiled roof. Outside the gate, two bodyguards in dark suits sit on a concrete culvert. More mill around inside. After being out of the country for a month, since the first round of elections, evading death threats and lobbying African leaders to his cause, Tsvangirai looks exhausted. He has a large, round, slightly pockmarked face, with deep-set eyes and a ready smile. Today he wears an open-necked checked shirt.

He tilts back in his office chair in the converted garage at the back of the house and yawns heavily. He tells me that his wife of thirty years, Susan, a stalwart of the party, has remained behind in Johannesburg with the two youngest of his six kids, fourteen-year-old twins, until the security situation up here improves. But, he says, "Susan has been unwavering."

Despite the pressure and danger, he is clearly relieved to be home. "Zimbabwe is special," he says. "When you compare it to other places in Africa, it has such potential, the infrastructure, the people—compared to the chaos in west Africa.

"In the last eight years there has been such anti-white rhetoric from Mugabe, but we Zimbabweans are non-racial now. It's unlike

South Africa—here the racial barriers have been broken down. There is really no desire to settle old scores."

But much of the pressure on Mugabe from the West has been counter-productive, he admits. Because Mugabe and his cronies champion anti-white attitudes, support by the West of the Zimbabwean opposition can backfire. "Which is why we have been trying to work through African institutions."

In many ways, Mugabe's nemesis is also his antithesis. Physically Morgan is a bear to Mugabe's mamba, his face round, his smile quick. Always a good performer in Shona, he has become an increasingly articulate and charismatic speaker in English too.

After almost toppling Mugabe's party in several finagled elections, in 2000, 2002, 2005, he stumbled over the decision whether to participate in elections for the senate. Tsvangirai favored a boycott, but two of his top MDC officials, Gibson Sibanda and Welshman Ncube, disagreed. In the end Tsvangirai bulldozed his way through, but Sibanda and Ncube split from the party as a result. They formed a new group, composed mostly of the MDC's Ndebele leadership, under Dr. Arthur Mutambara, a Shona Rhodes scholar, with an Oxford doctorate in robotics, who later taught at MIT. Confusingly the offshoot is called MDC-M, M for the Mutambara faction.

Notwithstanding Tsvangirai's refusal to be overruled in this case, he appears to share none of Mugabe's messianic entitlement.

"This has been an evolution for me," he tells me. "I was politically conscious, yes—but never in my wildest dreams did I expect to be in this position."

This afternoon Tsvangirai attended the funeral of Tonderai Ndira—the thirty-two-year-old MDC official who headed the party's security department for Harare, and who had been arrested more times than anyone else in the party, the man they called Zimbabwe's Steve Biko. "I'm so saddened by these indiscriminate, callous killings—there's no ideology to it," he says. "It's just state-sponsored violence against defenseless citizens."

But even the savage spasm of violence won't cow the people, he believes. "ZANU-PF cannot beat people into submission. Matabeleland proves it—they *massacred* people down there, but *still* those people vote against Mugabe."

What does he think motivates the man he has worked so assiduously to unseat, the man who has turned Zimbabwe into his personal fiefdom? "Robert Mugabe is an enigma—he evokes conflicting emotions in people. Liberation hero versus cruelty; the unleashing of violence, in Matabeleland, Murambatsvina, and now this post-election violence. I think he's driven by power—nothing else."

twenty

Canon War

A FEW HUNDRED YARDS from Dandaro clinic, where Denias Dombo lies with his broken limbs encased in plaster chrysalises, and Gandanga nurses his tumid legs, crushed under the truck wheels of Mugabe's agents, Bishop Sebastian Bakare lets me into his apartment, one of those that make up Dandaro's gated retirement community. After my father died, this is where we hoped my mother might live, before we lost that plan to the cancer of hyperinflation.

While his tall German wife, Ruth, makes tea, Bakare, who is a black Zimbabwean from Manicaland, explains how he was brought out of retirement to head the Anglican Church in Zimbabwe, after a schism engineered by Mugabe. Like the farms here, the Anglican Church has been jambanja'd, with most of its buildings illegally confiscated. "We have no premises, we are seriously displaced." He smiles.

This strange state of affairs began after the Anglican Church publicly condemned Mugabe's actions, and one of its priests, Bishop Nolbert Kunonga, a Mugabe apologist, broke away.

The matter is in court, sighs Bakare, though he has no faith in the country's pliant judges. "We say that Kunonga left the Church, committed schism, to found his own Church, and he has no claim on Church property.

"When I was appointed, I wrote to all our priests and asked them to declare themselves. All but seven of them stayed loyal to the Province of Central Africa. Since then, Kunonga has elevated four of those renegade priests to bishops.

"He put St. Mary's Cathedral under siege on the day of my installation," says Bakare, "supported by hired thugs, hooligans. I was supposed to be taking a service, but Kunonga was inside and wouldn't budge. He was sitting up at the altar with his miter on his head and a crozier [the heavy, hooked staff that is a bishop's symbol of office] in his hand—it looked unreal—he was on his own, with no congregation."

When Bakare tried to begin his service, Kunonga "charged at me with his crozier, using it as a weapon, and said I had no right to be there, that he was the only bishop. I told him he had been stripped of his office. He screamed at me, snatched the missal from me, and threw it on the floor."

He swung his crozier at Bakare again. The image of rival bishops dueling with their croziers seems ludicrous, but that is almost what it came to. Even the police officer was embarrassed, says Bakare. "He said, 'Look, this is no good, priests fighting in front of the congregation, let's go into the office.' But Kunonga wouldn't budge, so in the end we had to hold our service in the hall, while he stayed inside the cathedral."

Kunonga also busied himself sanitizing the cathedral of its history—it was built around a capstone brought from St. Paul's Cathedral in London, damaged by fire during the Nazi blitz in 1941. But now he ordered the ripping out of plaques to those killed in action in World War II. And the removal, too, of memorials to white pioneers.

"Then," continues Bakare, "the riot police started turning up at dozens of our churches and beating and chasing away our congregations. When we challenged them, and said they had no legal basis to evict us, they said, 'We are getting our orders from above.' We said, 'What, above *God?*'

"Kunonga has been campaigning for ZANU-PF, and when they lost the first round, they attacked us as scapegoats, just like they attacked people in the rural areas.

"At a recent gathering at St. Michael's of three thousand two hundred members of the Mothers' Unions from all over Mashona-land, the riot police came again. Kunonga was with them, hanging back, directing them."

The congregation was forced to disperse, and as Bishop Bakare drove slowly away, the women worshippers, in a gesture of support (meant to echo the palm fronds placed under the hooves of Jesus's donkey), laid their jackets and sweaters down on the road for his car to drive over. I find myself thinking of Gandanga, a few yards away in Dandaro hospital, a human frond beneath the devil's wheels.

ON SUNDAY, I go to Christchurch in Borrowdale, where my father's funeral was held, thinking of attending a morning service. But Sokiri, the church gardener, explains to me that the Rev. Harry Rinashe, the pastor, has defected to the rebel side. None of the Christchurch congregation has gone with him, and they are now led by the assistant pastor, Blessing Shambare.

It's all starting to make sense now. Rinashe had seemed oddly hostile at the prospect of my father's ashes being interred here. First, he claimed the church cemetery was full, which was patently untrue. Then he said that there was no record of the burial plot I'd reserved for Dad, next to Jain, and he was somewhat annoyed when the parish secretary duly dug out a receipt that proved otherwise. Even then, he insisted that I produce written statements from other prominent parishioners that my father had attended services there.

"He doesn't want any more white people in the cemetery," Sokiri murmured to me at the time, but I didn't believe him.

I wait outside for the service to begin; the only other congregant, a solemn black man in a tightly knotted tie and a lumpy tweed jacket, several sizes too big, clutching a crumpled felt trilby, is studying the parish list on the vestibule notice board. He approaches me, and pours out his predicament. "I used to be the gardener of Mr. Roderick, but Mr. Roderick went away to Australia, and I have lost his address, I used to keep it always in my pocket and then my wife washed my trousers and the paper, it got wet so I cannot read it now, I want to write to Mr. Roderick, for him to help me, but I no longer have his address." He looks crestfallen. "He used to attend this church, so I thought to come here. Do you have his address, please?" he beseeches. Together we scan the parish list, but there is no Roderick.

"Is Roderick his first name, or his surname?" I ask.

He thinks for a while, scrunching his eyes, and pressing his temples in concentration. "I don't know," he says, miserably. "For me it was his only name." He walks away, muttering to himself, and furiously beating his leg with his old trilby.

When the service begins, I slip into a pew at the back. With Mr. Roderick's gardener gone, there are only four congregants besides me. All are members of Rinashe's family, says Sokiri later, and they swing round and peer at me as I enter. Then they begin to sing. The only musical accompaniment is the desultory susurrus of a solitary maraca, deployed by Rinashe's wife. Recently elevated by Kunonga, Rinashe now wears a scarlet and gold bishop's miter on his head, and holds a crozier of his own. His new position obviously agrees with him — he seems to have put on more than fifteen pounds since I last saw him.

Today he preaches a sermon about turning the other cheek. "Human nature prompts me to want to hit back — to revenge — but we must not."

Afterward, I slip away to find that the loyalist congregants, about a hundred of them, black but for a couple of white pensioners (who soon depart), are standing in all their Sunday finery on Crowhill Road, outside the church, with Rinashe's former assistant pastor, Blessing Shambare. They wish to hold their service next, but their way is blocked by a dozen blue-helmeted riot police, armed with batons and whips and pistols. The congregation mill around for a while, their resolve hardening.

"What do we do?" one black middle-aged lady asks aloud.

"I've been worshipping here for thirty years," replies her friend, Charity Murandu, the deputy churchwarden, who wears a bright-pink angora sweater with matching trousers. "Let's just hold hands and go in."

"You know we will probably be savagely beaten?" says the first woman.

"Yes," sighs Charity, "very probably."

But they clasp hands and start to walk toward the church anyway, singing "On Jordan's Bank." As I'm about to leave, Charity turns, holds out her hand, and looks at me expectantly, and I feel a sudden surge of shame. I should stay away from this; my position is far too perilous as it is. But as these black women, middle-aged and elderly, in their careful Sunday clothes, their cardigans and cork wedge sandals, prepare to confront the riot police in order to go to church, I am ashamed to walk away, ashamed to let them do this on their own. So, to my own surprise, I find myself reaching for Charity's hand.

At first, the riot policemen are taken unawares and fall back, but they quickly regroup on the steps of the church itself, blocking the entrance. Their sergeant speaks urgently into his cell phone.

Prevented from getting into the locked church, Father Blessing Shambare decides that he will hold the service right there, on the lawn in front. He ducks into the parish office and returns in his cassock, with a bottle of communion wine and a plastic bag of communion hosts. Someone else brings a conga drum, and begins beating it as the congregation strikes up, "Stand up! Stand up, for Jesus!"

The riot police stand impassively on the steps, awaiting orders.

"Bless those who persecute you," Martin Murombedzi the churchwarden says to them. "If we fight, we fight on our knees."

A truck pulls up and more riot police spill out of it, commanded by a very small, angry inspector. He surveys the congregation and shouts at us to disperse, but his words are barely audible above the drumming and the singing, and no one budges. Then, though I am at the back, trying to stay out of sight, he spots me, the sole white, and points with his brass-topped swagger stick.

"*Bata murungu!*" he orders. "Grab the white man." The riot police swarm in to snatch me. But Blessing Shambare interposes himself, and links his arm through mine. "He is part of my flock, I am responsible for him, you can't arrest him."

The policemen try to pry him away but he will not let me go.

"Arrest him too," orders the inspector, pointing at Blessing.

Then Stanley Nikisi, the subdeacon, intrudes, so they grab him as well. And when Martin Murombedzi steps in front, they also seize him. And suddenly the whole congregation is pushing in, saying they will not allow us to be arrested, that we are all together.

"We are one," says Charity, furiously fending off a policewoman.

The little inspector, annoyed to begin with, is really losing his temper, but so are the congregants. One takes the inspector to task. "We have a court judgment that allows us to worship here. *You* are breaking the law."

"Fine," shrieks the inspector, his voice cracking into a falsetto to be heard above the melee. "Arrest all of them! All, all, all!"

So everyone is arrested, surrounded by the ranks of riot police, and herded out into the car park. And because they don't have enough transport, they form us into a long column, and march us down Crowhill Road for several miles to the Borrowdale police station. As we walk, we continue to sing hymns. Traffic slows to gawk at this strange spectacle, an entire church congregation surrounded by riot police, being marched at gunpoint down a main road.

As they walk, the congregants taunt the riot police. "You are being used by the higher-ups to do their dirty work," they say. "You should be ashamed of yourself, arresting church-goers." Others shout, "Judas!"

Some of the policemen argue back. They are just following orders, doing their duty. But others just shrug and look ashamed.

"We need the jobs," says one quietly, so as not to be overheard by his colleagues. "Our families must eat too."

In my little red backpack, hastily borrowed when I left New York from my son Hugo, to bring me good luck, there is a half-filled notebook and a cell phone with addresses of contacts, sources, and victims. I mention this quietly to Blessing, as we walk. Soon I sense a church lady walking very close behind me, and the zip being opened, and an item surreptitiously removed. Then another lady takes her place, and another, until all the offending items are gone, stuffed down the bras and underclothes of the church ladies.

Finally, the raucous congregation arrives at the police station. The priests and I are interrogated, separately and alone, sometimes by the small inspector, and sometimes by another policeman, who seems to be the same rank. They ask me why I was at the church — am I a journalist? I tell them I had simply wanted to attend the service, and that my family is buried there. The questions and answers have to be shouted, to be heard over the Christchurch women in the courtyard, directly under the window, who keep up a continuous round of "Onward, Christian Soldiers" in Shona, ignoring the angry shushing sergeants.

In a separate office, we can see "Bishop" Rinashe, who seems to be running the operation. The man who buried my father is now, it seems, responsible for my arrest.

The two senior officers are clearly at odds. One is embarrassed and ashamed that his police station is filled with hymn-singing middle-aged ladies, arrested for going to church. This is clearly not what he joined the police force to do. The other, the little inspector in charge of our initial arrest, seems determined to lock me up, and charge me, with Rinashe egging him on.

I am shuffled between offices and holding cells, and finally they take me in to be confronted by Rinashe directly. "You were at my earlier service," he says. I agree. "Who are you, why were you at my church, what business do you have being there?"

"You know me," I say. "My sister is buried in your churchyard, and so is my father."

He looks unconvinced. He turns to the small inspector. "He is a spy, or a journalist, or working for the opposition."

"You should remember," I say. "You buried my father yourself, you conducted the funeral service. And now you have me arrested for trying to visit my family's graves! What kind of a priest are you?"

He asks for my name again. I spell it out for him, and he sends a policeman back to the church to check on the gravestone inscriptions, the ones that we have filled with scarlet lucky beans.

While we wait for him to return, I am thrown back into the group interrogation, with Blessing and Murombedzi. And I find myself next to a man in shorts and flip-flops, whom I haven't seen before. He begins defending us rather articulately, and seems to know a lot about the law. When the police officer briefly leaves the room, he murmurs, "I'm a lawyer, the American embassy sent me."

So many people have seen our arrest and our public march that they have called it in.

The policeman returns to say that my gravestone has checked out, there is indeed a George Godwin in the churchyard. I can almost hear my father chortling over it—that he is protecting me not so much from beyond the grave, but from the grave itself.

The small inspector, however, remains determined to hold me. He is trying to get through to CIO, but because it's the middle of a three-day weekend, in honor of Africa Day, and it's also the launch of Mugabe's "run-off" election campaign, which is preoccupying senior members of state security, he can't get through to anyone on the phone. Finally, I hear him tell his colleague that he will drive over himself to speak to them, and return shortly, and I see him walk to his vehicle and set off.

The other priests have now been released, though no one will leave without me, and they are still milling around the charge office.

The seriousness of my situation now sinks in. So far, the police haven't worked out my identity. And I have a perfectly legitimate reason for being at the church. But once CIO get involved, my gig may well be up. As I sit there, listening to the Christchurch ladies singing themselves hoarse, I can't help but spin through the parade of images of the torture victims I've seen so much of recently. Deep in my stomach, I feel a hernia of panic rising — polyps of fear threatening to burst out of the abdominal wall of my calm.

It's odd really, but when I'm here, I mostly do a pretty good job of suppressing the thought of what might happen to me if I am picked up by the police. But at some level I know even a routine police stop can play out in any of four possible ways for me.

It can be, and usually is, a bit of banter at a roadblock and I'm sent on my way.

It might end up, as has happened to some foreign correspondents recently, with a week or two in cells — with friends or embassy staff permitted to deliver take-out pizza and bottled water — followed by expulsion from the country, with nothing worse than some head lice and a good story.

It could, I suppose, end up with the resuscitation of spying allegations against me, originally leveled after my news reports of the Matabeleland massacres (after which I was accused of working for British or South African intelligence), and following a trial before a pliant Mugabe judge, years in a ghastly, shitfumed Zimbabwean prison.

Or, as seems to be happening more these days, I suppose it could end with being blindfolded and driven to some waste ground outside the city to be shot in the back of the head, and dumped there, doused with kerosene and burned, like rubbish.

But if you went around imagining that, you wouldn't do anything; you'd be paralyzed by the fear of it. It simply doesn't bear thinking about.

My forebodings are interrupted by a summons from the other officer in charge, the one who seems fed up with his role of religious inquisitor. He closes the door behind me so that we are alone, and settles back into the office chair behind his desk.

"Sit," he says, nodding me into the hardback chair opposite.

He pauses for a moment to allow a particularly full-throated chorus of "Onward, Christian Soldiers" to recede.

"You are in trouble," he announces.

I nod.

"My colleague wants you to stay in jail."

I nod again.

He pauses once more, places his hands together, fingertips to fingertips, and glances over at the side wall where there is a large chart graphing burglaries in Borrowdale.

"He suspects you are lying to us," he says. "And so does the priest, Rinashe."

I nod, noncommittally this time, trying to look penitent without looking guilty, a somewhat subtle expression to try for, I realize.

His cell phone rings and he flips it open. I fear this is the small angry inspector, calling in the disquieting results of his inquiries at CIO.

"*Herro? Herro!*" shouts the policeman. But the call has been dropped. "This cell service is *useless!*" he says.

"Yes," I agree, secretly glad. "It's very frustrating."

He snaps the phone closed and places it on the desk in front of him, and we look at it for some time, both expecting it to ring again. When it remains silent, he finally looks up.

"I have decided to release you from custody," he says slowly, examining me closely.

"Thank you." I grin foolishly. But almost immediately, I fear a trap. I don't want to be set up for "attempting to escape."

"What about the other inspector, he said I was to be held here."

"It is *my* decision to make," he says irritably, and I sense a history of tension between the two. "And these women"—he gestures wearily at his window where the hymnal medley shows no signs of abating—"are giving me a headache."

He grows grave. "But you must leave the country as soon as you can. During this weekend. It will not be safe for you to stay here any longer. Okay?"

"Okay." I nod vigorously.

I leave on the next plane out, to Johannesburg, early the following morning. And when the captain announces we have reached our cruising altitude, my hands start to tremble uncontrollably. So much so, that the steward has to put the drink on my tray table for me.

twenty-one

They Laugh While You Burn

THE SITUATION THAT GREETS ME when I arrive in Johannesburg is hard to believe. The place is in the grip of the most ferocious attacks on foreign migrants. It is chilling to behold. Starting in the gritty squatter camps of Alexandra township, the pogroms quickly spread to the grim dormitory townships of the East Rand. Hunting parties of residents are summoned by eerie, high-pitched whistling, as though being piped aboard a warship by the bo'sun. They jog through the streets, armed with pangas and chains, spears and sjamboks (long tapered whips), axes, knobkerries (cudgels), knives, shovels, and metal fence posts. A few have golf clubs, and one even has a tall carved wooden giraffe. From time to time, hunters will squat down to sharpen their blades, drawing them back and forth over the asphalt, with a sinister rasping.

But the target of the mobs' anger is not the rich folk next door in the plush garden villas of Sandton, with hadedas cawing by the pool and Weimaraners lounging on the lawn. These rich folk live behind tall walls crowned with razor wire, chaperoned by pistol-packing patrols.

The targets are poor black migrants, from Mozambique and Angola, Nigeria, Somalia, Malawi, and Zimbabwe, especially from Zimbabwe—because they are here in such great numbers now, well over three million by some estimates, fleeing south from the violent collapse of their own country.

The mobs pulse with a primal hatred of the interloper, and they flourish their weapons to the sky, in rhythm with their stride and with their chant, "*Awuleth' umshini wami*" ["Bring me my machine gun"], the anthem adopted by Jacob Zuma's supporters from the ANC Youth League, as they seek out *makwerekwere*—the foreigners. Those they find, they attack and kill, and they loot their shacks and burn them down. Sometimes the hunting parties set fire to their victims too—it all reminds me of the 1980s when as a correspondent here I covered the township protests. Then, a favored mob punishment for suspected *impimpi*, collaborators, was to "necklace" them with burning tires.

This appalling echo is immediately recognized too by the diminutive Nobel Peace Laureate Archbishop Emeritus Desmond Tutu, who distinguished himself then, in an act of real bravery, by wading into a lynch mob to rescue a man from being necklaced.

"These are our sisters and brothers," he implores now. "Please, please stop!" He tries to remind the mobs that during apartheid, Zimbabweans and Mozambicans and Angolans risked attack by apartheid forces, by giving shelter to South African refugees and guerrillas. "We can't repay them by killing their children."

But they pay him no heed, and the rampage continues. In one image I wish I'd never seen, a burning man writhes slowly on the ground for long, agonizing seconds, the clothes searing off his back, before a policeman finally arrives with a fire extinguisher and douses his cinder-crusted body, coating him in white foam, a grotesque snowman. This white apparition sways weakly on its hands and knees, with the tentative gait of a chameleon, and then topples over to die.

"They set you alight…and laugh at you while you are burning," says Teboga Letsie, a local photographer. "It's so shameful right now to be a South African, seeing all these things happening here, while claiming to be a rainbow nation, after all the struggles that our parents have gone through."

Once the blood lust has the mobs in its savage clutches, there is an almost carnival atmosphere—the cutting and the killing seem so casual, the hunters high on it, psyched, excited, and they are indiscriminate, attacking schoolgirls and old men, anyone who can't speak the main local languages, or does so with an accent.

Sometimes the hunters challenge you to count in Afrikaans, to prove to them that you are truly South African, a bizarrely ahistorical reversal: it was black school pupils' protests at being taught in Afrikaans that triggered the June 1976 Soweto massacre and ignited international revulsion at apartheid, yet now you must pass an Afrikaans test to fend off the asphalt-sharpened blade at your throat.

Xenophobia, they are calling it—the fear of strangers, an intense dislike of those from other countries. But there are uneasy questions about these "spontaneous" pogroms. Why do they seem coordinated? How can they spread so quickly throughout Gauteng to KwaZulu-Natal and even the Western Cape, places hundreds of miles apart?

The Methodist Bishop of Johannesburg, Paul Verryn, for one, is suspicious. "I was called and warned the day before it started," he tells me. His Central Methodist Church on Smal Street in downtown Johannesburg is choked with Zimbabwean refugees, three and a half thousand at the last count. The desperation shows on their sweat-beaded faces; they are sleep-deprived and scared; they have lost everything and their trust in their fellow man is shattered. "It's like living with a wild beast," says a man with a bandage around his head, who's too anxious to give his name. "It has turned on us once, and it may turn on us again without notice."

Down in the chapel a black Zimbabwean pastor is preaching about xenophobic attacks in the Bible, on Joseph, on the children of Israel. "They had a difficult time in Egypt," he says, "making bricks with their own saliva, it was tedious. But God wanted to deliver them to their own land."

For these people that land is Zimbabwe, but not tonight. Tonight they will sleep here, dossing down on pieces of sackcloth — mattresses take up too much room — squeezed, slave-ship tight, on every available berth of floor space. At the chapel door, under the sign of a handgun deleted with a thick red diagonal line, a man in a trench coat is handing out stickers to the exiting congregation. He gives me one too. It reads, *Xpress Yourself. Go Vote.* He's an engineer with an MBA, and works for the Zimbabwe Diaspora Network. For now he goes by the name of Chester, because he's worried about Mugabe's CIO agents. "Even down here, we are not safe from them," he says. Forty buses will leave this weekend from Johannesburg, to take Zimbabweans home. "Our message to them is, 'Go home and vote, and change things there so you can repatriate permanently.'"

He wants to address the refugees here, to appeal to them to board the buses, rather than stay to be attacked by hostile locals. "They need to go home and vote, to make a difference. At the end of the day it's up to us, no one else will help."

But Bishop Verryn disagrees, and won't let Chester make his address tonight. "There's no guarantee of their safety if they go back," he says. "What if they are brutalized again there? I'm not prepared to cooperate with sending them back to their deaths."

I find Verryn in his eyrie at the top of the church, surrounded by great mounds of donated clothes that rise to the ceiling. To get here I've had to walk up four flights of stairs in the dark, stepping over prone bodies on almost every step. *"Pamusoroyi"* ["Excuse me"], I apologize, as I accidentally nudge the bundled forms. *"Ehoyi"* ["That's okay"], come the muffled replies from beneath blankets and coats.

I FIRST ENCOUNTERED Paul Verryn twenty-two years ago, after I'd written a profile of Stompie Moeketsi, a thirteen-year-old who had become the leader of anti-apartheid resistance in a tough black township in the Free State town of Parys. His mother, a poor washerwoman, arrived at my door, bearing the business card I'd given her a few months before, dog-eared and creased now, and asked me to help her find Stompie, who had disappeared. It turned out that he had initially found shelter, along with other refugees, at Verryn's Methodist residence. Then he had been snatched by the bodyguards of Winnie Mandela, Nelson Mandela's increasingly erratic wife, and hadn't been seen since. After a few weeks, his body turned up. Later, we found out that her bodyguards had murdered him.

Verryn has been providing sanctuary for Zimbabwean refugees at this church for several years now, much to the annoyance of the local authorities, who want them moved away before the 2010 World Cup. Three months ago the police raided this church and arrested hundreds of them, before a court appeal forced their release.

The church has never been this full before, says Verryn. He is brown-bearded, with glasses, a purple surplice and white clerical collar, clever and funny. When I use his episcopally correct title— Your Holiness—he hoots with laughter. But mostly tonight, he's angry.

"You can't have a nation that sanctions prejudice for over fifty years and then imagine it's a walk in the park out of it," he says. "But these xenophobic attacks, they're organized, I've got records. It's a combination of elements of the police, councillors, ANC, Inkatha. Someone came up to me on the first day and said, 'Watch out, this thing is going to spread.'"

And spread it certainly did.

Other, temporary, refugee camps have sprung up all over Gauteng and beyond. One of them is in the old town hall in Boksburg, on the East Rand. They call it the Pink House—its roof is a startling shade of salmon—and most of the Zimbabwean refugees crowded inside have fled from the nearby Angelo squatter camp. It is suppertime and they have formed a long orderly line for the beans and thick maize porridge they call *posho* here, being doled out at trestle tables.

In the line is Arthur Basopo, twenty-two, who has been in South Africa for fifteen months, working in a bed shop. At 11 p.m., a few nights ago, he says, "they broke down my door."

"Who?"

"Citizens of South Africa—they came in, grabbed me by the neck, searched me, took my money belt, stole my TV and my radio and my generator, and then started beating me, but I managed to run away to save my life. The next day, I went back there but my house was broken down."

Casper Mugano, twenty-one, from Rusitu, near Chimanimani (the area overlooked by Chris Lynam's old farm), has been in South Africa for sixteen months, working as a welder. He was also attacked, looted of all his belongings, and his house was burned down. Which was the fate of Godfrey Matanga, also from Rusitu, working here as a house painter. "The only solution is to go home," he says. "I'm too scared to stay here now."

Brian Maviso, twenty-six, worked as a freelance plumber and electrician. Ironic, I suppose, given that his shack had neither running water nor electricity. Ten people were killed in Angelo in those first attacks, which, he says, were launched by the Pedi (a Northern Sotho people, who were corralled by the apartheid authorities into the "homeland" of Lebowa), who dominate Angelo squatter camp. "The Pedi know us, they know who we are." He wants to go home too. "If only I could get my tools," he wishes, "so when I go back to Zimbabwe, I could keep working."

That's what's remarkable about these refugees. Although they're surrounded by jobless locals—South Africa's unemployment rate is over 25 percent—most of these Zimbabweans manage to find jobs, or to create jobs for themselves. Sure, this is partly because they're prepared to work for lower wages. But it's also because, like so many migrants, with the wolf at their backs, they are industrious, ingenious, indefatigable. And this has stoked the jealousy of their attackers, many of whom, complains Maviso, "sit around playing dice and drinking."

In return, South Africans blame foreigners for the high crime rate here—often unfairly.

For me, the irony of this all is completed by the sci-fi movie *District 9* (sponsored by Peter "Lord of the Rings" Jackson), now being shot on location in southern Soweto, at Chiawelo, during the worst of the xenophobic attacks. The director, Neill Blomkamp, a South African himself, says in interviews that the film is an allegory of apartheid and xenophobia, that the District 9 of the title is an echo of District Six, an old-established mixed-race inner-city neighborhood on the slopes of Cape Town's Table Mountain, which the authorities declared "whites only" in 1966. Police forcibly removed the sixty thousand mostly mixed-race "colored" residents to the Cape Flats, about fifteen miles away. Then they bulldozed the houses of District Six, and renamed it Zonnebloem — "Sunflower" — though no one ever called it that.

For years, District Six stood as a graphic reminder of the pernicious realities of the Group Areas Act, a flattened urban wasteland with only its churches and mosques spared, their spires and minarets rising like the few lonely teeth in a punched mouth.

In *District 9,* tall, wheezing, mucus-trailing, prawn-like aliens, whose giant spaceship has stalled in the skies above Johannesburg, are evacuated to Earth and confined to a slum outside the city. There they are hunted down by furiously xenophobic locals. Even as the actual residents of those slums are hunting down the human aliens who have landed among them. Blomkamp no longer has to reach back to apartheid days for his allegory. It has been horribly updated by today's South Africa. Life has imitated art imitating life.

Eventually, ten days into the attacks, with sixty-two recorded deaths, hundreds badly wounded (six hundred and seventy-two officially recorded), and more than a hundred thousand foreigners huddled in churches and community halls, police stations, and tented camps, Thabo Mbeki finally does what he should have done at the start of the violence; he authorizes the army to go in and restore order. By now, the harsh hymn of hate has been clearly heard: aliens, especially black Zimbabwean ones, will never feel completely safe here again.

AMONG THE ZIMBABWEAN refugees in South Africa are many of the MDC's most senior leaders, driven south of the Limpopo in fear for their lives, during these last few weeks of state-sponsored attacks up north. They include Tsvangirai's top two lieutenants, Tendai Biti and Roy Bennett.

Tendai Biti is an old friend, a former student leader, now a lawyer and secretary-general of the MDC, and its chief election strategist, Tsvangirai's tactical wizard, who clearly relishes the detail in the poll data. But as the level of state-sponsored violence has risen, he realized that Mugabe has no intention of giving up power at the ballot box.

The last time I saw Biti, we were on the same team in an IQ2 Debate at the Royal Geographical Society in London. The motion we were asked to support was: "Britain has failed Zimbabwe." We won, largely because of Biti's bravura performance and contagious enthusiasm.

Today we meet at the five-star Michelangelo Hotel in Sandton, a world apart from the Angelo squatter camp out in Boksburg. Biti takes off his Kangol houndstooth flat cap and through angular, post-modern German glasses looks around uncomfortably at the faux-Renaissance opulence. "It's a convenient place to meet." He shrugs. He fields calls on his constantly buzzing BlackBerry, and taps away at his laptop.

Both of us are reeling at the xenophobic pogroms, which, he admits, took him by surprise.

"I didn't expect their anger to be channeled against foreigners, rather I thought it would be directed at the state, as the freedom train has passed most black South Africans by. I think that given the poverty levels in those communities, juxtaposed with obscene wealth, there has to be anger, pent-up frustration in knowing that you are a fourth-class citizen, that for the poor, the geography of apartheid is still intact. I mean, what have these ANC guys been *doing* since 1994?"

Like Verryn, he too suspects that the violence was not spontaneous. "The magnitude of it, the extent of the displacement of entire communities—fifty thousand people uprooted at a stroke. This thing is being done on a large scale, it has to have some backing, planning. You know, the definition of genocide includes displacement. And wherever there's genocide, there's a plan. In Rwanda there was a plan."

He warns that it won't stop with foreigners. "Once you let the genie out of the bottle, next time the South Africans will be doing it to each other."

Biti flew down to Johannesburg the week after the elections, nearly three months ago, to address a press conference and go straight back to Harare. But while here, he was tipped off that Mugabe's regime intended to assassinate him on his return. "They want to make an example of me. If they can attack me, then anyone is at risk.

"Nobody wants a run-off," sighs Biti. "It means more suffering for our people, more deaths, murders. The number of those already displaced in Zimbabwe is over a hundred and thirty thousand.

"A run-off," he predicts, "means you are creating conditions for a war. Mugabe will lose, so he will resort to guns and bullets. If we win and he does that, I wonder to what extent we can rein in our youth, the radicals in the MDC, we might not be able to control them.

"Zimbabweans down here are saying, 'We are ready to go in at any time.' At a public meeting at Wits [the University of the Witwatersrand], the biggest applause was for a guy who said, 'There's only one thing dictators understand — the gun.' We've tried everything else, courts, elections — we won and yet..." He trails off, suddenly dejected.

"Mugabe is demented. He genuinely believes that we are puppets, he genuinely believes he's in a grand fight with imperial lords and that the country needs him more than ever, it's a reflection of his insanity, his disconnectedness."

And even Mugabe's death is unlikely to deliver us, he says. The delusional psychosis spreads throughout his henchmen. General Constantine Chiwenga, the head of the army; Emmerson Mnangagwa, the head of the Joint Operational Command (JOC); Gideon Gono, the Reserve Bank chief; and Augustine Chihuri, the head of police: "these are his courtiers who depend on the king for everything, so even if he dies, they would stuff his body and prop it up on the throne. Just these few courtiers are holding the rest of the country to ransom."

Biti intends to return to Zimbabwe next week. Apparently, the South Africans have intervened, and now assure him that he won't be assassinated by Mugabe's men.

"But you'll be arrested," I warn.

"I know," he sighs. "But I have a mandate from the people. I must honor that."

ROY BENNETT, the party's treasurer, has been continually arrested and assaulted and threatened with death. He famously lost his temper in parliament, when the Minister of Justice, Patrick Chinamasa, taunted him, calling his forefathers "thieves and murderers." A shoving match ensued, and instead of the small fine that such a fracas would normally attract from the court, Bennett found himself sentenced by parliament to a year in Chikurubi, the country's maximum-security jail—where he was forced to wear a shit-encrusted uniform and routinely humiliated.

On his release, in mid-2005, his hair now turned polar white, he sought refuge down here. It took a long court battle to make the South African government grant him asylum. Today he sits in Bryanston, northern Johannesburg, at the MDC office, like a caged bear, out of place and uncomfortable behind his desk, clearly pining for home. He spends his time trawling the diaspora and other sympathizers for donations to keep the MDC going.

"You know the worst thing for me during my exile here," he says, "is to go to a restaurant, and the waiter is a Zimbabwean lawyer, or an accountant, or a lab technician—we simply have to restore their dignity."

Roy shows me a sheaf of documents that have been leaked from inside the government. One is a CIO overview of the coming presidential run-off elections, marked SECRET. After a very pessimistic assessment of the real mood of the electorate, it answers the question, Who is likely to win the run-off? "President Mugabe will lose the election as the people now have the confidence to come out and express their feelings without fear." This newfound confidence, it urges, should be broken. It ends with a section headed "Covert Operations to Decompose the Opposition," which recommends, among other things, "harassing MDC activists and driving MDC supporters out of ZANU-PF strongholds, and massive rigging by any means possible, e.g. manipulation of postal votes in ZANU-PF's favor and reduction of polling stations in MDC strongholds..."

Like Biti, with whom he works closely, Bennett believes that Zimbabwe is now on the brink of full civil war. When I ask him about Mbeki's attempts to cobble together a Kenya-style composite government of national unity, a GNU, of all parties, Bennett won't even let me finish the question.

"We won't touch a Government of National Unity—over my dead body, under no circumstances. The people will never accept a GNU. They saw what happened to ZAPU."

Instead, he lays out an apocalyptic scenario.

"If Mugabe steals this election, what's our option? There'll be a war, we'll be forced to go violent. They'll underestimate us. If we mobilize, you'll see what will happen. It'll be vicious. The people will slaughter their oppressors if they get the upper hand. We've already decided, Morgan Tsvangirai, Tendai Biti and me, that if Mugabe steals this election, we'll form a government-in-exile, delegitimize his regime, and move to a military confrontation."

And then, he says, there will be no middle ground. "Those making money out of the regime—whites too—are real bastards. I phone them, and say, 'People are being murdered and tortured—you've got their blood on your hands, for what? A few pieces of silver?' I'm gonna phone them now and tell them to choose—we're heading to war—you side with the people, or with the regime. You answer to some colonel, or to the people of Zimbabwe. I'm gonna phone them myself."

As I leave for the airport, to catch my flight back to New York, he is trawling through his contacts list, doing just that, calling Mugabe's backers directly, and warning them that their time is nigh.

JOHANNESBURG'S Oliver Tambo International Airport judders with jack-hammers, part of an ambitious project to vastly expand it in time for the 2010 World Cup. I find myself wondering what the slogan will be for the ad campaign to attract foreigners to a country where rampaging mobs have spent the last fortnight hunting and killing black foreigners. I think of the image of the burning man, now identified as Ernesto Nhamuave, as he slowly topples over to die. *A Warm Welcome awaits you in South Africa…?*

twenty-two

The Final Battle for Total Control

TENDAI BITI does just as he told me he would—on 9 June, he goes home. And it happens just as I feared. When he arrives at Harare airport, he doesn't even make it to passport control. As he steps off the plane, ten armed security agents in cheap suits seize him. They handcuff him, bundle him into a car, and speed him away. Biti vanishes. MDC colleagues worry that he is being tortured. They send lawyers to police stations to look for him, and prevail on a judge to issue a habeas corpus order, declaring he must be produced in court.

After two long, anxious days, the police finally comply. They have been interrogating Biti at the Goromonzi torture center just outside Harare—a facility nicknamed by former inmates, with gallows humor, "the swimming pool," because the cement floors of interrogation rooms are hosed down to keep them wet, in order, they say, to boost their conductivity, facilitating electric-shock torture.

Biti is moved to Chikurubi maximum-security jail, and police spokesmen announce that they are charging him with treason for writing a document (which Biti says is fake) describing how a transition of power to the MDC would work, and also for revealing the results of elections "prematurely"—the equivalent of announcing exit poll results. These charges carry a maximum penalty of death, so he will stay in prison while awaiting trial.

IN THESE LAST WEEKS before the 27 June election re-run, Mugabe's men clamp down on Morgan Tsvangirai, making it almost impossible for him to campaign. He tries to launch a country-wide tour in his bright red battle bus, the Morgan Mobile, which has huge pictures of himself on the sides, grinning over the motto *Morgan Is the One*, and signs on the fenders declaring it to be a *Victory Tour*. But riot police follow him wherever he goes, dispersing well-wishers and canceling his rallies. They arrest him three times in a single day and finally confiscate his campaign buses.

Meanwhile ZANU-PF rallies become compulsory, turning into all-night *pungwes*—indoctrination sessions. In Harare, behind the Triton gym, in which the diplomats and fat cats pound their running machines, the open patch of land where Georgina used to ride Top Ace is turned into a ZANU-PF base. The nannies and cooks and gardeners of the northern suburbs are herded there by Mugabe's youth militia, forced to sit on the ground and chant themselves hoarse until dawn, in praise of the octogenarian dictator.

The pace of violence picks up around the country as Operation Ngatipedzenavo—"Let Us Finish Them Off"—gets under way. Mugabe's election strategy has been completely militarized. The securocrats have taken over the day-to-day running of the campaign. The team that Mugabe has put in charge of the operation is led by the Minister of Defense, Sydney Sekeremai, working with Air Marshal Perence Shiri and General Constantine Chiwenga, out of Joint Operations Command. It's the same dream team that carried out the Matabeleland massacres twenty-five years before, when Perence "Black Jesus" Shiri commanded the North-Korean-trained Fifth Brigade, alongside Chiwenga, under the then Minister of

Defense, Sydney Sekeremai. They are all architects of a previous genocide.

MDC officials are besieged: arrested, beaten, and chased from their homes, murdered.

In Zaka, near Masvingo, a dozen of Mugabe's youth militia, now dressed in army fatigues, driving a pick-up with no plates, arrive before dawn at the rural home of Elias Mudzuri, a former Mayor of Harare, and now the MDC's national organizing secretary, and an MP. He is an old friend of mine, whom I hosted in New York. The militiamen shoot his brother in the leg and savagely beat his eighty-year-old father, before looting his homestead.

In Chipinge, the family of Lovemore Madhuku, another friend, who heads the National Constitutional Assembly, a group promoting a new constitution, is also in the line of fire. Addressing a pro-Mugabe rally there, a senior police officer, Deputy Commissioner Godwin Matanga, threatens to kill him. "We have dealt with Tendai Biti," he warns. "Madhuku is next."

He's as good as his word—soon afterward, Mugabe's militiamen burn down Madhuku's rural home, and those of twenty-two surrounding villagers, for good measure, and the police throw his brother into jail.

In Chiredzi, CIO agents seize five prominent young MDC supporters, drive them into the bush, force them to lie face down, and shoot them in the back of their heads. Four of them die instantly. The fifth, Jacob Ngirivana, though grievously injured, survives to bear witness.

In Harare, Mugabe's men murder an MDC official's wife, Pamela Pasvani, who is five months pregnant, burning her to death in her house, together with her six-year-old son.

In Mhondoro, less than a mile from the home of "Notso" Bright Matonga, Mugabe's spokesman, CIO agents arrive in their signature white pick-up trucks looking for Patson Chipiro, an MDC electoral organizer. Finding him absent, they grab his wife, Dadirai, forty-five, a former nursery-school teacher. They hack off her right hand and both her feet, drag her into her house, and set it alight with a petrol bomb. When Jan Raath, Rita Harvey's brother-in-law, attends her funeral, he finds that Dadirai's relatives have been unable to close the lid of the cheap wooden coffin. Her arm, charred, rigid, and handless, protrudes, as though imploring for the help that never arrived. The village women who swept away the cinders of her burned house have found her missing hand among the ashes, and placed it inside her coffin.

"These youths are taught cruelty," her grieving husband tells Jan. "They get used to murdering. They enjoy murdering."

The body count rises toward a hundred, with another five thousand missing. Bodies are being found bobbing at the spillway of dams; others are discovered in the bush, dumped by their murderers, miles and miles from where they were abducted. In some particularly gruesome cases, the victims have been castrated, their testicles stuffed in their mouths, or their eyes gouged out. Many will never be found. Some ten thousand people have been tortured. Twenty thousand have had their houses burned down—up to two hundred thousand are now displaced.

Genocide Watch, the Washington DC–based monitoring organization that specializes in recognizing the signs that group killings are imminent, issues a chilling "politicide warning" on 19 June. Zimbabwe, they say, is now at a stage six, "the preparation stage immediately preceding political mass murder."

They recognize the growing instances of murder and torture victims having their ears, lips, and sexual organs cut off "as one of the surest signs of dehumanizing of target groups during genocide and politicide." The killings of opposition leaders' families is also a prelude, as is the phenomenon of "mirroring," "a strange but common psychological mechanism of denial used by mass murderers," whereby the perpetrators accuse the victims of doing what perpetrators themselves are doing.

Tsvangirai is in despair, powerless to stop the killings of his aides and supporters. His party makes a last attempt to hold a rally, in Harare's showgrounds, but it is invaded by over a thousand of Mugabe's men, armed with iron bars, who break it up and beat opposition supporters. Harvest House, the opposition headquarters, is surrounded by a force of two hundred and fifteen policemen. They arrest over sixty people there, mostly women and children fleeing violence in the rural areas, and they seize documents and computers.

Tsvangirai meets his party executive, and after reviewing the mayhem, they realize that they cannot go on. So a week before the 27 June election re-run Tsvangirai finally calls a halt, announcing his withdrawal as a presidential candidate. He cannot ask his supporters to come out and vote for him "when that vote would cost them their lives." The bullet, he says, has replaced the ballot. He cannot participate in what has become a "violent, illegitimate sham." And he makes a plea to the international community to "intervene and stop the genocide." That night, just ahead of a raid on his house by General Chiwenga's soldiers, he flees into the Dutch embassy, in fear for his life.

MUGABE's election slogan in the violent presidential run-off is "The Final Battle for Total Control"—a chillingly totalitarian clarion call, as Orwell might have imagined it. When fighting Rhodesia for universal suffrage, Mugabe had used the mantra "One Man, One Vote." And now that Tsvangirai has been bludgeoned out of the running, and Mugabe is the only man left to vote for, he has finally achieved a grotesque version of just that—there is only one man left to vote for, the dictator himself.

To make sure voters do just that, and turn out in support of their glorious leader, the Generals in Joint Operational Command launch one last operation. They call this one Operation Chigunwe Chitsvuku, "Red Finger." To prevent multiple voting here, your little finger is coated in a special red dye, indelible for several weeks. So the red finger is a sign that you have voted. Now Mugabe's men put out the word that they will be inspecting hands after the election. Those without a red little finger will have the finger cut off.

LESS THAN an hour after the result is announced, Mugabe has himself sworn in as President at a hastily organized inauguration. It is boycotted by McGee, Pocock, and the rest of the Western diplomats. The African ambassadors stay away too.

Even the observers from the fourteen nations of the Southern African Development Community, who have been pliant to Mugabe, finally balk at his terror tactics. The one-man election, they concede, "did not represent the will of the people," and they condemn the "politically motivated violence, intimidation and displacement." But crucially, they fail to back this with any action.

Looking subdued and pensive, Mugabe holds a black Bible aloft and swears himself in for another term, his sixth. Around him at State House are only his family, his judges, and his generals. Most of all, his generals, with whom he shakes hands, one by one, Chiwenga and Shiri at the vanguard, the men who have bathed this path to prolonged power with the blood of their people.

Later that same day, Mugabe jets off for the annual African Union summit, held this year in the Egyptian seaside resort of Sharm el-Sheikh. Mugabe continues to command residual respect from this audience, as Zimbabwe's original liberator. And as the continent's oldest head of state, he is still politically priapic. When the subject of his stolen, blood-soaked elections comes up, in closed-door session, he challenges the assembled African presidents, many of whom—thirty-two of fifty-three—preside over authoritarian regimes themselves. Those of you without electoral sin, he says, in effect, cast the first stone. I may have unclean hands, but most of yours are dirty too.

So they shrink from any direct action, handing off the Zimbabwe conflict once more to Thabo Mbeki as "facilitator," though the South African remains Mugabe's prime protector.

One of the few African leaders—in addition to Botswana's Ian Khama—bold enough to stand up to Mugabe's harangue is Zambia's president, Levy Mwanawasa, who is due to sit next to him, according to the alphabet of Africa. Mwanawasa has been preparing to mount a spirited attack on Mugabe. But his chair remains empty. The evening before the meeting is due to begin, in a bitter stroke of cosmic irony, Mwanawasa is felled by a massive heart attack. He falls into a coma and dies six weeks later.

Attempts by the UN to impose sanctions against Mugabe for his bloody election crackdown fare just as badly. The proposal before the Security Council includes an arms embargo, and a travel ban and a financial freeze on Mugabe and a dirty dozen of his top officials who are considered to be the main architects of the violent campaign there, including Chiwenga and Shiri. But it is vetoed by two permanent members, China and Russia, together with Vietnam and Libya. South Africa, to its eternal shame, given the support that the ANC received from the UN in its struggle against apartheid, joins them in voting to protect Mugabe.

twenty-three

Where Do Tears Come From?

Back in New York now, it seems to me that the palsied grip of Zimbabwe's gerontocracy is unbreakable; the country's transformation into a dystopia, complete. That Mugabe's moral dementia is simply a reflection of the wider ideological dementia of African post-liberation movements. It is yet another mask for the exclusionary greed of a medieval patronage system, with its bloody barons arrayed around the autocrat, all of them locked into a ferociously fixed-frame world view, one in which fairground mirrors line the corridors of power, where giants are reflected back at strutting moral midgets.

In a small way, I am trying to draw attention to the Zimbabwean tragedy. I sit at my study desk writing up the tales of torture for a *Vanity Fair* magazine article; I appear on cable news shows, and speak to the White House fellows in DC. I go on the public radio WNYC's *Brian Lehrer Show* with a Zimbabwean DJ, Chaka Ngwenya, who used to be a media personality back home with Georgina, but fled in 2000, and founded an Internet radio station, SARFM, "The Heartbeat of Africa," which he broadcasts from a tiny room in a Salvation Army Church in Harlem.

In a *New York Times* op-ed, I point out that South Africa could use its economic power to end Zimbabwe's suffering in weeks, but instead, the vacillating, dithering, morally compromised figure of Thabo Mbeki has protected Mugabe. In order to nudge his cost-benefit calculus, I suggest that maybe Zimbabwe should become to the South Africa–hosted World Cup what Tibet has been to the Beijing Olympics — the pungent albatross that threatens to spoil every press conference with its insistent odor.

The newspaper accompanies it with a woodcut of a football boot, which has skulls for cleats.

The South African embassy releases a furious riposte. Unable, I suppose, to lose apartheid's old obsession with racial categories, they quickly establish mine: "Mr. Godwin," they write, "whose family immigrated from England to Zimbabwe in the early 1950s," and they go on to call me rash, flippant, irrational, privileged, protected, emotional, subjective, and hypocritical. "It is highly unlikely," they conclude, "that Mr. Godwin will be sharing in the pain of Zimbabweans or South Africans, for that matter, from his high-rise apartment in Manhattan." I consider a one-line reply, which would read: "How dare you impugn me — I live on the ground floor..."

But our efforts have little effect. My wife, Joanna, who edits a fashion magazine, suggests that this is because we lack a celebrity cheerleader, a Clooney, a Farrow, a Damon, Jolie, or Pitt. Indeed, the truth is that in the race of African moral outrages, Zimbabwe's body count earns us a mere bronze to Darfur's gold and Congo's silver. They are both classified as civil wars, so have achieved international peace-keepers. Ours is not, because the opposition has not yet picked up weapons. Ours is a war with only one side.

For as long as Zimbabwe's victims stick to the pacifist path of MLK, rather than the AK, we cannot expect blue helmets in Harare. As Tsvangirai had rued to me: "If we took up AKs, the UN would rush in here, but we are penalized for being peaceful."

Perhaps now that democratic avenues have been exhausted, the moment has come, as Roy Bennett had suggested it might, for Zimbabwe's frustrated democrats to fight back, to follow Thomas Jefferson's exhortation that the tree of liberty must be watered from time to time with the blood of patriots and tyrants.

Tsvangirai continues to insist, "I won't have the blood of our young men on my hands." But it seems to me that in the last ten years, the body count has been higher *without* a fully fledged uprising. Millions of Zimbabweans have perished from the repression, from AIDS, from starvation, and from the collapse of health care.

We are also trying to help build pressure to prosecute Robert Mugabe and his colleagues. In what court could they be indicted? The craven courts in his own country are a charade. But there are other avenues. Under international law, torture, "when committed as part of a widespread or systematic attack directed against any civilian population, with knowledge of the attack," qualifies as a crime against humanity. It's pretty obvious to me that Mugabe and his cohort clear this bar: the atrocities in Zimbabwe have been widespread, systematic, and committed on the express order of a central dictatorship through the Joint Operations Command. The hierarchy of terror is clear, with no smokescreen of anarchy to blur the blame. The fact that almost no one has been prosecuted shows that the abuses are centrally condoned. And they are probably the best-ever documented in Africa—gavel-ready.

Under the new legal principle of "universal jurisdiction," South African courts could prosecute any of the perpetrators that come onto its territory, but the National Director of Public Prosecutions there has so far resisted requests to investigate torture in Zimbabwe. The UN Security Council could task the International Criminal Court to investigate and prosecute the perpetrators of Zimbabwean crimes against humanity—but that's unlikely because those two trusty human-rights champions, Russia and China, are bound to veto it, just as they vetoed previous action against Mugabe. But the International Criminal Court Prosecutor has the power to initiate proceedings on his own. Raising awareness of the horror of Mugabe's crimes will help in both these efforts.

As well as the torture itself, a case is being made by a Boston-based advocacy group, AIDS-Free World, that the mass rape in Zimbabwe also rises to the level of a crime against humanity. The extent of these gang rapes takes longer to emerge—the stigma so great, the victims so deeply ashamed, and in danger of being rejected by their husbands. AIDS-Free World is assisted by the international law firm DLA Piper, one of the few to have a dedicated international pro-bono department, New Perimeter. They have donated U.S.$1m of billable hours to work on the Zimbabwe rape cases, and sent lawyers to South Africa and Botswana to take detailed depositions from victims who have fled there. They cannot do it in Zimbabwe.

Later I meet a group of them, young women in their thirties, in DLA Piper's Washington DC offices, a smart new sandstone-clad building on 8th Street. The corridors are lined with blond wood and original art. In the sunny cafeteria, lawyers ladle muesli into little clay bowls and pump fair-trade coffee into gleaming white mugs before returning to their glass-walled offices overlooking an airy central atrium.

Sara Andrews is the team leader for the Zimbabwe project. Like the other young lawyers who made the trip, she is haunted by the women they have met there, some of them refugees in Bishop Verryn's church. The trip, she says, has changed them forever. "It's very surreal afterward, to return to a comfortable world, where people complain about the trivial."

"At the end I didn't want to leave," says her colleague Kristen Abrams. "There was so much more to do, and people to talk to. I still think about it constantly, the stories, the women's faces. I had a hard time coming back and re-engaging with my life here, laundry, preparing dinner..."

Syma Mirza tells me that "going in, you assume that the victims' primary concern is the trauma of the rape—when in fact it's just day-to-day survival. They don't have the luxury of healing yet."

"I was okay for the first couple of days of interviews," she says, "but after the third day of hearing it all first hand, I was just thinking how humans could be *capable* of all this deliberate violence and hurt." The story tattooed on her mind is from a twenty-year-old woman who was raped while listening to her father screaming just outside the room as he was beaten to death. Before he died, they rubbed dirt in his eyes. "In the trade-offs involved in transitional justice," says Mirza, "I used to be on the peace side, but after this, I want accountability more."

Another woman she deposed, who ran a small business selling vegetables, proved that Bishop Paul Verryn's concerns for the Zimbabwean refugees sheltering in his Johannesburg church were valid. She intended to go back for only forty-eight hours, just to vote in the run-off, but she was abducted by Mugabe's men. "We know you're back to vote for the MDC, you are on our list as an activist," they said before gang-raping her.

Brenda Meister is haunted by the story of a woman who went out with one of her year-old twin boys to run errands, leaving the other baby at home with his father. When she returned, she found her husband dead on the floor next to her son, who had been decapitated. The Mugabe thugs who had done this then grabbed her and gang-raped her next to her headless baby and her husband's corpse, while her other baby sat crying nearby.

She was quite composed and matter of fact as she explained to Meister what had happened. While she talked, her surviving twin played quietly on the floor with the toy trucks and the plastic fruit provided by the lawyers.

"I've done Afghanistan and India," says Meister. "But I've never heard anything this horrific. As they described their experiences, it struck me that there was never anyone to help them at the time, no police, no health care. They were totally on their own."

On her last day in South Africa, Meister bought six cuff bracelets made by Himba women in Namibia from sections of recycled PCV. The women carve designs on them, which they rub with ocher. Back in DC, she had a local jeweller paint on the inside of each bracelet the name of one of the babies of the women she'd interviewed. Each morning she wears a different one, "just to remind me, every day, that those babies are still there." Today she has a blue bracelet on. The baby's name is Owen.

The women deposed by the DLA Piper lawyers are just a small sample of the victims. Betty Makoni, director of the Girl Child Network in Zimbabwe, has compiled a list of over eight hundred names, and these, as they say in Zimbabwe, are just the ears of the hippo. There are many, many more beneath the surface. Women who will never get help, and most of whom will die, untreated, of AIDS. And no one has been prosecuted for these rapes.

LIKE THE YOUNG lawyers who find it hard to re-engage with their lives when they return, I struggle to compartmentalize my life. Shaken by what I have seen in Zimbabwe, I'm acutely grateful that my family is safe here in New York. That we aren't awoken by the shattering of glass, the reek of kerosene and the room in flames, that we don't have to run out into the night carrying our sons, pursued by Mugabe's henchmen. But I feel guilty and ineffectual too, maudlin and distracted and angry.

Unable to sleep, I flick listlessly through the cable TV spectrum. Mostly, I watch natural-history shows, but they only feed my preoccupation. A show about mole rats—which tells me that so long as the queen rat lives, all other females are intimidated into remaining infertile, but once she dies, they all become fecund again, and fight for her role—reminds me of the political caste system in Zimbabwe, with Mugabe's potential heirs sublimating their ambition until the dictator dies and a war for succession erupts.

A show that tells me how starfish eat, by thrusting their stomachs out through their mouths secreting gastric acid onto their proposed meal, reminds me of our leaders too. I imagine them revealed that way—their bellies bulging out through their mouths to squirt corrosive effluent onto their threadbare constituents before gorging on them.

I find myself trembling for no reason, getting flashbacks to the parade of torture victims that lines the halls of my memory. Though I am no longer there to witness it, their misery continues.

I want to hug my sons to me now, spend all my time with them. They can sense something changed in me.

One morning, newly back, I am playing with them on their bedroom floor. Hugo and I are defending a wooden fort with a force of small plastic dinosaurs. Thomas is attacking us with large U.S. soldiers. The rallying cry of our army of diminutive dinos is "We may be small—but we are many!" To which Thomas's giant GIs retort, "We may be few, but we are large." In the middle of the game, I reach to move a little *T. rex*, and suddenly I see the little boy, Sampson Chemerani, lying in hospital with his eye hanging out, and the *T. rex* picture the nurses had taped to his medical chart, to cheer him: "The truth about killer dinosaurs."

"What is?" asks Hugo. "What's the truth about killer dinosaurs?"

Without realizing it, I have spoken aloud.

I haven't told the boys much about Zimbabwe this time. Nor have I shared the details with Joanna, who is just back from the Paris collections. "When two worlds collide," I joke, "couture versus torture." She suggests that I may be suffering from some form of PTSD by proxy.

Now I tell Hugo a diluted version of Sampson's story, how I met a little boy in Zimbabwe who had been hurt. But Hugo is at an incontinently curious age. He wants more detail. "Did he cry?" he demands.

"Yes."

"Can you run out of tears?" he segues.

I draw breath to answer, but he's already serially speculating. "Do you have a little reservoir where tears are stored, and when it's empty, you can't cry anymore? How does it fill up? Where do tears come from anyway? What are they made of? Did Alice really swim through her own tears in Wonderland?"

That night he comes into our bedroom in tears himself. He has been awoken by a bad dream. "I was kidnapped by a man in a snake suit," he sniffs.

"You've upset him with your war stories," Joanna chides.

"But then I woke up," says Hugo, rallying, "and I realized that it was just a fake life."

A fake life. Maybe that's what I'm living. But which is my real life and which is my fake one? Zimbabwe seems so real while I'm there. But even while I'm there, I'm not really. Soon I leave and it fades into my past again. It reminds me of working as a foreign correspondent, shoulder to shoulder with photographers and cameramen. How they became so integrated with their cameras, they feel they aren't really there in the flesh. You have to hurry them away as the danger grows.

And I remember one cameraman, George D'ath, a friend who was killed that way, years ago by the *witdoeke*, the "white cloths," a vigilante force used as surrogates by the old white South African police. It was in the black squatter camp of Crossroads outside Cape Town, and George was filming them for ITN as they *toyi-toyi*'d past him, brandishing machetes. Right at the end of the jogging column, one of the *witdoeke* attacked, flicking his blade to slice George's throat. The last image on George's camera, before he fell in a pool of his own blood, was the face of his murderer. The cops took his videotape "as evidence," but when they returned it, they'd deleted those last images, so that his murderer couldn't be identified. There but not there.

Hugo's bad dream, his first in ages, has come because his dreamcatcher is full, he reckons. His sleep used to be stalked by a malign character he calls "the fat lady," who taunted him and threatened him, though didn't appear to do him actual bodily harm. But the bad dreams stopped once he made us buy him a Mohawk dreamcatcher from a farm stand in the Greene County in the Catskills. He hung it on his bedside light from its leather thong—a suede-bound willow ring with indigo beads strung on a twine web within it, and feathered tassels twirling slowly below—and the fat lady went on sabbatical.

"My dream-catcher needs to be emptied," he announces now. "You have to shake it over running water." Apparently, you can't just release bad dreams into the air, or they will escape to plague someone else. "It's like *Ghost Busters*," he says, "the way they have to store the captured ghosts in that special tank." So we walk down to the Hudson River and solemnly empty his bad dreams into its fast olive water.

I wish it were that simple. I wish that I could commit all the horrifying images and stories—things that will live with me forever now—into the dark currents as they slide swiftly under the twisted metal hulk of the old New York Railroad pier, and have them borne away, past Ellis Island and the Statue of Liberty, and out into the gelid gray sea.

twenty-four

Like a Candle in a Dungeon

ALTHOUGH MUGABE dodges the bullet of UN sanctions, the U.S. and many other countries, as well as the EU, refuse to recognize the legitimacy of his continued rule.

Even Mugabe himself appears to realize that his regime is now widely regarded as profane. He has been shocked by the extent to which his own people have turned against him. Fewer than 12 percent now support him, according to a Freedom House MPOI poll. His government is bankrupt, inflation is exploding exponentially, and now cholera has broken out. The failed state is here; there is little left for even Mugabe's elite to loot.

So he tasks his ministers to seriously explore plan B, a way to survive by co-opting his opponents, via Thabo Mbeki's hitherto moribund inter-party negotiations, his so-called "quiet diplomacy," which has formerly served the chief purpose of fending off further international action, with the pretence that there is a negotiated option in the works, one that robust action would derail. Now

Mugabe has to grasp the cactus of "power sharing," though, of course, he doesn't want to share real power at all.

The opposition, for its part, is exhausted—bankrupt, battered, traumatized, intimidated. Its structures are shattered; thousands of its tortured officials have fled their homes. Their only other option is war, something that Morgan Tsvangirai still recoils from.

To many, going to war is preferable to sharing power with a blood-drenched Mugabe. And in the senior ranks of the MDC there is resistance to any joint rule. Roy Bennett, who had told me in the MDC office in Johannesburg, where he was in exile, that a Government of National Unity would only happen over his dead body, and Tendai Biti remain the two main hold-outs. Stop-start negotiations drag on for months.

A South African friend of mine, Vincent Mai, now a New York–based investment banker and philanthropist, who knows Tsvangirai, and once rescued him when he got stranded at JFK, calls me in late January with the news that he's just had a long phone conversation with him. "Morgan says there's absolutely no way he'll agree to any coalition government with Mugabe," reports Mai. "He says that day has passed—the only way it would work is as part of a complete transfer of power, because no aid will be freed up otherwise."

"These talks are just symbolic," he told Mai, "because of the tremendous pressure the South Africans are putting on him."

"Don't worry," Morgan assured him, as he concluded their chat. "I won't sign anything."

A few days later he signs the so-called Global Political Agreement to enter into a power-sharing government with Mugabe.

THE GLOBAL Political Agreement is a nebulous deal. Mugabe is to continue as President and chairman of cabinet of a Government of National Unity, GNU, with Tsvangirai in the newly created post of Prime Minister and Arthur Mutambara, from the other MDC wing, as deputy PM. But the shape of a new constitution is postponed. Like the power-sharing deal reached between rivals in Kenya, Zimbabwe's deal shelves any real resolution.

Jim McGee emails me: "Tendai [Biti] is saying this is the worst day of his life. Morgan is upbeat and looking forward to being PM. I think he's being set up for failure. We'll see."

I am on my way to midtown Manhattan to take part in a panel hosted by the Global Center for Responsibility to Protect, R2P (the principle that the international community has a duty to intervene to prevent crimes against humanity), to discuss how to invoke the R2P principle in Zimbabwe, when I hear the news of the deal.

Mugabe's envoys are usually allergic to these events, but today Chrispen Mavodza, the chargé d'affaires of the Zimbabwe mission to the UN, shows up. He listens politely to the graphic evidence of human-rights abuses in Zimbabwe, and when he speaks, it is not to deny the evidence, but just to hope that it is all over. Afterward, he seeks me out. "I hope we Zimbabweans can all come together now, Peter," he says. "It is time for Mugabe to stop hunting enemies, real and imagined," and he proffers his hand. But I can't bring myself to shake it. Not yet, not so soon after what they have done, after what I have seen. So I glance away, pretending to be looking for something inside my briefcase.

Tsvangirai says the agreement is just a transitional arrangement, that he will quickly sign off on a new constitution, under which free, international-monitored elections will be held. It is, he says, "like a candle in a dungeon."

My worry is that he has given Mugabe a reprieve, time to draw breath, re-appraise, and reload, that this GNU will be nothing but an interlude, a short intermission in the repression.

And indeed it quickly becomes apparent that Mugabe doesn't anticipate that the deal will ease him out; quite the contrary. Selling the power-sharing plan to his party Central Committee, he castigates them that if they hadn't blundered over the elections, "we wouldn't be facing this humiliation." Then he quickly rallies: "Anyhow, here we are, still in a dominant position which will enable us to gather more strength as we move into the future. We remain in the driving seat."

*　*　*

THE INAUGURATION of this "hybrid" government is something I want to witness for myself. Georgina does too. After conferring with friends in Zimbabwe, we calculate that the changed political situation there should mean that, despite my hurried exit last time, we can now go back without being arrested. But as I am about to leave New York, my mother calls me, in tears. Georgina is in hospital with bad pneumonia. She was diagnosed at her doctor's, who ordered her a taxi, straight to hospital, as she might be developing a pulmonary embolism, says Mum. The taxi driver squeals across North London to the Royal Free Hospital in Hampstead, and pulls up outside the casualty department — where a security guard curtly informs him that Georgina may not disembark there, because of building work.

A row ensues, and eventually Georgina gets out and promptly collapses onto the pavement. Now the hospital staff heatedly debate whether she is already in Casualty, in which case they must admit her, or still on the street, in which case they will need an ambulance to take her there. Mum, meanwhile, is trapped inside the taxi, between the traffic and Georgina's prone body on the pavement.

Finally, Georgina is loaded onto a stretcher and wheeled inside, while Mum retrieves her walker from the trunk. Georgina is seen by a nurse, who inserts a shunt into her arm but doesn't connect it. They sit there for four hours, when the staff from the respiratory ward come down themselves to find her. She still hasn't been X-rayed or assessed by a doctor. My mother can't get a signal to call Georgina's boyfriend, Dominic, to ask him to collect Xanthe from school. The hospital won't let her use their phone — no exceptions. Finally, another elderly lady lends her a phone. Then she waits forty-five minutes outside in the winter cold for transport home, and now she is racked with flu.

Later I get an email from Georgina from her hospital bed. She is on a drip and can't talk because she has an oxygen mask. When I call through to her ward, the nurse who answers has a distinct Zimbabwean accent. His name is Bright Makunde, and he used to be a teacher in Zimbabwe before retooling as a nurse in the UK, one of the flood of Zimbabweans fleeing to the UK. Bright promises to take good care of Georgina, and I feel happier knowing that she is being watched over by a compatriot.

I route my flight to Zimbabwe through London, and arrive at the tail end of the BIGGEST SNOWFALL FOR 18 YEARS as every newspaper shouts, and the city is paralyzed by it.

GEORGINA is out of hospital, still looking wan and ill. Xanthe comes bounding back from school, in her blue Hampstead Parochial sweatshirt and corn-yellow hair. "Where's Uncle Peter going to sleep?" she asks Georgina, looking round the crowded flat.

Georgina points to the wooden Swahili daybed in the sitting room.

"But he hates that," says Xanthe. "He says it feels like sleeping in a canoe."

"Well, at least this one won't sink," says Georgina curtly.

My mother is still unsteady on her feet and furniture-surfs around the flat. She only goes out now reluctantly. She finds living in England as an elderly person one long parade of indignities: being shoved on the pavement because she walks too slowly, tutted at when she takes too long to retrieve change from her purse at the till, or to step up onto the bus, or climb the stairs on the Tube. It has resulted in her becoming agoraphobic. Outside, there lurk only dangers and rudeness. When she does venture out, she often returns offended and querulous, armed with tales of her latest brush with boorishness, and many slights.

When I try to change the subject by mentioning that I saw the playwright David Hare walking down Church Row carrying his Tesco bags, this only fuels her theme. "His wife, Nicole Fahri, the designer, was followed home by a couple of thugs who tried to wrench her necklace off her, at her own front door, and nearly strangled her," she says, presenting this as crowning proof of the lethal world out there, where yobs lay in wait for easy marks. "She's Persian," she adds.

The impatience and discourtesy with which the elderly are

treated here is in sharp contrast to the attitudes in Africa. My theory—quite untested—is that it's not so much cultural in its origins, but arithmetic. In developed countries like the UK and the U.S., growing old is common, and there's a big demographic bulge of the elderly. In Africa, very few are lucky enough to live into their fifties or sixties, never mind their eighties—Zimbabweans are usually dead by thirty-five—so the grizzled are a statistical rarity there, admired and venerated for their life experience, and their sheer survival skills.

MY MOTHER asks me to sit in on an interview she must give to be assessed for charitable help. Her last few interrogators have been foreign, she says, and she's struggled to decipher their accents. She has found them to be peremptory and dismissive, and the whole experience humiliating. I try to tease her about the irony of her returning to England from the Third World only to find that the Third World has followed her here. "It's revenge for colonialism," I laugh, but she finds it quite unfunny.

There is something bizarre about the spectacle, though. Partly, it's that despite (or maybe because of) her fifty-year life in Africa, my mother still speaks in a now quite unusual antebellum upper-crust English accent. Xanthe does an amusing imitation of it, dancing around Mum chanting: "Heylio, it's Hillin. Would you like some parsta in a plahstic berl and a glahrs of miylk out on the payshio," which translates as: Hello, it's Helen. Would you like some pasta in a plastic bowl and a glass of milk out on the patio?

The examiner today is a chic middle-aged lady wearing a sloping black beret, a red jumper, leather boots, and plum lipstick, her smooth mocha neck coddled by a turquoise scarf. She opens her briefcase to begin, while I make coffee. But my mother tries to keep the conversation all about the examiner, Georgette Emilieu. She is from the Seychelles, off the east African coast, where her brother is the vice-president. Her husband came to the UK to join the British army. She volunteers for four charities, and acts as a translator in the courts.

Georgette tries to steer the conversation back to my mother's situation.

"Well," Mum says finally, looking stricken. "I'm so embarrassed to seek charity, but I was in the war, the Wrens, the Royal Navy, you know, and then I worked as a doctor in Africa for over forty years. And then, and then, we lost everything..." She trails off and begins to cry. "I'm so ashamed," she says, dabbing at her eyes.

"Don't be ashamed," says Georgette. "You *deserve* this help. I know how you feel. We've paid our taxes for twenty years, we've never been on the dole, and yet people come here and as soon as they arrive they get a council flat. I was disgusted the other day," she says, "when a Somali lady tried to sell food vouchers to me. 'Take them,' she said. 'I sell them to you for less than their face value.'"

She places a comforting hand on my weeping mother's forearm, and repeats gently, "You deserve it."

THE NEXT DAY my mother would like me to meet her friend Hildegard Weinrich, who, she says, together with her companion, Anne, was very supportive of her when Georgina was in hospital, bringing a goodie basket. "Not just fancy things, bonbons and stuff," says Mum, "but things you really need at a time like that—bread and eggs and things. So nice of them."

I'm intrigued to meet Dr. Hildegard Weinrich because as Sister Aquina, a Dominican nun, she played a significant role in the rise of Robert Mugabe. We go for tea at her house in North London, where she now practices as a Jungian analyst. In the corner of the front room is a large raised sand tray, and along the walls are shelves stacked with hundreds of small figurines, people, animals, and other *objets*. This is where she carries out sand-play therapy, she explains. The patient chooses figures and arranges them in the sand, in the re-creation of a world that illuminates their inner state, in much the same way as dreams do. "It gives me a better diagnosis than oral alone," she says, speaking with the Teutonic precision of a German aristocrat. Her grandfather used to hunt with the last German emperor, Wilhelm II. And she remembers being taken to see Hitler's motorcade as a child.

Hildegard became a formidable figure in Rhodesia, a liberation theologist, who decided by 1970 "that the conditions for a just war of liberation had been met." She worked on the Catholic Justice and Peace Commission with Dieter Scholz and tasked Fidelis Mukonori to infiltrate the "protected villages" into which the Rhodesian security forces had herded black civilians, to gather evidence of the poor conditions there. She remembers hiding documents in her underwear, to avoid detection.

When Mugabe was put into detention he wrote to her asking her to get him books he needed to study for his MA thesis on education in Rhodesia. He signed himself "Your brother in Christ, Robert Mugabe."

She started visiting him in detention, and on his release in 1974 a close friendship continued. She imitates the way his voice cracks when he gets excited, and shows how he used to thumb the rosary his mother, Bona, had given him.

One day she received a message from Mugabe, that he was in hiding and needed to escape the country. "Robert believed that I was the only person he could trust..." she says. She suspected that Mugabe's hiding place, in a presbytery in Rhodesville, northern Harare, had been compromised, so she raced there in her old gray VW Beetle, running through red lights to warn him.

Mugabe fled to a commune in Chief Tangwena's district in the Nyanga Mountains. She tells me that, just as the police arrived there at the front door, looking for him, he scrambled through the refectory hatch at the back, and over the border.

Later, Hildegard clandestinely assisted guerrilla recruits. Tipped off by a Catholic member of the police Special Branch in June 1975 that she was about to be arrested, she was ordered to leave by her Dominican superior, much to her chagrin.

"I felt that my heroic aspirations had been opposed by opportunistic Church leaders. While I was ready to sacrifice my life for a cause, the local Church decided that it had to be prudent. Hence I had to be silenced; and how better could they silence me than by whisking me out of the country?"

Hildegard was invited back by Mugabe in 1980, she says, "to serve on two commissions: one to change the capitalist into a socialist system, and the other, under the Lord Chief Justice, to work out a nation-wide voting register for the indigenous population." Mugabe also asked her to help teach parliamentary procedures to the new black MPs, and to assist them in writing their speeches.

But when she decided to establish a Center for African Culture, Socialism and Practices in Early Christianity, "as described in the Acts of the Apostles," one Catholic bishop complained to the leadership of her congregation, and Hildegard was ordered to drop socialism from her agenda. She refused. "There was a clash," she says. "I had a nervous breakdown and was ordered back to the UK."

The day before she left Zimbabwe, she visited Mugabe in the State House. In the context of a discussion on South Africa's attempts to undermine his government, Hildegard said to Mugabe: "Robert, I want you to have power." At that, she says, he exclaimed in a crazed falsetto: "Yes, *power*, I want power! Power! Power!"

"He was like a demon, punching the air with his fists," she says. "It was a revelation to me. I had never seen him like that before."

Six months later when his wife, Sally, came to London for kidney dialysis, Hildegard visited her. "Sally called Robert and handed the phone to me—and he just screamed at me. I think he was still furious that I had left." Hildegard shakes her head sadly. "That was the last time we spoke. I don't know what happened to him. I'm deeply distressed at the way the political situation of Zimbabwe has evolved."

THE NEXT DAY, as I prepare to leave London, my mother hands me two documents. One, which she asks me to post, is a letter. This is a ploy. The pre-printed address is the General Medical Council's. "What is it?" I ask, as she expects me to.

"They are forcing me to renounce my retiree's honorary membership, which I was awarded in 2004, after having been a member of good standing for fifty years," she says. She gags on her words and her eyes well up and spill over. "It's just my thyroid imbalance," she says, angrily wiping away the tears. "Pay no attention to them, they're not real tears.

"The European Court ruled that it is age discrimination *against the young* for the General Medical Council to continue giving retired doctors honorary membership. If I don't pay the new £500 [about $900] annual fee, or formally resign *in writing,* they'll register me as 'dishonorably leaving.'"

I take the envelope from her. But once in the mini-cab to the station, I tear up her resignation letter, and put in a check for £500. It's more than my flight to Harare, but I can't bear to see her break her last link with her profession. It would seem a formalization of her inutility.

THE MINI-CAB DRIVER taking me to Paddington to catch the Heathrow Express is Ugandan. So we talk about things there and soon I start boasting about how I once knew the President, Yoweri Museveni, how as a foreign correspondent I had accompanied the young guerrillas of his National Resistance Army as they had taken Kampala and fought their way north, against General Tito Okello's forces. And how I'd been wounded in the face by shrapnel from a rocket-propelled grenade when they counterattacked.

He listens patiently to all of this, and when we finally pull up at Paddington Station, he says quietly, "Myself, I am from the north. I am an Acholi, same as General Okello. We were the ones that were overthrown by Museveni. That is why I am now driving a mini-cab in London." Feeling mortified, I over-tip him and flee onto the Heathrow Express, and back to Africa.

twenty-five

The Day of the Wildebeest

5 February 2009

I ARRIVE IN A CITY once more on the brink, a city hoping to be delivered from the jaws of oppression. That strange atmosphere of euphoric despair has taken hold again. Real change, which seems so certain a prospect when you view this place from outside through the lens of the foreign media, seems suddenly less likely from within—a sort of parallax syndrome.

For the last few months, the parties have jostled over the distribution of cabinet posts, who will control the treasury, the military, the police, the justice system, the media. And even as Mugabe ostensibly prepares to share power, his men continue to seize the last few white-owned farms, and to arrest civil-rights activists. Jestina Mukoko, from the Zimbabwe Peace Project, has recently been dragged from her bed in the middle of the night and hauled to jail, barefoot, in her nightdress, without her essential medication. She is one of at least thirty political prisoners.

Already there are many naysayers of the new Government of National Unity, the GNU, which some have nicknamed the wildebeest, after its acronym, an animal so ungainly—with its huge, broad muzzle and humped shoulders, its back sloping sharply down to a disproportionately small hindquarters and oddly dainty legs—that it, too, could only have been created by warring parties.

Tsvangirai is calling it another animal, "a union of donkey and a horse…a mule—not very pretty but functional." Which also implies that one party is screwing the other. It looks likely to me that it's the MDC that's getting shafted. They won the initial election, even after all the fraud, yet they have been bludgeoned out of their victory. And Tsvangirai doesn't pursue his analogy—that mules are sterile.

Two other animals come to my mind, from an old Shona saying: *Manjeni, kuona ingwe ichitamba nembudzi*—"It's astonishing to see a leopard playing with a goat." What it means, really, is that it's suspicious, unnatural, that it will not end well—for the goat.

PENNY BEATTIE, my architect friend, picks me up from the airport in her little red Suzuki, and drives me across to their house in Borrowdale, where I'm staying. The city is even more disheveled since my last visit. The rains have been more plentiful than usual and the whole place is overgrown. Water collects everywhere, except in the city's leaking dams. It spills out of clogged storm drains, and pools on the broken pavements. And the roads, the runoff tears at them, creating jagged edges and huge potholes, new ones almost daily, so that you can't remember the geography of them well enough to slalom around their minefields.

No one likes to travel at night now. Between the potholes and the lack of street lights and the broken traffic lights, people prefer to lock themselves into their houses by the fall of darkness.

And as the surrounding farmers have been evicted, and their lands fallen fallow, the bush has encroached, and is re-colonized by wildlife. Eagles wheel overhead, adjusting their wingtips for sudden plunges onto rodents below. Snakes slither through the thickening undergrowth. There are more insects: scorpions and mosquitoes, flies, bees. A man stands in the middle of the road, unperturbed when we drive within inches of him, holding a placard on which he's scrawled in large red letters: BEE REMOVAL. Monkeys and even baboons have reappeared in the city, scampering through the suburbs, rustling through the trees.

Working street lights are rare now, and at night bats flourish, as the city grows profoundly dark, in a way that no modern city ever really does. Without light pollution you can see the stars pulsing, limpid and glistening, unusually near. And the luminous craters on the moon are startlingly clear even to the naked eye. With most industry closed and traffic dwindling, the city's background hum, that urban tinnitus, has relented, and at night it falls eerily silent.

Most people survive without electricity now. Women walk the streets carrying thick bundles of wood on their heads, their backs and shoulders perfectly straight, the posture so sought after by Western debutantes, perfected here in the impoverished streets of Africa.

And the natural rhythms of the bush have started to return to a capital of two million people. Hungry residents now plant maize on every available patch of land, even along the highway medians. And you see the soft glow of fires as people cook their meals in front of their houses, and on the curbside. And they come to work in the morning, those few with jobs, reeking of wood smoke, as though they have been camping. And in a sense, they have. They've become urban foragers, hunter-gatherers reverting to a pre-industrial rhythm of life, maximizing daylight, walking miles to collect untreated water, to cook with it and to bathe in it, and to flush their stagnant toilets. Their lives are returning to the old way, the way people used to live out in the countryside, a hundred years ago.

The country is being ravaged by an epidemic of cholera, an utterly preventable medieval disease that hasn't been seen on any scale here in modern times, and is symptomatic of acute poverty. But of course it has nothing to do with the collapse of water supplies and sewage systems and medical facilities. No. According to Mugabe's current information minister, Sikhanyiso Ndlovu, it is a "serious biological chemical war...a genocidal onslaught on the people of

Zimbabwe by the British...Cholera is a calculated racist terrorist attack on Zimbabwe by the unrepentant former colonial power which has enlisted support from its American and Western allies so that they can invade the country..."

He has deduced all this from the public warning issued by Jim McGee of the likely spread of cholera, after the first cases were reported, and the need for urgent preventive action. (Although why McGee would choose to reveal his dastardly secret plot, pre-emptively, is not immediately apparent.)

Before it ends, the epidemic will have stricken a hundred thousand people—killing four thousand of them, to add to Mugabe's roster of deaths. Cholera kills fast, through extreme diarrhea. People are just keeling over in the street and dying of dehydration. The hospitals are overflowing with their corpses.

The extent of the government's response is to tell Zimbabweans to stop shaking hands. When you meet now, you use a special cholera handshake, which is either a fist bump or even—by the particularly cholera-phobic—an elbow or shoulder bump. The public-health ads by the WHO, warning you to boil your water, render cholera in Shona as "*korera,*" the language having no resident "L"—so they morph into Rs.

The Borrowdale shopping center is even more faded; the banks there are almost empty. I look at the uneven brick plaza and see the ghosts of the long line outside the Standard Bank, in which I used to accompany my mother, and where once she took a terrible tumble, even though I was holding her arm at the time. Everything has now moved over to U.S. dollars, and no one here wants Zimbabwe dollars, not even the freshly minted trillion-dollar note. Enterprising Zimbabweans in the diaspora are selling it on eBay as a curiosity—the world's largest-denomination note—for more than its black-market face value here.

An elderly white man totters up clutching a check to deposit, made out in Zimbabwe dollars. "How much is this number?" he asks me, his rubber-tipped aluminum stick clattering onto the par-quet floor. The check has twenty-one zeros before the decimal point. I try to calculate. Six digits is a million. Nine digits is a billion. Twelve is a trillion. Fifteen is, a quadrillion? Eighteen is... hmm. "About five U.S. bucks," I say, and he chortles. The cashier slides across a handy laminated chart. Twenty-one zeros is a sextillion.

"One of my friends who emigrated left me this," says Penny Beattie, showing me a bulging backpack. "Go on. Open it."

Inside are wads and wads and wads of money, in ever-ascending denominations. Like the lines of sediment in a geologist's drill bit, they represent each phase of the Zimbabwe dollar's hurtling collapse—the fastest currency collapse of a nation not at war the world has ever seen. "Bloody worthless," she says.

Richard Beattie drives me over to his office to access email, and on the way we look in at what had been one of the main safe houses, when I was last here, a low rambling green-roofed complex in Highlands. It belongs to a church group, and today they are preparing to screen a film about Angus Buchan, the "miraculous South African farmer who grew a bumper crop of potatoes in a famine, on faith alone," says Wendy, the white woman running the church. "Do stay for it."

She has adopted a quadriplegic black baby, Richard says, and to support themselves she makes jewelery. She hands him a small bag of tiny silver earrings in the shape of an open hand, the sign of the MDC.

When I was here last, dozens of fearful and wounded political refugees cowered inside, fed by John Worswick's group, Justice for Agriculture (JAG). But as the successful torture campaign wound down, all the refugees were dispersed. Well, almost all.

"Shame," says Wendy, wringing her hands, "one lady we had here with her small baby, she came back, saying she couldn't find anywhere else to stay. We told her we no longer operated as a safe house. We gave her some food and she left. I just heard that she and her baby have both died of cholera."

When we reach the gate of his architectural office, Richard honks. "I have a security guard now, ever since I was shot at here," he explains as the guard unlocks. There are twenty-six architects left in Zimbabwe, down from a peak of about two hundred and fifty in the 1970s. Richard and Penny struggle to keep going, with little new work in this shattered economy.

While Richard battles to get online, I notice a Scientology DVD set on his desk. "Who's dabbling in this?" I ask.

"Ah that," he says, arching his brow. "We're supposed to be converting an office block they bought on First Street. But they left it empty for nearly three years and it was totally vandalized, picked clean of all fittings and fixtures. Anyway, we've done six months' work for them and they haven't paid us a bloody thing. In the initial contract, there was a confidentiality clause saying that every time we said anything at all about the Scientologists, they would fine us $20,000," says Richard. "I just deleted that bit.

"Did you know that each Scientology church has to have an office for L. Ron Hubbard—just in case he returns? We went down to their HQ in Johannesburg, which used to be a golf club, and there are portraits of Hubbard in every room, it's worse than bloody Mugabe."

Hubbard, Richard tells me, came to Rhodesia to try to advise Ian Smith on how to resist majority rule, but after two years, Smith chucked him out of the country. The Scientologists bought the house on Gun Hill (the suburb where Mengistu now resides) where he lived, and turned it into a museum.

Heinrich von Pezold calls to say he has two horses running at the Borrowdale races on Saturday afternoon. His wife, Amanda, now heavily pregnant, is staying at home, and Heinrich has brought his little boy, Christof. The races are a little better patronized than before as the bets are now in U.S. dollars. Both Heinrich's horses win—one is unbeaten in Zimbabwe, "which isn't saying much, these days," he hastens to add. He poses in the trainers' enclosure for photos, with the horse and jockey, a tiny white man, dressed in the von Pezold colors: yellow with a giant black polka dot. Behind them a double rainbow appears, ending in a flame tree behind the Mashonaland Turf Club.

With Christof still on his hip, Heinrich gives a TV interview to a young black dreadlocked commentator. Christof is fractious, frowning, and pulls his dad's arm, but Heinrich blithely continues. Then he glances down in distaste as a wet patch grows across his white shirt and down his pants. Christof is peeing on the 1,337th in line to the British throne—on national TV.

Upstairs, in the members' bar, Heinrich toasts his victory with JC Le Roux "champagne." "The champagne made to be shared," he declares, grimacing, "so you never have to drink more than one glass yourself."

"Still hanging in there at Forrester?" I ask.

"Yes, it's tough, but we're still managing to farm."

"What currency are you paying your labor in now?" I inquire.

"Food," he says. "We pay them in food. More than they can eat, and they barter the rest. They're very happy with that."

DINNER IS AT Paula Worsley-Worswick's house. Her marriage to John has collapsed under the strain of everything, his campaigning work on behalf of farmers at JAG, the continued invasions, the never-ending uncertainty—and they haven't seen each other socially for months. Tonight, I think, I am there as a sort of domestic blue helmet. But after a few glasses of wine, we get into a political row.

"People like *you* are responsible for Zimbabwe's terrible situation," Paula suddenly declares.

"Who?" I ask. "People like who?"

"You," she says. "You and John and your whole bloody generation of men, it's all your fault. You're responsible for the continuing political hostilities because of your confrontational, hair-trigger aggressiveness, born of war. You've been trained as soldiers," she maintains, "trained to fight in wars, and you've never bloody gotten over it—you just don't see it in yourselves, you're blind to your own conflict psychosis."

John is spluttering in protest, cataloguing more deserving culprits, but Paula has made up her mind.

"You're past help," she says. "Compared to you, the next generation is gentle and spiritual. They're indigo people — with peaceful auras, not like your violent ones."

The dinner ends early.

"What are indigo people?" I ask John, as we walk to our cars.

"Buggered if I know," he mutters. "Some New Age crap."

BACK AT THE BEATTIES', Henry Chimbiri, a former high-school teacher, drops by, looking thinner than ever. Henry is the Zelig of Zimbabwean opposition politics with elements of Forrest Gump and the Scarlet Pimpernel. He was active in the union movement, held various posts in the MDC, then stood as parliamentary candidate in Mount Darwin South. While trying to campaign, he was beaten and imprisoned, during which his mother died. On polling day, as the candidates were waiting for the ballot count to begin, they heard the results being announced on the radio! Unsurprisingly Henry had lost.

He moved across to the Mutambara wing of the MDC after a falling-out, and then, as a freelance photographer and cameraman, he covered almost every significant event and meeting. He has been arrested so many times he's lost count — more than sixty. Put it this way: the human-rights lawyer who represents Henry (Alec Muchadehama) is on Penny's speed dial.

Also, Henry is funny as hell.

"I am still trying," he responds, as he always does, when I ask him how he is.

"He's been in trouble *again*," says Penny, sighing like a worried parent. "Only recently got out of prison, didn't you, Henry?" Henry smiles. "This time for trying to investigate the cholera situation."

"Well, I heard that at Parirenyatwa Hospital, they were throwing bodies out of the windows," he says. "There were so, so many bodies, because of the cholera, and it took too long to get them out of the hospital to the morgue below, because the lifts were broken.

"So I went to the hospital pretending to be a visitor, and I saw it was true. I was outside and suddenly from above bodies came tumbling out of a window on the third floor. Some were in plastic body bags. Others were not. One and then another and another, at least nine of them! I got my camera and started to film it. I was shocked. I mean how can one human being throw another human being out of a window like that, even if he is dead. It's taboo.

"But I had been spotted filming, by a CIO agent in a security guard uniform, I didn't realize that sometimes they disguise themselves as security guards."

Henry was tailed and eventually pulled over.

"Four guys surrounded my car and told me to open the door. I refused, so two of them pulled out pistols. One of them started to screw another barrel onto the barrel of his pistol, you know this thing called a—a silencer? Yes, that's it, a silencer. So, remembering my James Bond, I realized that these guys are killers, so I got out of my car."

They took Henry to Morris Depot, where police officers are trained, where I once trained myself, as a young conscript. In the grounds there is a wooden cabin all draped with vines, so it is almost invisible. Henry was locked inside.

"They put handcuffs and leg irons on me, and started interrogating me. They asked why I was at Parirenyatwa, and I told them I was visiting a sick relative."

They slapped him repeatedly across the face until he was bleeding, then they left him there for five hours, when suddenly the door swung open, "and then this giant of a man, with very long arms so his hands hung down past his knees, came in. His hands were huge, one hit from those palms, man, you were sent reeling! I knew who this guy was. His name was Makendenge. He's behind many of the political abductions.

"He looked at me sitting in cuffs and leg irons and said, 'You, give me your phone.' I stood up and gave it to him. He placed it on the ground, went outside, and returned with a large rock, which he smashed down onto the phone. It burst apart, and he smashed each piece, the battery, the phone, the SIM card, smashing, smashing, smashing, until it was in tiny little pieces. Then he looked down at me, and said, 'You, you are a nuisance. What were you doing in the hospital? I have three minutes. After that, if you don't talk, you won't be alive.'

"'Okay,'" I said—I believed him—"'I'm a freelance journalist. Sometimes I don't know if what I'm doing, if it's allowed or not.'"

Makendenge left the cabin, and the three policemen returned and beat Henry with truncheons and kicked him with their boots in that small room, hidden beneath the carpet of vines. And when they grew tired, and Henry was covered in blood, they allowed him to go, but first he had to wipe the blood off himself with an old mutton cloth.

Henry hobbled back into town; he had no phone and no money and his face was covered in blood again. He asked several people for help, and no one would. Finally he made it downtown and staggered into an office and used their phone to call CSU, who sent a car to take him to Dandaro—where he was admitted with internal bleeding, cracked ribs, and concussion.

When he was discharged, the irrepressible Henry went to Harare Central Police Station to ask for his cameras back. They shoved him into a police van and dumped him in the Remand Prison on Enterprise Road. After several days, during which Henry went on hunger strike, a sympathetic prison guard lent him his cell phone to call his wife, and she called his lawyer, Alec Muchade-hama, a veteran now at representing him.

"I was charged with trespassing in a public place likely to cause public alarm," says Henry. "But the case was dismissed."

With no money, Henry walked all the way back home to Budi-riro township.

"I was covered in lice and fleas from prison, so I shaved off all my hair and had a hot shower..."

He grins again, and shrugs: "And that's how I spent my Christmas and New Year."

ON MONDAY morning, I have an appointment at the American embassy. It's on Herbert Chitepo Avenue, but don't try parking there—the road is lined with hefty concrete planters to prevent car bombs. I park around the corner and walk through Harare Gardens, annual home to HIFA. This far end of the park is rundown now. Nestled in the corner is an overgrown playground with rickety swings, a wobbly roundabout, and a half-subterranean concrete submarine, angled in the midst of coming up to the surface, its fore gun pointing at the embassy.

Inside the embassy, which sits adjacent to its old Cold War rival, the Russians, a marine in camouflage fatigues and forage cap sits in his teal-tinted bullet-proof glass pen, like a seal in an aquarium, the light from his computer screen playing across his downturned face like sun dappling through the sea. The ambassador will see you now, he says.

No matter how long it's been since our last encounter, I always seem to take up with Jim McGee in mid-booming conversation, as though I've just popped out of the room for a minute. He sits there with a shelf of Schulz cartoon books on one side and Old Glory behind him, telling me how he's been trying to get his embassy driver released—the same one who drove the decoy car that day we went on the torture road trip. The minister concerned had promised he'd be out this week, "now he won't take my calls."

He's also working the phones to get Jestina Mukoko and the other abducted activists out of prison. There is evidence that they too have been tortured, and Mukoko is gravely ill. He feels that the MDC should use the leverage they have now, to refuse being sworn into the new government until all the political prisoners are freed. "But apparently the folks in prison are not a showstopper," he sighs. "The inauguration of the new government will still go ahead. That's just the way it is, unfortunately.

"There are no losers, apparently, in African elections—just a tie," he says. "I fear we've given Mugabe a life-line."

twenty-six

After Forty Years in the Desert

Aᴏ ᴛᴇʀ ᴛʜʀᴇᴇ ʏᴇᴀʀs in exile, Roy Bennett has flown back into the country last week. His wife, Heather, will follow once she's packed up their house in Johannesburg.

"Not exactly incognito." I smile when he collects me from the Beatties' in a cherry-red Jeep Cherokee.

"I have South African guarantees," says Roy. "When I came back in, President Motlanthe [who has now replaced Mbeki as interim South African president, until Jacob Zuma takes office] told Mugabe's people, 'Touch Bennett and this whole thing's off.'"

Roy is in his town gear, in so far as he's not barefoot. He's wearing Timberland deck shoes with white ankle socks, khaki chinos, and a gingham-checked short-sleeved shirt. A tattoo of a dove curls into the crook of his elbow. Next to him is his pale-blue-eyed son, Charles, twenty-three, and just back from Cirencester Royal Agricultural College. Charles has the impeccable manners of Zimbabwean youth. Over my protests, he calls me Mr. Godwin. He presses the remote and the metal gate slides open to admit us to Roy's sister Cynthia's house. There's a small boat on a trailer in the drive, and at the back, Cynthia's husband, John, is using a gap wedge to chip golf balls down the lawn for their German Shepherd to fetch.

Inside the house, beneath prints of English fox-hunting scenes, we drink tea while Bennett talks at a torrent about how amazing it is to be home. He is giddy, high on it.

I remind him that when I last saw him he was swearing he would never agree to a power-sharing deal with Mugabe. "You know, Peter," he says, "had Morgan not signed it, this country would have been plunged into war. Morgan took this country back from the precipice. Of course, it's a shit deal, Morgan understands that — he told me that to my face — but it was the only way forward. He phoned me from the airport and said, 'I wanted to tell you and Tendai last,' because he was scared of us, because we were both seen as hardliners. SADC forced both sides into this. They told Robert Mugabe, 'If you don't accept this, we'll close all the borders and switch off the power.' I sat with President Motlanthe and he said, 'You *have* to do this.'

"At our National Executive meeting, the first five speakers were dead against it, and then it was my turn. I got up and I said, 'We have to do this — to keep SADC onside and for Zimbabwe. It's our only option.' Of the eleven speakers, eight were against, and I swung it. When they saw that I was in favor, they conceded." (Tendai concurs — but was annoyed with Roy for changing his mind to support the deal.)

Roy talks of a new constitution, with accountability and transparency and a neutral police and army. But he warns, "We're entering into a very dangerous phase. ZANU-PF will do everything it can to stall, to undermine. Man, I've got a headache just thinking about it."

One of his three cell phones rings, a retro bell. "That was Morgan," he says, when he hangs up. "I'm going to be Deputy Minister of *Agriculture* in the new cabinet — phew!" He shakes his head. "I told Morgan, 'Mugabe's guys are going to go *berserk*.' But he said:

'Listen, you know about agriculture, so that's why I'm appointing you.'"

As news of the announcement spreads, all three of Roy's phones begin chirping, and he tends to them in quick succession, his message the same to all the inquiries: "No, no. I'm not going to Ministry of Lands—that's the one that deals with the former white farms—I'm going to be Deputy Minister of Agriculture, to help *black* communal farmers to get the inputs they need to feed the country."

In the background, Cynthia has put on ZTV news, which is squirming with the sensitive matter of how to portray the new dispensation. "Comrade Mnangagwa says all is set for the swearing-in tomorrow—a major feat of African diplomacy," says the newsreader. Then, with visible relief, he moves onto safer ground: a lengthy report on the anniversary of the Islamic Revolution in Iran. There is extensive footage of the birthday party at the Iranian embassy, complete with a towering cake in red, white, and green, the colors of the Iranian flag.

We switch off the TV and sit looking out over the garden. A pair of plump turtle doves are diligently pecking at the grass seeds, when suddenly, with a whoosh, a large raptor swoops down from nowhere, seizes one in its talons, and flaps away. "Martial eagle," says Roy, squinting into the sky. "That's rare." It leaves me feeling unsettled.

As I leave, he turns away from his chirping phones to wave a white embossed invitation at me. It's to the swearing-in of the new government, to be held at the polo grounds behind State House tomorrow afternoon. The invite says *Roy Bennett +1.*

"You wanna come?" he says. "It might be interesting."

ROY PICKS ME up the next day in an SUV with his security guy, a burly black man, at the wheel. Roy is dressed for the ceremony, squirming in his collar and tie, as though in sackcloth. He is sitting up front, not in the back as most do when chauffeured.

We roll down Borrowdale Road past Dandaro clinic, through whose wards Denias Dombo and Norest Muchochoma, Tichanzii

Gandanga, Tonde Chakanedza, Henry Chimbiri and all those shattered people have passed. They are the "collateral damage," the
price paid for this "power-sharing" ceremony today, which, depending on your faith, is either the final way station to real democracy,
or just another sleight of hand by Robert Mugabe, in his violent
game of political poker. Roy's cell phone begins its familiar retro
chime. Something about his tone of voice, a mixture of intimacy
and respect, makes me realize that he's talking to Morgan Tsvangirai. I lean in. Morgan is telling him not to come to the inauguration,
to turn around immediately.

Roy is flabbergasted. "Why?" he asks.

"Because they are planning to arrest you, to disrupt the ceremony. They have placed roadblocks around State House and you
will be picked up there, Roy," says Morgan. "We have good information that's what they are going to do."

Roy begins to argue. There are many reasons to do so. "We can't
let them dictate how this will work, if we set out like this, they will
have the upper hand, it's a bad precedent. If they're going to arrest
me, then let them do it on the day when all the VIPs, the foreign
leaders, are here, for maximum impact."

But Morgan cuts him short. "I'm not asking you, Roy," he says
gently. "I'm telling you." Roy concedes and instructs the driver to
do a U-turn. He is already yanking off his tie, undoing his collar,
and shucking off his jacket.

He calls Tendai Biti, who agrees with Roy's reasoning that he
should have gone ahead, and Nelson Chamisa, who agrees with
Morgan. "We have to think strategically," he says. "Wait until you're
sworn in as Deputy Minister of Agriculture, then they'll be arresting a *minister*..."

Roy's theory is that Mugabe's securocrats are divided about
what to do with him. There's a renegade faction, he's heard, led by
Mnangagwa, who want to arrest him as a show of strength, even if it
means disrupting the birth of the GNU.

Back at Cynthia's, Roy sits with some Manicaland friends,
who've come up to welcome him home: from Chimanimani, Bad

Hair Day Birgit and Allen Radford, owner of Heaven, the backpack-ers' lodge there; from Mutare, Belinda Sharples, an MDC activist, and Brian James, that city's newly elected MDC mayor.

We're watching the inauguration on ZTV—via a SATV feed. It's running late, very late. The chiefs of staff are boycotting the event, balking at saluting Morgan, their bête noir. The war vets have put out a statement saying they will only support the unity government if all three leaders "respect the values of the revolution."

As the last-minute hitches are papered over by South African mediators, the police brass band plays on and on. Inside the VIP marquee, white against the brilliant blue sky, Mugabe reclines in his wing-backed armchair, laughing at some bon mot from Grace, who lounges next to him in an orange headscarf, white-framed sunglasses, a multi-stranded pearl choker, and a leopard-print dress—the leopard eyeing the goats.

The first goat Mugabe swears in is Arthur Mutambara, a large jocular presence in a beige shirt, dark suit, striped tie, and fulsome grin. Then it is time for him to read the oath for Tsvangirai to repeat. Mugabe's eyes dart from side to side, refusing to meet the steady gaze of his nemesis. When it is done, the raucous ranks of opposi-tion MPs and their families applaud and whistle. The two men shake hands and stand together for photos, Morgan a genial bouncer under Mugabe's raven-hard eyes. Even Mbeki, midwife to this dubi-ous deal, smiles through his pensiveness.

Roy's mood has darkened and is overlaid now with flashes of anger. "These guys," he says, "they'll never give up voluntarily. Look at who they are, how they behave, and what they've done, even to each other."

As the camera pans across Mugabe's senior henchmen, Roy keeps up a dyspeptic commentary. Chihuri, the police commis-sioner, "was held by his own people in a pit in Mozambique for some transgression during the guerrilla war..." Vice-President Msika "is on my farm, in partnership with the Russians, looking for dia-monds." Gideon Gono, head of the Reserve Bank, "told the interior designer who did his house: do what you like, there are no restraints on your budget," he claims. "The landscape gardener was given a luxury Pajero as a tip!" And when we see Mugabe and Grace again, Roy says, "An Air Zim guy told me that a big box of cash goes with the President's entourage whenever they travel overseas. They had fifteen *tons* of personal baggage when they last came back from Singapore."

A young Zimbabwean student ends the event with a lengthy poem she has penned for the occasion. "Arise and shine, Zimbabwe," she exhorts, "for a new era has come."

After the inauguration, I pile into the pick-up truck with Roy's son, Charles, and his cousins, and head for the MDC rally — the first they've been permitted by the police in many months. Tellingly, there is no equivalent ZANU rally; their leaders retreat to their mansions to strategize. Roy too stays at home — grounded by the party to prevent his arrest.

The rally is at Glamis Stadium, in the agricultural show grounds (though there's little real agriculture left to show) on the western side of town. The MDC have instructed that there be no party regalia — this is to be "a national event." But apart from the Zimbabwe flag hung from the podium, this event is entirely partisan — a victory parade of the MDC party faithful. They come in open trucks and in buses, but mostly they come on foot — chanting phalanxes jogging down the middle of the streets from the "high densities," the townships that are the repositories of black working-class Zimbabwe. They are smothered in MDC regalia: party T-shirts and flags and posters. Some have fashioned the posters into tall stovepipe hats, emblazoned with Morgan's grinning face. Wearing any of this would have brought them beatings, home burnings, imprisonment, and torture just a few months ago.

We are swept along in the human current, through the turnstiles, frisked by party marshals, and deposited in the arena. In a holding pen, just below the VIP stand, stand seven plump black bullocks, a traditional gift to Tsvangirai from his supporters, for the feasting that will follow. High above the sun-bleached billboards for Coca-Cola, Blue Circle cement, and Castle Lager ("Africa's finest"), supporters are clinging to the lighting gantries for a better view. At the very top they unfurl a banner: *New Zimbabwe—New Beginning.* For several hours they wait, with the uncomplaining patience of an African crowd.

When the newly elevated MDC political gentry eventually percolate in, fresh from the inauguration ceremony, women kneel at their feet with clay pots of water for the ritual washing of hands. Overhead, heavy clouds gather. Party marshals stand at the red-and-white-striped tape that separates the crowd from the sheltering canopy of the VIP stand, with its chairs cloaked in white covers, tied at the back with peach bows.

I am next to the VIP section, in an area populated by party organizers and journalists, many of whom have come up for the first time in years from South Africa, the closest they could get hitherto. At the moment Tsvangirai is scheduled to take to the podium, the bulging clouds finally release their payload and bright umbrellas blossom in the crowd below. But most are unprepared, and just stand there, in the rain, regardless.

The cloudburst is short-lived—and soon the plastic sheeting is peeled back off the loudspeakers and the crowd is singing and dancing along to "Makorokoto [Congratulations] Zimbabwe!" The marshals throw sweets into the crowd. Paul Madzore, known as "the singing MP," urges, "However rough the road of democracy, we should never look back," and sings "The Battle of Jericho."

Thousands of open hands are raised—turning the crowd beige. A hefty man in a red baseball cap and checked shirt shuffles to the mic and begins crooning—it is Raymond Majongwe, President of the Teachers' Union.

Tendai Biti, the party's crown prince, now in the key post of Finance Minister, waves to the multitude and they ululate back at him. "*Chisa,* MDC, *chisa!*" yells Nelson Chamisa, who has masterminded the MDC's media effort, and the crowd bellows back, "*Chisa!*" It means hot.

"The power has been transferred from President Robert Mugabe to Prime Minister Morgan Tsvangirai," he announces. "This is the beginning of our new identity. You can meet anytime you want. Even in the middle of the night!"

Rev. Dube, a blind pastor, blesses the event and quotes Deuteronomy, the passage that ends with the summons: "Enter the land that the Lord promised your forefathers in the desert for forty years." It's only about ten years off in our case, but who's counting now.

Tendai Biti invokes those who fought so hard to get us to this point — so that we celebrate today those who sacrificed so much. "Cognizant of the protracted struggle we have gone through ... Let the people of Zimbabwe be free to associate with whomsoever they wish — it is a God-given right. We plead for transitional justice. Yesterday we visited detainees languishing in Chikurubi — we demand the immediate release of these people. There can be no reconciliation without justice, no reconciliation without truth."

Finally, Morgan rises, both hands aloft, and the crowd swells with noise. He gestures at his wife next to him, and she obliges by standing. "I want to recognize *amai* Tsvangirai, my better half," he says. "We are opening a new chapter in our country, we are starting afresh. On this day nineteen years ago Nelson Mandela walked free from Victor Verster Prison. It was an historic day. But freedom was not achieved on that day. For far too long Zimbabwe has endured violent political polarization. This must end today. For too long our people's hopes for a bright and prosperous future have been betrayed. Instead of hope, their days have been filled with starvation, disease, and fear. A culture of entitlement and impunity has brought our nation to the brink of a dark abyss. This must end today."

He promises that the political prisoners will not stay in "those dungeons a day more than I can manage." That emergency aid must be distributed regardless of tribal and political affiliation. All schools must reopen, he says; all civil servants must be behind their desks on Monday. "I will ensure that there will be a distinction between party and state, that there will be an open and transparent government." He ends with an invitation "to walk with me on this promising phase of our journey to a true and lasting democracy."

As we chug slowly away through the crowds after the rally, our pick-up truck filled mostly with young white Zimbabweans, the black crowds cheer and give us open-handed salutes. "Go back to the farms now," they shout. "Go back and grow food."

AND YET, despite all Tsvangirai's fine words, the noose around Roy is tightening as state agents fan out across the city looking for him. He insists he's not really in hiding. He's staying openly with his sister in Borrowdale.

Kerry Kay, the MDC's welfare officer, calls to say that the CIO has just visited her — six agents bursting out of a Mercedes. "We are here to look for Bennett," they tell her. A veteran of dozens of such encounters, Kerry is now a little volatile. "Search. Go on search! Search the whole damn house — I'm sick of you people," she says, and storms from room to room, flinging open cupboard doors and flicking up bedspreads.

They go on to other houses looking for him, but not to this one in Borrowdale, which doesn't appear to be on their radar — yet. That's the tricky thing about dealing with Mugabe's spies, who, like all spies, are paid to be professionally paranoid. They are so hard to predict — there are islands of competence (backed up by Israeli Web-monitoring software, and Chinese-installed surveillance systems) within a sea of bungling, dim-witted, racist bullies, who rely indiscriminately on a vicious, smash-mouth MO.

With Charles, Roy discusses escape routes from the house if CIO arrive. There is thick foliage along the back fence and a hole through into the neighbor's yard. They discuss his other options. He could ask friends still out on the farms to hide him, though he would be putting them at enormous risk. But he also hates the danger in which his presence is putting Cynthia and her family. Roy's mood oscillates from pugnacious to resigned and back.

"I'm sick of hiding," he says, exasperated. "If they're gonna arrest me, let them come." He turns to Charles. "I dunno. What do you want me to do? I'll do whatever you want me to." Charles concludes that of the options, the best is an offer from the new German ambassador, Albrecht Conze, to stay at his residence, which will offer Roy a safe house with minimum risk to his host. They phone Albrecht. "Good. We'll have bratwurst," he says. "Where else would you be declared a minister one day, and be in hiding from the secret police the next!"

GEORGINA arrives the next day, a week later than planned, having finally shaken off her pneumonia. She unpacks and lights up a Madison on the Beatties' veranda. "Yes," she pre-empts me, "I'm smoking again. So sue me."

"But the pulmonary embolism scare..."

"Well, I'm not on LighterLife powdered food anymore either," she sighs, turning away to exhale.

Lance Dixon, a young Zimbabwean with an IT business in Dubai, is here for tea. He has flown up from Johannesburg in a rented plane for the inauguration, with a bunch of others in MDC Support, who help with logistics, and will fly back late this afternoon.

"We're holding a seat for Roy," he says. "The swearing-in of deputy ministers has been delayed. Tomorrow is Valentine's Day and it's his birthday on Monday, so he wants to go down for a long weekend to be with Heather." Morgan has met with Roy today and okayed the trip.

After Lance leaves, I let Georgina sleep off her flight, while I go foraging with Richard. There are rumors of meat in Marondera, that—"Alleluia!" cries Richard—turn out to be true. Dougie's butchery has actual red meat. Word has spread and a line has formed. Men in white coats and rubber gloves are cutting it up. The whirring of their saws changes tone as they encounter bone. They pass back and forth through fly curtains of plastic ribbons, carrying sharp instruments, and I almost expect a stretcher to burst through, laden with a corpse, a label tied to its big toe. At the desk, a large black man taps fluently on calculator keys so worn that they have no numbers. We pay in U.S. dollars and Richard packs the cuts methodically into his cooler box.

Back in Harare, Lance Dixon calls on my cell phone. He sounds panic-stricken. "They've got Roy!" he says.

"What!"

"We were taxiing on the runway, with Roy on board, when suddenly a white Toyota single cab—reg AAP 4581—came hurtling onto the runway and the next thing we knew, the tower ordered us to abort take-off. These plain-clothes guys, who said they were from the President's office, came on board and pulled Roy off and drove him away. Now we're under arrest here at Charles Prince Airport."

I drive out to the airport in Penny Beattie's red Suzuki, while next to me Georgina phones lawyers, journalists, MDC people, anyone she can think of. By the time we get there, the Pilatus plane, from Sefofane Air Charters, is standing silently on the apron, chocks wedged under its wheels. Grizelda, the pilot, and her passengers are no longer under arrest, and have repaired to the bar of the Mashonaland Flying Club. But they're worried that if they leave now, the CIO will allege that Roy was trying to "escape arrest," by attempting to sneak out of the country illegally.

"Did he go through immigration?" I ask Grizelda.

"Yes," she assures me. "I gave them a full passenger list, with all the passport numbers. Including Roy's."

I walk out to the small immigration shed to find the immigration officer. It turns out that he is an MDC member, who was arrested himself during a previous election. He shows me his original of the departure document. Roy's name is number three on the passenger list. And it is all duly stamped. He even lets me photograph it.

Meanwhile we are getting calls updating Roy's whereabouts. Charles has followed him to Goromonzi, the infamous "swimming pool" interrogation center. Then Roy is bundled into a different vehicle, a silver Vigo twin-cab, and driven away on the Mutare road, fast, very fast. MDC spotters follow his vehicle, and others sit along the way to see if it turns off.

"What do you think?" asks Lance.

The day is fading fast, and Charles Prince closes at sundown, as it has no runway lights. They must leave now if they are to get out today.

"I don't want to abandon Roy," says Lance. He is almost in tears.

"There's nothing more you can do here now," I say. "You can do more back in Johannesburg."

Grizelda swings into the cockpit and runs her final checks. The rest of them climb up into the Pilatus. Lance waves from the top of the stairs, and the door swings shut. Grizelda feathers the prop and eases the plane out onto the darkening runway. We watch as she lifts off due west, directly into the bulging yolk of sun, just as it slides below the edge of the Earth, and then the plane banks sharply to the south.

twenty-seven

Lassoing the Moon

W ell, that didn't take long to go wrong, did it?" says Georgina, unsurprised to hear that Roy has now been thrown into the cells of Mutare Central Police Station. We will go down on Monday morning, once we have surmounted all the logistical hurdles. But for now, we are hyped up, frustrated, dismayed, confused, worried. The MDC condemn Roy's arrest, but beyond that we wonder how they will respond to this instant challenge to GNU? It makes a mockery of all Tsvangirai's fine words at Glamis Stadium, and of the South African guarantee to Roy, "Touch Bennett and the whole thing's off."

We sit drinking with the Beatties, at a place called Thai Thai. You enter it through a concrete drive-through supermarket, stocking the most random selection of stuff, jelly pops, spare-rib marinade, Quality Street, three choices of Carex condoms ("rough 'n' tough," ribbed, and strawberry flavored), samosas, honey, biltong, cans of "freshpikt" baked beans, dog food, and local plonk called Bon Courage.

Inside, Thai Thai has a nautical theme. Wall-mounted marlin, tiger fish, and barracuda arch above a makeshift stage. The propri-etress, Wanphen MacDonald, a young Thai woman with a bird of paradise tattoo settled on her left shoulder, supervises the clearing of the tables and chairs to the sides, as the restaurant morphs into a night club. The place is already heaving, keeping the butch staff in perpetual motion. Wanphen explains to Georgina that lesbians make the best bartenders. They can lift heavy crates; they don't steal, drink to excess, chat up the customers (or get chatted up), have child care crises, or provoke fights, but can break them up pretty well.

"Who are the clientele?" I ask Georgina. She does a quick tour d'horizon.

"Divorcées in poly-cotton with sun-beaten faces, blond high-lights and bingo wings, smoking Berkeley extra-mild, drinking cane-and-Coke, chatting about their last shopping trip to Joeys. A divorced father, out with his underage son on access day. Some medical NGO types, hating it, and hard-core fans of the Tourette's," she concludes briskly.

The band—yes, it's Tourette's, like the syndrome—are refu-gees from other bands, from the Nouveau Poor, the URJ, the Herb Boys, the Rusike Bros. The guitarist used to be a professional Zam-bezi River guide, until one sweltering day when his clients took a dip in the river and one had an arm bitten off by a crocodile. They're doing a creditable job, covering Alanis Morissette, Natalie Imbrug-lia, and the Grays, Macy and Dobie.

Calls start coming in about trouble in Mutare. Several hundred activists have gathered outside the central police station, where Roy is being held in the cells. Singing and dancing, they are determined to keep up their vigil all night, to make sure he isn't spirited away to a secret location, as is the CIO habit. By the end of the evening, the police have attacked the demonstrators with dogs and tear gas, baton charges, rubber bullets, and live ammo. Several people are badly hurt.

On Sunday we prepare to travel east, and in the evening we go to supper in Glen Lorne, right out on the city limits. It is already dark as we drive, and with almost no traffic, I become aware that we are being tailed. I speed up, slow down, make a series of illogical turns, and double back down dark empty streets, but the headlights behind stick to us. So I head back into town, toward the U.S. ambassador's residence, where there is a guarded gatehouse; as we approach, our tail peels off, and I loop back north, driving fast, to the supper.

"I need a *drink!*" announces Georgina as we finally get inside Kundisai's house, both of us feeling quite unnerved. Kundisai Mtero is a talented a cappella singer and ophthalmologist, and her companion, DJ, is a Dutch tour operator. We sit round a low table on their flagstoned patio, lit by an elaborate Liberace candelabra. The barbecuing ends up being done by Jordan, the only other local white there, "because he's a Boer," jokes Kundisai, "so he knows how to *braai.*"

An old friend, Beatrice Mtetwa, is here too. A feisty human-rights lawyer with sharp post-modern glasses, she is representing Roy. Last time I saw her, we were in New York, being buffeted down the icy canyon of 29th Street, after she'd accepted another of the many human-rights awards she's garnered for continuing to defend Mugabe's enemies—political activists and journalists mostly—despite being harassed and beaten by police herself. Her other growth area, she says, is divorce. "The diaspora splits couples, and so the divorce rate has soared—there's a huge cost to family life because of this crisis."

Beatrice is fifty-one; she's originally from Swaziland (she came here after marrying a Shona Zimbabwean she met at university), as Mugabe's mouthpiece, the *Herald,* never tires of pointing out. And when she speaks Shona with a Swazi accent, Mugabe's people do mocking imitations of her. Her father, a prosperous Swazi farmer, had six wives and more than a hundred children. Beatrice is the eldest, and the first in her family to go to university.

During the evening, she's frequently interrupted by calls. From Mutare, she hears that ten activists have now been arrested. From South Africa, the lawyers with whom she's working Roy's case want to refine legal tactics. When she hangs up on them, she fumes, "They just don't understand, this is not about the *law*, it's about *politics*."

On the other side of a few beers, and distressed about what's happened to Roy, and how once again a white man is being used by Mugabe as a pretext to attack his opposition, I suggest we should just butt the hell out, leave, move on. "Maybe it would be better for all of you."

Beatrice leaps from her chair and draws herself up to her full five foot one. "Nonsense!" she cries. "Whites have been here for a hundred and twenty years. You're as much a part of this place now as anyone. If you all go, then who's next? You guys have to stay involved, for the sake of *all* of us."

We leave early for Mutare. So early that the squads of police recruits are still jogging through the city streets near Morris Depot, in their white shorts and singlets and heavy boots, chanting. The low sun dazzles through the web of cracks in our windscreen, and it reflects off the Superman shields of white fur on the skinny sternums of the local dogs, and the white shirts and blouses of the kids straggling along the roadside to teacher-less schools, and off the white banner flapping across the road in Rusape, advertising last week's Valentine's dinner dance. To the northeast, the saw-tooth skyline of the Nyanga Mountains draws near, where Hildegard Weinrich, as Sister Aquina, had helped Robert Mugabe escape all those years ago, across into Mozambique through Chief Tangwena's land.

Just before Nyazura, on the right, we pass Tikwiri Hill. Its name means "Let us climb." I've always loved its history, and I used to think about it on my way to boarding school when the Harare-bound sleeper train stopped at Tikwiri siding to pick up urns of milk, and mail. Tikwiri Hill, I had been told, was sacred to Chief Chiduku's people, who lived here. When the more powerful Chief Makoni pressured Chiduku to move further south, Chiduku replied that his people would not leave their sacred hill. An irritated Makoni said, "Then take it with you."

So they tried to. They erected scaffolding on the summit of Tik-wiri, and they dug a trench around the base to "loosen" it. They plaited tree bark into ropes and then they waited for the next new moon, and when it rose low in the sky they climbed the scaffolds, to cast their ropes up around the horn of the crescent, like lunar cowboys, hoping it would tow the sacred hill south to their new territory. But the scaffolding collapsed, and many were killed.

I always loved the story, the poetic lunacy of it all, Chiduku's celestial cowboys trying to lasso the moon. The story may even be true—you can still see diggings at the base of Tikwiri Hill, and Chiduku's people do live some distance to the south of it now…

On the brink of Mutare is Christmas Pass, where a monument used to stand to Kingsley Fairbridge, a local settler and poet who founded a scheme to ship poor British children out to new lives in the bastions of empire. It featured the young Fairbridge standing with Jack, his black companion, whose arm is protectively around him, and his dog, Vixen.

Of all the settlers in this corner of the country, none lived larger and more eccentrically than the Courtaulds, Sir Stephen and Virginia. Up the Penhalonga road just a few miles north is their châ-teau, La Rochelle, left in death to the National Trust, and run today as a thirty-bed hotel by Simon Herring, in his genial early forties, key bunch hanging from his belt, pen clipped to the front of his polo shirt. Tea is served on the veranda under an ornate Islamic wall mosaic, which reads, in Arabic script, "Allah Is Great," while Herring tells me of this extraordinary couple.

Stephen Courtauld was the youngest of six, born into a family that had made dizzying wealth manufacturing artificial silk— rayon—and he was left a fortune. Shy and reserved, he met Virginia on the piste at Courmayeur in the French Alps. An Italian-Hungarian divorcée, ten years his senior, impulsive, stylish, racy, with a tattoo of a snake coiling up one leg, and a belief you could chat to extra-terrestrials, she was most unsuitable. He was immediately besotted. They embarked upon a three-year honeymoon, much of it on their steamship, *Virginia* (later to become the presidential launch of Liberia), accompanied by their ill-tempered ring-tailed lemur, Mahjong, purchased at Harrods, where else?

After renovating Eltham Palace, in South London, they grew bored of England and began scouring their favorite continent, Africa, for somewhere suitable to settle. One day they were flying over eastern Zimbabwe, near the Mozambique border, and saw below them the enchanted Imbeza valley, and they were smitten.

Stephen had wanted to call his new African home La Rochelle, in homage to his family origins as French Huguenot silversmiths, who fled to England to avoid persecution in the seventeenth century. And when he and Ginnie saw the property deeds, they were amazed to see that it already bore that name. If she was smitten before, Ginnie was now convinced this was predestined, and they set about designing and building their dream house—a French-style château in the lush bush of the African highlands.

They shipped in three Welsh tilers and had the roofs laid in imported Welsh slate. They installed radiant heaters within copper cupolas in the ceiling. Lady Courtauld's boudoir looked out onto a conservatory teeming with orchids, and beyond to the swimming pool. The cabinetry was of swirling honeyed bird's eye maple, the rings from her G&Ts still visible on the bedside table. Cedric Green, a young South African architect who had fled that country after the Sharpeville uprising, designed Ginnie's studio—her folly, she called it—which, at her request, riffed off Great Zimbabwe, complete with curved walls and chevron borders.

And the gardens, they were splendid, fifty acres of exotic plantings gathered from across the world, roses and sweeping lawns, and a lake. People came from all over the land to see them, even the blind, for it had a Braille trail. Fifty-two full-time gardeners toiled to trammel the fecund.

But they didn't just spend on themselves; the Courtaulds were huge philanthropists, favoring the arts and progressive, multi-racial institutions. Simon walks me over to the large drawing-room window, on which many of the guests etched their signatures, using

Ginnie's diamond-tipped stylus. It's a who's who of Zimbabwe's leaders, black and white.

In the snuggery bar, Simon reaches up and pulls down one of the hidden wooden screens on which once hung Sir Stephen's collection of thirteen Turners, to protect them from the harsh African sun. You can still see the faded rectangles where the landscapes used to be.

Together we inspect the château's tower — it was supposed to be one of a pair, but the other was never built. Ginnie would be proud to know that it's the site of an extra-terrestrial encounter. "La Rochelle is cataloged as the second-best UFO sighting in the country," Simon tells us. "Seriously," he says, parrying our grins. "In August 1981, there was a bright ball of light at the top of the tower, which was already derelict by then, and the staff thought it was on fire and came running, only to encounter three figures in silver jumpsuits, who dazzled them with some kind of ray, and they then fell down and were unable to move."

We walk the gardens now, past the stone obelisk, set among the rose beds. Carved into its base is a likeness of Mahjong, the temperamental lemur, who appears to be biting his own tail, with the inscription *Companion in our travels over many lands and seas.* "It's hard to run an inn," sighs Herring. Where once there were fifty-two gardeners, now there are two. "And we've had power for only six out of the last thirty days. They keep stealing the wire, we've lost five miles of wire."

And though the property belongs to the state, via the National Trust, he has to keep explaining that to various war vets who want to take it. "The whole thing is sheer craziness," says Herring. "While Pete Hurrell, seed-producer and farmer-of-the-year, was in the USA looking into advances that enabled satellite-directed fertilizing, his farm here was jambanja'd and looted by machete-wielding Mugabe mobs — from the space age to the medieval!"

During the first round of the election, he says, Lieutenant Colonel Tsodzai, in charge of the national vote-count center for

Manicaland, stayed here. He was a ZANU-PF guy, but a day after the count he shook his head, and told Simon, "There's no way Mugabe's back in. He has been resoundingly defeated." He was upset because many of the junior soldiers were already giving MDC open-hand *chinja* salutes.

But a few weeks later, when the violent re-run campaign was launched, the one they call the Fear, Air Marshal Perence Shiri (a.k.a. the Butcher of Matabeleland) rolled into La Rochelle, with his soldiers and vehicles full of AKs. The men stayed in the cottages here while Shiri holed up in Lady Courtauld's old boudoir. Simon was away then, but the staff say that each evening, as darkness fell, Shiri and his men would leave La Rochelle and wouldn't return until the next morning, their fists swollen from having spent the whole night beating people up in Nyanga for voting the wrong way in the first round. When he left, instead of signing the guest book under his real name, which in Shona means bird, Shiri wrote *Nyoni*, which means bird in Ndebele, the language of the Matabele people he decimated.

He returned a week later, when Simon was back, and asked how much the rooms were. U.S. $400 a night, Simon told him, which was ten times the previous rate. "Why so high now?" demanded Shiri. Herring looked at him evenly and said, "Because there is so much uncertainty here as people have been badly beaten up."

twenty-eight

Don't Trade Me for Anything

WHEN WE ARRIVE in Mutare, the opposition vigil is gathered outside the central police station where Roy Bennett is in the cells—without access to a lawyer, or food from the outside. The crowd of supporters stands across the wide, flame-tree-lined Herbert Chitepo Avenue, which slopes northward up toward Cecil Kop. In the day their numbers swell, and they surge over into the street itself, singing and chanting. When darkness falls, most of them gather at the small MDC office up on the ridge by Cross Kopje overlooking Mozambique. Two impressive young local MDC MPs, Pishai Muchauraya, a former teacher, and Prosper Mutseyami, who used to be a fitter and turner, struggle to contain their frustration. Roy's arrest has completely shattered any illusions these people had about the new "inclusive government." "It's like sleeping with the devil," says one man, to cheers.

"Isn't that supposed to be 'supping'?" Georgina asks me.

"Not if you're getting screwed," I say.

Their placards stacked there sum up their feelings. *Free Our Roy*

Bennett Today, Happy Valentine's Day Roy — We Miss You!! and *Roy Is Our Hero.*

Soon, even the police reinforcements brought in from outside to contain the situation start to soften. When they complain of hunger to Kurt, a displaced farmer who has come down from Harare to join the vigil, he promises to get food for them.

"It's like feeding your own executioner," I laugh. But Kurt says, "Maybe they won't bite the hands that feed them." And Memory, another opposition member, is giving loaves of bread to the local cops. "So they can be strong to beat you later?" I joke. "No," she says, "they told me they would give us tear-gas cans to throw."

The local police do seem torn — uneasy at the confrontation that has been dumped in their lap. One cop says to us: "Now I'm going to speak to you harshly, and you must move away," while he was watched from a distance by superiors, and he winked. "But then you can come back as soon as I leave."

His superior, the local police boss, Chief Superintendent Kasika-kore, is more hard-line. Flanked by armed paramilitaries, he walks over to the crowd with a rolled-up copy of this morning's *Herald* tucked under his arm, like a swagger stick. It bears a banner head-line hailing the Government of National Unity, *A New Beginning.* One of his men hands him a megaphone and he orders us all off the street. Then, noticing a young man at the back taking photos with his cell phone, he dispatches a snatch squad to seize him. They sprint down Main Street after him, beat him to the ground, and haul him away.

The crowd whistles and boos and surges forward around us, and I become aware of a tapping on my shoulder. "Will you please get off my foot," Georgina says. "I just put sparkly nail polish on it, to remind myself not to take myself too seriously."

LATER I WAIT AT the barricaded main entrance to the police station to visit Bennett. I am with Brian James, the new Mayor of Mutare, a slim, compact man, with silver-framed glasses and a mild, unflappable disposition—a good man in a crisis, which is just as well, because in addition to trying to get Roy out of jail, he is also trying to stop the cholera outbreak here. Brian's phone rings, with a sonorous chant: "O Great One, how may we serve you?" "That ring was downloaded by mischief-makers." He grins, embarrassed. "I'm not sure how to change it." It's George Lock, Roy's lawyer, who's accompanying us. He is tall and blond, with a mustache, and the lanky wide-shouldered physique of the ace tennis player he was when we were classmates at St. George's.

We have brought food for Roy, sandwiches, a bunch of bananas, groundnuts, a bottle of water, corn curls, and a box of premium Swiss chocolates, a gift that the EU ambassador, Xavier Marchal, has asked me to give him.

The inner courtyard of the police station is crammed with luxury cars, Mercs and Beamers, mostly, confiscated from diamond-dealers. We squeeze sideways between them to a small, grimy concrete cellblock. Though it's not yet 4 p.m., the captives have already been herded back into their cells for the night. The jailer unlocks a door, and Roy and his cellmates emerge into the small caged area, blinking in the sunlight. Roy wears shorts and a T-shirt with the slogan *Climbing Around the World*. He is barefoot.

Through the blackened chicken-wire fence, he tells us that initially there were twenty-five people crammed into a tiny cell, and he had refused to go inside, so they summoned the riot squad to force him in. The lavatory is blocked so they must use a bucket, which frequently overflows. "It stinks so bad in there," he says, "that it gives you a headache."

We hand the food to the jailer, who takes it through, and Roy distributes it to his cellmates, those arrested at the protest, demanding his release. He saves a single banana for himself. The rest, they fall upon and devour.

George briefs Roy about his forthcoming appearance in court, but Roy interrupts him to ask if we can do something about one protester who was bitten by a police dog, and whose wounds are badly infected. He still hasn't been allowed to see a doctor, says Roy. And then we are told the visit is at an end, and we are escorted away.

We have also brought a can of insect repellent, which Roy had requested, as the cells are infested with both mosquitoes and fleas. As we leave, I turn to see that instead of applying it to himself, Roy has dropped to his knees and is spraying the legs of his cellmates, one by one, as they scarf the food. It is a striking scene, Bennett on his knees, spraying the legs of these black men, outside their fetid jail cell.

I realize, in that moment, why Roy Bennett, more than anyone else, scares and appalls Mugabe and his party, why they see him as such a threat. Black MDC members, they reason, can ultimately be co-opted, bribed, or brought within the collective umbrella of the same racial and historical back-story, a narrative of colonial subjugation that can be hammered into a common political identity.

But Bennett — a white man behind whose back you cannot talk, one whose chiNdau accent is so unnervingly authentic that his race is undetectable over the phone — is the champion of a rural black peasant constituency, with a strong provincial base here in Manicaland. He has black populist appeal, yet a Rhodesian back-story. He has not reached his pre-eminence as a politician through the usual route of white liberalism. His is not the Albie Sachs, Joe Slovo, comrades-in-arms story. And this, for Mugabe, is more than just an affront. It shatters his own mythology. His whole framework of control is rocked by Roy's very political existence. Roy exposes the lie of what Mugabe pretends to be.

And I realize, too, what I have missed in all these years of looking at it: that despite appearances, the Roy Bennett story is no longer about race; it has moved beyond that.

ON THE WAY OUT, George asks Inspector Florence Marume if we can send a doctor to see the injured prisoner. But she refuses. "He will see our police doctor, if necessary," she says curtly.

"We will hold you responsible if he dies," I say, ludicrously — as if she cares. She just shrugs with monumental indifference, and shifts her huge haunches on the creaking plastic mushroom of her old diner stool.

WE ARE STAYING with Belinda and John Sharples in Fairbridge Park, named after Sir Kingsley, the pioneer of child emigration to the British colonies. The streets here, more eroded gullies than roads, have the names of poets — Kipling, Shelley, Keats. The Sharples got the bard himself: they live on Shakespeare Drive.

Belinda escaped to Texas for ten years but returned to Africa after her divorce. In 2002, when Zimbabwe had already gone into its tailspin, she turned down another opportunity to get away, this time to Australia, and instead joined the MDC. "More care to stay, than will to go," concludes Georgina, quoting from *Romeo and Juliet*. She is on a Shakespeare riff, in honor of our address.

Effervescent and indefatigable, Belinda has coordinated much of the monitoring of the political violence here, and it motivates her with a quiet rage. After supper, she flips open her laptop, and shows us a sickening sequence of torture victims, some dead, and some barely alive. She's also worked a lot with the women gang-raped by Mugabe's men.

"There was this one woman, Memory," Belinda tells me, "who was raped twenty-one times by Mugabe's youth militia, and basically lost her mind. She was in a terrible way, a cage of silence." Belinda started visiting her every day in hospital. "She had rosary beads and a Shona Bible, and if you stroked her hand she eventually relaxed, and over time I got her to tell me the names of seven of the men who'd raped her."

Belinda wrote up the case in detail, including the perpetrators that Memory could identify. She shows me the list:

> *Pepukai Magera*
> *Trymore Magera*
> *Tavaira Gavazi*
> *Chipo Muyapwa*
> *Trymore Pinukai*

Sorobi Musa

Nowell Musa

"I wonder if anything will ever happen to those names," she says.

IN THE MORNING, we sit on the balcony on Shakespeare Drive watching the mist burning off Christmas Pass. "And jocund day stands tiptoe on the misty mountain tops," declaims Georgina, in her best drama-school voice, from *Romeo and Juliet* again. Vervet monkeys drink from the birdbath on the lawn, and then leap up into the branches when the yellow Labrador puppy yaps at them and the Maltese poodle pogoes up and down below. The gardener sweeps bright yellow cassia blossom off the driveway and off the cover of the "Bushbaby," a plane that John, a pilot, is building from a kit. "The wings are in our bedroom," Belinda complains mildly.

THE COURT, that first day of Roy Bennett's trial, 18 February, is packed with his supporters, crammed together on the benches, and standing, lined against the wood-panelled walls. I sit sweating in my borrowed jacket and tie, trying to look like the lawyer I was, briefly, a lifetime ago.

On the wall behind the magistrate's chair is the coat of arms, with its motto *Unity, Freedom, Work*. Zero for three, by my score. Twin eland hold up a shield, which bears the conical tower of Zimbabwe ruins, the stone Zimbabwe bird that guards its walls, and a red star (all that's left of the communist DNA of the liberation movement). But presiding above that, in the totem pole of state symbols, is a lopsided portrait of Robert Mugabe, not the geriatric one we see today, his eyes rheumy with cataracts, but a youthful, plum-faced one, with one hand placed fastidiously upon the other. The clock above him has stopped at twenty to twelve. "It's been like that for the last thirty-odd years," says Brian James, following my glance.

Roy is escorted in by prison guards. He bows to the magistrate and smiles at his supporters. He is still in the same T-shirt and shorts, though they have allowed him to wear leather flip-flops for court. I notice that his right hand is closed around something. It is the little silver cross that Brian James smuggled to him through the chicken wire of the police cage, a gift from his friend Monty Hunter, a talisman of his faith.

Trust Maanda, Roy's lead lawyer, starts by arguing that Roy was arrested illegally, in effect abducted. That he had a gun put to his head by plain-clothes agents who seized him on the plane, and wouldn't identify themselves, and so he should be released immediately. The magistrate, Livingstone Chipadza, his eyes owlishly magnified behind thick black-framed spectacles, promptly overrules that, so Trust then complains about the conditions Roy and his fellow inmates are being held in, overcrowded and food-deprived. The prosecutor, Mr. Nkunda, tall and thin, with a black suit that hangs off his shoulders, says, "Roy Bennett is not being singled out, the whole nation is starving, not just the prisoners." The other prosecutor nods vigorously. He is as fat as his colleague is thin, and the prosperity rings at the back of his neck tremble as he nods, somewhat undermining that argument.

Chipadza takes copious notes by hand (there is no court stenographer), while the prosecutor outlines the state case against Roy. He is charged under Mugabe's infamously draconian POSA (Public Order and Security Act) with possessing weapons intended to be used for "insurgency, banditry, sabotage or terrorism." The maximum sentence is life imprisonment. The charge centers on an alleged plot to assassinate Mugabe when he visited Mutare on 6 March 2006. And Roy's coconspirator is alleged to be Mike Hitschmann, the local gun-shop owner, who, the prosecutor outlines, was found in possession of an "arms cache," and an email from Roy to him, detailing the plot. Apparently they were to pour engine oil on the road down Christmas Pass so that Mugabe's cavalcade slid down it, at which point (unknown) assassins would open fire on him.

There are so many holes in the case that Trust Maanda struggles to know where to begin. But the elephantine one is that Hitschmann was *acquitted* of this very same "plot," yet the state is relying on him as their main witness. They have approached him in jail, where he is locked up on other charges, and offered him a deal: his testimony against Roy, in return for his own freedom. So far, Hitschmann is refusing.

There's also the small matter of Hitschmann's torture, already proved at his trial and as such, *res judicata* — accepted as fact by any court.

Throughout the back-and-forth, there is, however, a worrying sign. The judge only writes when the prosecutor speaks, which he's careful to do at dictation speed. When Trust Maanda lays out the defense case, the judge's pen remains mostly still.

My pen is soon stilled too. Constable Magaya, the court cop, comes over and peers crossly at my lap, where I am jotting in my notebook. "Why are you writing?" she inquires. "It is not allowed. If you do it again, I will throw you out of court," and she shuffles back to her high chair.

The second charge against Roy presents me with a dilemma. As I'd suspected they would, they are accusing him of trying to leave the country illegally. It's a charge that's useful in denying him bail, by showing he's a flight risk. I have the photographed departure forms, correctly filled out, to refute this. But to give evidence, I will have to break cover and appear as a defense witness. I'd much rather not do it, with all the risks it entails, the CIO scrutiny, and the consequences that may unleash. But surrounded by people making such overt sacrifices of their own, how can I possibly refuse? So I tell Trust I have the photos, and he is elated. We download and copy the departure forms, and Trust duly introduces them as evidence, and adds my name to the witness list.

THAT NIGHT we repair to the Mutare Club. Founded in 1890, it occupies on old colonial house on Herbert Chitepo Street. "London Bridge Is Falling Down" chimes when you press the door bell. A framed letter from Churchill, thanking the "Royal" Mutare Club, as it was, for "your kind thought of me on my ninetieth birthday," hangs on the wall, and a photo of the bunting-strewn "Steam Engine Number One," the "Cecil J Rhodes," in Umtali, prior to pulling the first train to Salisbury. The banner on the front declares: *"Now we shan't be long to Cairo."* In the event, of course, they still haven't made it. The dress requirements, prominently displayed, specify "Smart Casual at all times—shorts may only be worn with long socks. No T-shirts, boxer shorts."

When Georgina arrives, the barman sheepishly points out another large sign. "Gentlemen Only. By Order of the Committee." He smiles and shrugs. "It is not my rule," he says. "I am not on the Committee. Women are allowed on the veranda." So, we all troop out to the veranda, and the power promptly cuts out.

Over beers in the dark, Brian James traces his curious political trajectory. He used to be a "mainstream white," no great liberal or activist, he says. "During the war, I thought a gook was a gook, and that they were going to stuff the country up." He served in the Police Reserve, running patrol boats up the Zambezi. Now he's found himself pretty far upriver again, the white mayor of a black city.

His politicization began when ZANU-PF minister Oppah Muchinguri (once Mugabe's secretary) decided she liked the look of his poultry farm, the Grange, near La Rochelle, and decided to jam-banja it. James joined the MDC, and helped provide logistical support to Oppah's rival candidate, Giles Mutsekwa, who trounced her in the following election. Their victory party was invaded by a crowd of Oppah's supporters, who took James hostage.

When the MDC members tried to mount a rescue, Oppah's vets tied James up, doused him with petrol, bound him to a fuel tank, and placed dried grass underneath him, threatening to set him alight and explode the tank.

"The police did nothing. They just watched. I was lying there, praying that the local matches wouldn't light, 'cos they're so shit! Eventually the war vets allowed me to call George Lock, my lawyer, and I asked him to bring a ransom or I was going to be burned alive. He arrived with Z$90,000." He takes a swig of his

Zambezi, and his voice lowers. "Later I found out that my neighbor, Tom Martin, had cut a deal to feed the 'war vets' on my farm," he says, bitterly, "on condition they stayed off his."

Mugabe appointed Oppah Muchinguri, roundly rejected by her own people, as Governor of Manicaland. James was taken hostage a second time and forced off the Grange. "Oppah gave a TV interview posing on a tractor on my farm, declaring that she would wear down the *mabhunus* [the Boers] and kick us out of the country." James hasn't been back to the farm since March 2003. "Whenever we drove in the vicinity, I would say to Sheila, my wife, shall we go through the farm, and it was always a venomous 'No!'"

Both their adult children left Zimbabwe, for Australia and New Zealand, but Brian and Sheila wouldn't go. "You know, I was determined not to cower," he says. And then he was approached by Roy and other senior local MDC leaders, and asked to stand for Roy's position as MDC Manicaland treasurer (because Roy was going up to Harare). "After much deliberation and, more importantly, having been accepted as a Zimbabwean by the people, I accepted the challenge." And from there he was voted in as a Mutare city councillor, and finally, in March 2008, its mayor. He still seems somewhat surprised at the turn of events. It was also overshadowed by personal tragedy—Sheila, his wife, was killed in a car accident just months after his mayoral election.

"O Great One, how may we serve you?" his cell phone strikes up again in the dark. It is a friend in Harare to say that the person who had given Grizelda and Lance Dixon a ride out to the airport, when Roy was arrested, has now been picked up by the CIO. They are systematically going through the airport sign-in sheet from that afternoon. "Well," says Georgina, "it'll only be a matter of time before our names come up, then." I call Penny and warn her to expect a visit by the CIO, because we were in her little red Suzuki at the time. She is sanguine. Richard has been arrested before.

Pete Musto, another of the MDC logistics guys who comes down once a week with boxes of MDC newsletters to distribute, takes up from Brian. He was hardly a blushing liberal either, especially after losing his brother in the war, at seventeen. "He had just come back from boarding school for the hols, and took the dogs out for a walk, and he was killed by *terrs*," the guerrillas, he recalls.

"In all my life, I've never been as close as I am now to the people," he says, meaning black people. "Before, there was an us-and-them gulf—but that's been bridged now. I've become very close to Pishai and Prosper. It's changed my attitude. I think this applies to a lot of us. This process, as tragic as it is, has brought us close together. The population must understand that they *can* change the government. Having a common enemy and facing common threats, we are on the same team, rely on each other. They feel safer to have a *murungu* there, among them, it's that much harder for them to be knocked off."

THE NEXT DAY we reconvene at the court. Roy, now in his khaki prison uniform of baggy shorts and shift shirt, is led to his little wooden pen, and the Hon. Livingstone Chipadza reads from his handwritten notes. "The state," he decides, "has succeeded to establish the reasonable suspicion" that "the accused person, acting in concert with Hitschmann, had unlawful possession of weaponry intended to be used in insurgency, banditry, sabotage, terrorism." Roy turns to us, and seeing us crestfallen, he gives a broad wink. *He* is trying to cheer *us* up. The judge tosses out the other charge of trying to skip the country illegally. Still, he remands Roy in custody, initially for another two weeks, while awaiting trial. Roy is led back to prison.

Now Pishai Muchauraya must take the news to the waiting crowds lining the street under the stucco overhang of Frank Gammon House, against the wall of Mutare Toyota and Duly's Nissan. The cops are grouped together nervously behind the fence of the police station, tear-gas canisters hanging from their stable belts. A troop of Support Unit officers wait near their vehicles, rifles at the ready. And police dogs sit panting under the flame tree.

Bruise-dark clouds have gathered up over the Bvumba, and lightning flickers restlessly between them. And then a perfectly sharp rainbow develops just as the convoy bearing Roy to prison drives out of the police station, with paramilitary cops and water cannons front and back. The crowd all cheer and bay as the vehicles grind by, down past the Courtauld Theater and the Museum, to the Mutare Remand Prison.

Later, with Brian James, I visit Roy there. We talk to him through the iron bars, worn smooth by the grip of many captive hands. "Leave me here for as long as it takes," he instructs. "Don't trade me for anything."

twenty-nine

Blood Diamonds

GEORGINA AND I are waiting outside Meikles Park in the center of Mutare early on Saturday morning, waiting to meet the Hon. Lynette Kore-Karenyi, another of the new crop of local MDC MPs. She thinks she may be able to sneak us into the Marange diamond fields. Control of these diamond fields is now the key to the country's future. With the economy shattered, the farms looted, and the death of the Zimbabwe dollar snuffing out the black market in foreign currency, diamonds—*ngoda*—are one of the very few remaining sources of wealth. Mugabe and his men need to keep control of them to finance their political machine.

The granite obelisk in the center of the park is plastered with AIDS sensitivity posters, part of the "Zimbabwe National Behavioural Change Strategy: 2006–2010." I rummage beneath the accretion of posters, to find the original carved inscription, *For King and Empire 1914–1918.*

One of Brian James's orange-uniformed municipal street-sweepers methodically works her way past us, down the runnel of the road, assembling little mounds of detritus, scooping them up in her dust-pan, and emptying it into her hand-cart.

Above us, the Bvumba Mountains are still wreathed with cool morning *guti*. Yet, here, along the central island of Herbert Chitepo Avenue, deferential ilala palms sough softly in the sunny breeze. Georgina is window-shopping across the road in the tragically under-stocked Meikles Department Store. Behind the glass, frozen in time, stand naked white mannequins under twirling yellow smiley-faced cardboard discs declaring, "Going Summer!"

A soldier strolls down the road and stops at the bus stop. He is tall and straight-backed, in his early thirties, wearing a sharply ironed one-piece camouflage jump suit with the insignia of a Zimbabwe bird within a laurel wreath looped through his epaulettes. "How are things in the army, Major?" I ask tentatively.

"We are happy since yesterday"—he grins—"when we were paid for the first time in Usahs. We got $100 each."

"Where did it come from?" I ask disingenuously.

"From Tendai Biti, and the MDC," he laughs, and high-fives me. He has trekked all the way from Harare to give some of his hard-currency bounty to his grandmother, who lives in Zimunya, the arid communal land at the foot of the Bvumba. In Harare, he is in charge of a Yugoslav-made artillery battery. "It has forty missiles," he says proudly, "with a range of twenty kilometers."

Lynette's husband drops her off, and we drive south, past Sakubva township. Its roadside market, where mounds of donated clothes end up for sale, is just cranking up. We drop down into Zimunya. On the left, freshly painted, is the New Cannibal Inn and Butchery. "What kind of flesh do you think they sell?" Georgina asks Lynette, and she giggles.

Lynette is thirty-four and wears cork wedges, a calf-length brown corduroy skirt, glasses, and straightened hair. Georgina is complaining to her about the sexist policies of the Mutare Club. "Shona men have a saying," replies Lynette. "*Mhamba inonaka nav-amai mudhuze.* It means 'Beer tastes better with a woman by your side.'"

Lynette was educated at a Catholic mission school, St. Patrick's, Nyanyadzi, worked as a doctor's PA and, in 2003, became the MDC's first woman local councillor. It was Roy Bennett who suggested she stand for national office. She comes from a political family—her mother had worked for Ndabaningi Sithole's party, for years the sole opposition voice in parliament, but still, she had reservations about Lynette's candidature, "in case I lost, and people laughed at me." But Lynette didn't lose, and she was reelected in the recent elections.

She's had a tough time of it, though. As well as fighting various recounts and court challenges, she's been arrested four times, and beaten up by the police. She's had to send her three kids—the youngest, a girl of eight—away to boarding school, for their own safety. "They're proud of me becoming an MP," she says, "but scared that I will be killed." The last time she visited her fourteen-year-old son at school, he said it was lovely to see her, but he'd rather she didn't come in her official MDC vehicle, in case he got into trouble.

Things got particularly bad for her two years ago, she says, when Inspector Marume, the hefty policewoman from Mutare, set the CIO on her. They raided her house, hunting for her, so she fled for a while to South Africa. She crossed the Limpopo and then climbed through the razor-wire border fence—ripping her clothes and slicing her back; she still has the scars—and then walked five miles, with a guide Roy had sent to assist them. Three times they had to fight off *maguma-guma*, robbers, armed with knives and iron bars, who prey on border-jumpers. "I had no idea getting across would be so *horrible*," she says. Finally, torn and terrified, she met up with Roy at a service station at 2 a.m.

Before Wengezi, at the spot we encountered it when we last came here on our way to the Chimanimani music festival, we arrive at the roadblock that marks the entrance to the diamond district, the first of five roadblocks we will encounter. This time, though, it is manned not by policemen, but by soldiers. Lynette leans across me to do the talking to the soldier sweating at my window.

"I am visiting my constituency," she tells him. "And these ones are my guests."

This seems to do the trick. As he jots down the vehicle details, I ask him, "Why don't you guys erect some kind of shelter from the sun?"

He shakes his head. "Ah, it is a shortage."

"A shortage of what?"

"A shortage of initiative," he says, without missing a beat, and waves us through.

As we head south, the land is parched and goat-wrenched, stony and thorn-treed. It's too dry here for maize, and sorghum, the ancient grain, is still grown. Many people here are only alive because of emergency feeding by Christian Care, says Lynette, though Mugabe interrupted that during the elections.

"How is the irrigation scheme?" I ask. The nearby village of Nyanyadzi used to have an ambitious project for black farmers, growing back-to-back crops. "It is no longer functioning," she says. "All is diamonds now."

We start to pass trading stores that service the diamond diggers. Babylon Investments, Luckyfields Enterprises, New Gift Store. But many seem in ruins. "During the run-off elections shop-owners in Nyanyadzi had vehicles burned, and houses," says Lynette. "The Nyanyadzi Training Center was turned into a ZANU torture base."

The way Lynette tells it, in 2006, a diamond-miner made his way home to Chiadzwa from the massive alluvial diamond fields of Namibia, known as the Sperrgebiet, "the Forbidden Territory." It's an area stretching more than two hundred miles along the Skeleton Coast (so called because it is strewn with the ribs of ships, wrecked in the lethal fog band caused when the cold Atlantic current laps the desert shore) and up to sixty miles inland that is off-limits to all but NamDeb, the Namibia De Beers Diamond Corp. Even carrier pigeons were banned as they've been used to smuggle out diamonds.

This returning worker saw something shining on the ground in Chiadzwa, recognized it as a diamond, and started looking for more. "Nobody believed that what he had found were really diamonds, there were no buyers and people were just throwing them away," she recalls. "But after six months, West Africans and Lebanese and Israelis came to buy them. Initially anyone could come and dig, then the syndicates started. The police would allow digging in return for half of the diamonds found."

Legally, the diamond rights belonged to African Consolidated Resources (who took them over from De Beers), but in 2006, once the rush began, the police chased them away, and they haven't got back since, despite High Court orders. Mugabe's ministers moved in and were soon making personal fortunes through the digging syndicates. Estimates put the potential haul as high as U.S.$1.2 billion a year. So it was unsurprising that people swarmed here from all over this paupered country, to try their luck. As many as thirty thousand miners were digging at any one time, working the main hundred-and-seventy-acre diamond fields. Conditions were appalling, with women and children digging too, often for a pittance. "There were lots of deaths from malaria," says Lynette. "No sanitation, no water supply—the diggers would buy water with diamonds!"

Alluvial diamonds, like the ones at Chiadzwa, have been eroded from their original kimberlite pipes and scattered close to the surface by rivers. In Africa, such deposits almost always result in conflict (hence the term "blood diamonds"), from the diamond fields of Kimberley itself, which helped cause the Anglo-Boer War, to the protracted war in Namibia, before South Africa would relinquish control, to Angola, Liberia, Sierra Leone, and the Congo. Zimbabwe has proved to be no exception.

In October 2008, just after his blood-soaked election, Mugabe decided to end the free-for-all in Chiadzwa and to control the diamond revenue more tightly. He ordered the army in, and they launched Operation Hakudzokwi, "No Return." Hundreds of soldiers, some on horseback, descended on the diggers at Chiadzwa, backed by helicopter gunships. Even by Zimbabwe's appalling standards, it was a scene of egregious brutality. They fired tear gas into the shallow diggings and when the miners emerged choking, they gunned them down, or released attack dogs to tear them apart.

In charge of the operation? Air Marshal Perence Shiri, the

butcher of Matabeleland, ably assisted by General Constantine Chiwenga. In a fit of nostalgia, perhaps, Shiri even shipped in some soldiers from the notorious Fifth Brigade, to reprize their main skill set: how bravely they can kill civilians. Human Rights Watch confirmed at least two hundred deaths, but the real toll is probably more than twice that number. Most were buried in mass graves in Chiadzwa and in Mutare. Thousands more were injured. Twenty-two thousand people were arrested, not just miners, but dealers and middle-men and smugglers too — anyone who was found with foreign currency or a nice car.

Now the army has taken control of the main Chiadzwa diamond fields, rotating new units through every two months, to keep them happy. They still use civilians to do the actual burrowing, including children, many of whom are used as forced labor — diamond slaves. The soldiers have cordoned off the entry points, and sealed the area to outsiders.

But Lynette knows of a new, subsidiary field, east of Chiadzwa, in a wild corner of her constituency where the army has not penetrated yet. To get to it, we turn down a very rough dirt road toward Mhakwe, past Chikwizi School, and after ten miles or so, we pull over at a kraal. Women are bent over, hoeing in the fields, babies bound to their backs. Lynette hails them, and they squeal with delight at seeing her. "This is my area," she says proudly.

Here we pick up a young man, who introduces himself as Ediclozi. It is only much, much later, when I ask him how it's spelled, that he says, "It is my nickname. Because my friends say I am clever, they call me after Ediclozi, who is too clever." I continue to look perplexed, so he spells it out for me: "Eddie Cross."

"Oh, of course!" I say, defeated once more by the Shona aversion for Rs. Eddie Cross is an MDC senator, and one of their chief strategists.

Ediclozi is eighteen, and has been mining, off and on, for more than a year now. In that time, he has found sixteen industrial diamonds. But his friend found a big gem-quality stone, what they call here a *maglass*, and got U.S. $2,000 for it. Four years' pay at the average annual income. "On this side," he says, "there are only police, but we bribe them."

We drive another few miles, past the rock they call Buwere Vasikana, "The Stone for Girls," where six girls were killed by lightning, and park at the bottom of a steep, conical mountain. Ediclozi points to the summit, where the ground is broken and piled with loose rock, the main diamond diggings. You can see ant-like figures up there. Georgina and Lynette take one look at the ascent, and decline to accompany us, so Ediclozi and I set off alone.

"The digging syndicates are usually three to six men strong, and we must trust each other because we share whatever we find," explains Ediclozi, as we clamber up in the pulsing heat. He has just finished a session up there, and has rotated out of his syndicate, but others have substituted for him, so the syndicate doesn't lose its digging place.

Once we gain height the view opens out onto a primordial topography of jagged mountains, furrowed with ridges like mastiff brows, thickly vegetated with gurugushi bird bush and mupangara thorn trees, and, in the Nyadokwe River valley, wide-girthed baobabs, silvered in the sun. From across the coulee, baboons bark. "There are too many animals here," says Ediclozi. "Leopard and kudu, mambas and puff adders."

We climb on, passing exploratory, zigzag trenches, about the depth of a man. These are called *hambakachana*—"the path you travel finding nothing."

As we climb we start to hear the *magweja*—the working diamond-diggers. The violent chime of pickaxes and sledge hammers as they strike rock. And behind that I can hear snatches of song. I squint upward into the sun, but I can't see anyone, nothing but wisps of smoke rising from the summit. When the diggers reach a boulder too big to break, Ediclozi explains, they light fires on it to crack it.

Not long ago, says Ediclozi, there was an attempt to flush the diggers from here too. A convoy of police paramilitaries arrived with guns and tear gas, he says. They started up the mountain, just as we are now. At that time, he estimates, there were four to five hundred diggers working up here. When the alarm call went up that the police were on their way up, the diggers, like defenders of a medieval castle, came to their ramparts and began hurling rocks down. The police fired back but the topography was against them. The diggers levered boulders that bounced lethally down the hill, and set off landslides. They taunted the policemen, shouting down, "*Muri imbwa dzaMugabe*" ["You're just Mugabe's dogs"] "*voetsak.*" The policemen took fright, "and they ran away," says Ediclozi.

On the ridge across from us, we now see the first syndicates, standing on the rim of their workings, silhouetted against the sun. They shout over to us. "They think you are a *mabhaya*," a diamond-buyer, says Ediclozi. Word goes from group to group up the mountain. Finally we reach the summit — which opens out into two extensive digs. As we arrive, men run over.

"You wanna buy diamond, mister?" they call out. They are rough, wild-looking. Their hands horned with carapaces of callus from swinging their smooth-shafted sledgehammers and picks. Many are dreadlocked, shirtless, reeking of ganja.

Soon we are surrounded. Ediclozi shadows his eyes with his hand against the sun, scanning the scree mounds for his syndicate. "My friends are not here," he says quietly. "These are new ones, *makorokoza* — gold-panners from Mberengwa. They are dangerous, these ones."

One of the men, his already considerable height augmented by a medusa's nest of fat dreads, comes to the front. He is the boss of one of the syndicates, he says, and his name is Dread. He snaps his fingers and calls Jealous, who is improbably wearing a houndstooth jacket and little else. From somewhere inside the shiny, sweat-infused lining, Jealous produces a tiny package, which he slowly unwraps. It's a billion Zimbabwe dollar note. He indicates that I should open my hand, and from the crumpled note, he drops into my palm a translucent stone. Jagged and irregular, it reflects the sharp Manica sun. The diggers' ranks draw closer.

"This is *maglass,* three, maybe four carat," says Dread, "the biggest stone we find here. The best opportunity you ever get—better even than Kimberley." He smiles brilliantly, though his eyes remain hard.

I admire the stone. It seems only polite to do so.

"How much do you think it is worth?" asks Dread.

"Well…" I glance over at Ediclozi, who is looking nervously at his feet. I can't decide which is more dangerous, to talk money, only to have to break it to them later that I don't actually have the money on me. Or to tell them up front that I don't have cash, that I'm not here to buy.

"I'm, I'm on a *recce,* just looking. I don't have money. I'm not buying today," I say.

"How much you think this one, it is worth?" insists Dread, his eyes narrowing. It's as though I haven't spoken. I've heard the going rate is about $2,000 a carat, but this doesn't look like three carats to me—two, maybe.

"Well, I think it's probably worth about U.S.$2,000," I say. There is wild jeering and shrill whistles of derision at my estimate, and the diggers' ranks contract again.

"Maybe $3,000?" I venture, uncertainly.

Dread looms. "A big one like this is worth *at least* 6,000 USAhs," he says. His tone is openly menacing now. "There are many of us and we have been digging a long time, and it is *dangerous* here. The army and the police, they shoot us and rob us."

"I understand. Then maybe it is worth $6,000, as you say." I reach out to hand the diamond back to Jealous, but he shrinks from me, and won't take it. Murmurs of confusion circulate through the crowd, and quickly congeal into outright hostility.

"It is your diamond now, so you give us the money. $6,000. As you agreed," Dread declares, with an air of finality.

"Look, I don't have any money on me," I say, and pat my empty pockets. "I'm not here to buy." I look over at Ediclozi again, for a cue. He looks ashen, and suddenly much younger than his eighteen years. The diggers are all shouting now. They surround Ediclozi, jostling him. I sense they are about to beat him. I raise my voice. "Look, I'm really not a *mabhaya.* I have come to see how you are doing here. I heard about the problems you had here, with the police and army, so I came with the MDC MP, Lynette Kore-Karenyi, to see how things are here."

They look thunderstruck. Not a *mabhaya*? Ediclozi and I are talking at the same time, placating, explaining that I mean no harm. But I can hear some of the men now suggesting that it is risky to let me leave this place alive. That I will tell others, cause trouble for them, inform on them to the police, not their local complicit ones, but the bosses in Harare. That maybe I even work *for* the police, or the CIO. They have used whites before.

I now realize how stupid I've been. Of course these men don't want any publicity; they don't want outsiders nosing around. They're outlaws, pirates, living this rough, violent life. Somehow, through a series of small, stupid decisions, I've ended up high on this mountain among these desperados. Ediclozi's mates were supposed to be here; I was coming with an insider, backed by the local MP. But up here, on top of this mountain, these men are now discussing whether to kill me.

If they kill me, will it draw more attention than if they let me go? That is now their debate. There are two schools of thought. Syndicates led by Dread, Abisha, and Jealous seem to favor killing me, because I will only bring them trouble. Obvious and Madhuku, on the other hand, think that killing a white man might bring even more police attention. No one is physically holding me, but diggers have moved behind me now, cutting off the path back. All digging has now stopped, and the men lean on their shovels and picks, lobbing over debating points. Several start rolling joints.

Baboons bark again in the distance, and kestrels wheel on the thermals, and I think of my boys. They will be just getting up in New York. Putting on their school uniforms, their blue-and-yellow-striped ties. Hugo drowsily trying to slick back his bed head, Thomas full of morning energy ready to wrestle the day to the mat. I think of them waiting for the M5 bus on Riverside Drive, playing tag around the triangular flower bed, doing their time trials to the Joan of Arc statue and back. What was I thinking, coming up here?

They are now discussing whether to hold Ediclozi hostage while I go down to get money, but quickly decide I'll just do a runner, and won't bother to return to bail him out, or worse, I'll return with the police or army. As Ediclozi might, if they did it the other way around, and held me hostage. It's clear that part of the problem is that they can't understand why I've come all the way up here, if *not* to buy diamonds? I don't want to tell them I'm a writer, or even some sort of human-rights monitor—and risk boosting the murder school of thought among these publicity-averse men. I try reminding them that Lynette is at the bottom of the mountain, waiting for me. But that has no impact on their calculations at all. Then I wonder if Bennett's writ can possibly stretch this far, into this wild world way off the grid. "I have been visiting Roy Bennett..." I start, and they all pipe down at the mention of his name.

"Pachedu, how is Pachedu?" call several men.

"I have been visiting him," I continue, "in prison."

In prison? They are aghast. They have no access to current affairs up here, relying on fresh diggers for second-hand news. They have no idea that Roy's been arrested. I launch into a detailed description of how he was picked up, and why. A blow-by-blow account of his court case, his conditions in Mutare jail, and speculation about what may happen next. They are rapt. I feel like an African Scheherazade, trading stories for my life.

They bombard me with questions about Roy's situation, and our relationship begins to change. Some of them sit down on the boulders. I sit too, and start inventing details, embellishing. Pachedu, I tell them, has actually tasked me to come up here to see how they were getting on. And this seems to make sense to them.

Finally, Ediclozi catches my eye and gestures that maybe we should try to leave. I look at my watch. "Well, we need to go now. I have to get back to Mutare in time for prison visiting hours, so I can take food to Pachedu."

I unfurl my hand from around the diamond, and offer it back to Dread. There is blood on my palm from gripping the jagged stone so tight. This time he accepts it. "It's a lovely diamond," I say. "Maybe next time."

"Okay, next time," he agrees, though we both know there will be no next time. They make no move to stop us from leaving. Many raise their hands in farewell, asking me to take their greetings to Roy. I follow Ediclozi over the top of the rocky parapet into the steep scree field, not bothering with the path this time, just scrambling down in a shower of loose gravel as fast as we can.

thirty

Witchwood

THE NEXT NIGHT we spend in the Bvumba Mountains above Mutare. I used to come up here from school in Mutare every week for riding lessons. At the time, it still had that feel of a sanctuary suspended far above the turmoil of Africa. Dr. Mostert's *Jumbo Guide to Rhodesia 1972* says the Vumba (as it was still spelled) transports you "back to the England of Constable; lush fields and quietly ruminating cows, a country scene softened by the vaguest hint of mist."

As we drive up the sole road, a steep, circuitous fifteen miles cut into the mountainside, Georgina's eyes widen and she points up the slope. It is infested with soldiers in camouflage, skirmishing through the bush toward us in staggered line, weapons at the ready. They drop one by one from the embankment onto the road, fan out across it, and disappear into the foliage below.

The route takes us through the mossy, fern-filled Bunga Forest, past hillsides thick with protea, and the botanical gardens, with its dozens of species of Jurassic cycads.

At the top, the land is mostly divided into small plots, orchards and market gardens, and the vernacular architecture seems to be the thatched cottage or the log cabin, with names like Shangri La and Sans Souci and Mon Repos, used mostly by retirees and weekenders.

The Queen Mother even stayed here, at Leopard Rock Hotel, on her last official visit in 1953, and looked in on Bvumba's very own castle, next door—a small hotel now, which boasts a lavatory perched on a granite boulder. "I see you have your own throne," she is said to have observed, upon viewing it.

During the height of the diamond rush, Leopard Rock was the favored haunt for the diamond-dealers. "Man, it was wild then," says Beefy Campbell-Morrison, the groundskeeper, over beers in the clubhouse, which overlooks the kikuyu-grass fairways of the hotel's award-winning golf course.

The diamond-dealers were vulgar and loud, and brash with cash, laying such huge bets at the hotel casino that it ran out of chips. There were flash cars revving in the parking lot outside and everyone draped in bling, hip-hop blaring from their car stereos, their baseball caps on backward, long basketball shorts flapping fashionably below their knees. They drank Johnny Walker Black Label, but mixed it with Sprite! And put their Converse high-top'd feet up on the sofas. There were sixty chefs, grilling Mozambican prawns as fast as they could.

Then the crackdown came—Operation No Return—and the diamond dudes fled or were arrested, and now the hotel is quiet again.

IF ANYTHING, the land grab up here has speeded up since the Unity government was established. "There seems to be a last-minute feeding frenzy," says Lynda, Beefy's wife.

The latest morsel in that feeding frenzy is Peta Hall, a seventy-year-old widow who lives nearby, on Witchwood. At the bottom of a deliberately ruinous drive we come, not so much to a gate, as to a portcullis across a stone tunnel. I honk, and she peeks from the front door, her movements radiating anxiety, even from this distance. She's a short, stout, capable woman, with gamine-cut blond hair and khaki Crocs, who's had one hell of a life.

"My mother came out from Holland already pregnant with me, and I was born in the Kalahari Desert. I grew up on horseback, cracking whips at livestock," she tells us as we walk through her almost empty house. Room after room has stunning vistas down into a broad valley four thousand feet below, with mountain ranges stretching beyond it. The mountains reminded British settlers of other ranges they had conquered, so they called them the Little Himalayas, and the land far below us they named Burma Valley, and planted it with bananas. Little clouds float by beneath us, and long-crested eagles glide in lazy spirals below, in a separate world almost, as though we are suspended in heaven looking down at the earth. It makes me feel giddy, lightheaded.

Beefy, whose family farm is next door, described how they used to watch the war from up here. They would see whole battles, the flash of rockets arching over the valley, and tracer bullets spurting back and forth, and then hear the distant explosions a little later up here on the mountains, like thunder following lightning. A Lilliputian war spread out below them on a map.

Peta Hall used to be Peta Kearns, married to Basil, a successful farmer in Mtepatepa, west of Harare, a talented polo-player and fluent Shona-speaker. Peta bred and trained polo ponies. Toward the end of the war, Basil was ambushed by guerrillas just near the farm. "He was shot in the head and the stomach, and died nineteen days later, never having regained consciousness," says Peta. "It was that fellow, Rex Nhongo, who killed him.

"Almost exactly a year since her father was killed, my daughter Debbie, who was seventeen, was also ambushed. She was driving along in her little beach buggy when she came to a tree they had felled across the road, and they all began shooting. Her jugular was severed and she bled to death..."

In time, Peta remarried, to Peter Hall, who commuted here at weekends from his printing business, Cannon Press, in Harare. Peter had bought Witchwood from Sir Edgar Whitehead, the former

Prime Minister, and the local myth was that it took its name from a tree that grew up through an old burial ground, dislodging human bones. They farmed coffee for a while, and macadamia nuts, and when Peter's health failed, they retired here.

Last year was their *annus horribilis*. Peter had a stroke and became paralyzed and bed-ridden. Peta returned to Witchwood one day to find the gate down, four vehicles in the garden, and the house full of war vets, chanting. "My husband was upstairs, Ruda, his carer, had locked herself up there with him. He was aware of what was happening." Their leader was a war vet called Francis Mazivikeni. The police refused to evict him.

The vets began to loot the house downstairs, loading furniture into their red truck and taking it away to the local auction house to sell. They found an old .303 rifle, plugged and rendered unusable, hanging on the wall as decoration, and took it, together with some dusty shotgun cartridges, to the police, who charged Peta with illegal possession of firearms, with intent to commit sabotage, insurgency, and terrorism, the same charges now faced by Roy Bennett. "The police said I was trying to create an insurgency in the Bvumba," says Peta.

Peter was ailing fast now, and Peta did a deal with the vets that they would let her stay until he died. Peter had chosen his grave six months before, near the house in a grove of trees, but when the war vets realized what it was, they became agitated. "Why don't you go to a cemetery, like ordinary people," said Francis.

The next day Peta heard the doors below being smashed, and then the vets trooping upstairs. Francis's bodyguard, Magaya, shoved his way in and grabbed me by the neck of my blouse. I was trying to call my daughter, Pebbs, in South Africa and he grabbed the cell from me, and she pleaded with him to let us go.

"They had drums and began to beat them and to dance around Peter as he lay in bed, about twenty of them banging pots and pans from the kitchen, and chanting, 'Out now! Out now!' They were all high and drunk too, having worked their way through the twenty cases of wine in our cellar.

"Peter was looking on in terror—he was in diapers by then, you know, and had only one leg—he lost the other in a car accident in 1995. His arms and hands were bent in permanent claws. But he could smile and he could understand and he could talk, too, in a slurred way, but that I could follow. He used to sing a lot too—as a youngster he had attended Chichester Cathedral School [the Pre- bendal School] and had sung in the choir there."

Now he groaned as they danced around him drumming and chanting and banging their iron pots together. "I really thought he wouldn't make it," says Peta, "that he was going to die then and there. Lynda and Beefy came, and were frantically helping me to get our stuff out." They put Peter on a mattress and slowly eased him down the stairs, while the vets watched and chanted, "Go! Go! Go!" each time Peter thudded down another stair.

As Peter was pulled out of the front door, across the lawn, he looked up at the house and said to them in a voice that was suddenly understandable, "Do you know how long I've lived here?" And lying there, in his soiled diapers, with his clawed hands, he began to sing in Latin, his voice strong now, clear and beautiful, the hymns of his youth. And he sang as Beefy and Lynda and Peta and Ruda dragged him on his mattress across the lawn and loaded him onto the pick-up, and drove him away through the broken portcullis.

The following night, Peta sneaked back to Witchwood, coming in the back way. Farnie, who had worked for Peter for twenty-five years, had arranged for her to consult the local *nganga*.

"I was pretty distraught at the time, so I thought it was worth a try. We sat in the dark, in a circle, four men, Ruda and me, with our arms crossed over our chests, holding hands, and the witch doctor murmured some incantations. In the middle there was a bottle of rock salt and a small pile of stones, quartz rocks, which we had found when we were digging Peter's grave. I picked out one of the stones, and the witch doctor blessed it, and the rock salt too. He said, 'Before you cross any new threshold, sprinkle the rock salt on it, for protection. And take the stone with you everywhere. Then the spir- its will keep you safe. No harm will come to you, Mrs. Hall.' Then we all melted away into the dark. He never asked for payment."

Peta produces the stone now — it is about the size of her fist, a pink-and-white-tinted quartz. "I keep it with me all the time," she says. "At night I put it under my pillow, or on the bedside table. When I go out, I keep it in my handbag. It's foolish, I know, but I believe in it."

In the meantime, her children had spoken to Roy and the MDC, and the next day the local MDC youth league chief told her, "What's happening to you is illegal. We'll sort it out."

"I was afraid," admits Peta. "I had had enough. I was worried about the consequences of fighting back."

As soon as the MDC supporters arrived at Witchwood that weekend, Mazivikeni and his entourage fled. The police escorted the MDC away the following day, but some hid and stayed behind, and the vets were too scared to return.

"Peter was in a terrible state that Sunday. I didn't think he'd make it through the night." But he survived, and early the next morning, Peta had to come down the mountain to be interrogated by the police again. "They spent all morning trying to get me to admit that I was the leader of the Bvumba insurgency," she snorts. When she got back to the Bvumba that afternoon, she found Peter had died. She was determined to bury him on Witchwood, as he had wanted.

"I got the doctor to issue a death certificate and he explained to me what I had to do with Peter's body — to bandage the jaw closed and bind his feet together, so that rigor mortis didn't distort the body position, and to plug the orifices. Ruda helped me. Then we wrapped him in a white sheet that was beautifully embroidered with roses.

"We loaded him into the back of the pick-up and brought him back home to Witchwood. We buried him that day. There were about ten people there. We laid out a table with drinks, and hit the gin and Scotch even before the service started! There was quite a funny moment when Pebbs, who had just flown in from Johannesburg, and was still in her Jo'burg clothes, wanted to get into the hole to see her dad — so I lowered her in, and then she couldn't get out.

"And while we were standing there, the police and the CIO, and the Support Unit and Canine Unit arrived in about four trucks. We had left the gate open for funeral guests, so they just drove straight in."

Peta just lost it. "This is a private service, get out now!" she yelled. Chief Inspector Chinyoka, the officer in charge, said that he'd had an anonymous call to say that she was conducting an illegal funeral. "He demanded to see the death certificate, and the burial certificate, but I had all the right documents.

"You know, they really didn't want Peter to be buried on the farm. Mazivikeni and his guys are very superstitious and they knew that once Peter was buried on Witchwood, his spirit would guard the place."

There was a power cut, so they played tapes of Peter's favorite hymns from childhood on the car stereo, with the doors open. "The Lord's My Shepherd" and "Abide with Me," and popular numbers he liked, "Kiss Me Goodbye," and "Send Me On My Way," by Petula Clark—they played that one just as the police convoy left.

"After that," says Peta, "my whole attitude changed. I'm fighting for this place for my family. If I have to die for it, I will. Peter's spirit protects this place." We are standing in the empty bedroom upstairs. His wheelchair is still in the corner by the window, facing the sublime view south into the Burma Valley, and the Little Himalayas beyond, and to the east, Chikamba Real dam down on the Mozambique flood plain. And for the first time in the telling of it all, Peta's eyes grow wet.

thirty-one

The World's Oldest Leader

WE ARE LOOPING SOUTH from Mutare, through Chimanimani, on our way to the Savé Valley to see our friend Rita, and then to the southern city of Bulawayo. I have heard that even while Roy is still in prison, diamonds have now been discovered on his farm, Charleswood, in Chimanimani. It seems too bizarre a stroke of irony, but Doug van der Riet confirms it. Russians came in with a thirty-ton bulldozer, he says, to take soil away for assay. It seems to be an oblique-angled kimberlite pipe, not a random scattering of alluvial stones, like Chiadzwa. The Russians are in partnership with Joice Mujuru, General Nhongo's wife.

Nestling into the base of the mountains, Roy's coffee bushes, those that haven't been wrenched out of the red earth, are now overgrown and choked with weeds and vines. The hillside above them, once thick with musasa and mjanji trees, has been shaved and prepped for invasive diamond surgery, and stands barren and eroded.

You can't see Roy's main house, Mawenje Lodge, until you are almost upon it. A forest has grown up in and around it, of musasa, fast-growing invasive wattle, ferns, and bracken, some of the trees already twenty feet high. The lodge is a ruin; only the chimney stack stands intact. Broken and charred ceiling beams jut from the walls. Georgina brushes away the cinders and leaves from the entrance, to reveal, etched into the threshold, a message.

GOD BLESS THIS HOUSE
ROY, HEATHER, CHARLES, CASEY BENNETT
1996

On another panel, a picture of the family dog (barking at imaginary intruders) and its name, *GUNNER*.

Georgina and I stand there with Tempe and Doug, looking at the indented blessing, now kohled with ash and open to the elements. No one speaks. There is nothing left to say.

The thatch on the guest cottages is rotting; there are holes in the baths; it has a forlorn, desolate feel, with the Haroni River rushing past, down into the Rusitu, past Chris Lynam's old farm and out over the Mozambique flood plain to the sea. Inside the cottages, the walls are darkened with soot from cooking fires that have been lit on the floors. And Mugabe's men have daubed crude graffiti that pillories Bennett, calling him an *mboro*—a dick. There are charcoal-drawn pictures of him—childish and unrecognizable, but you know they're supposed to be him because they have little arrows labeled "Bennett," pointing at the figures, drawn in shackles, as indeed he is once again, even as we stand here, in the ruins of his old farm.

THE FOLLOWING DAY we drive south to the Savé Valley Conservancy. The Savé River valley used to be a vast collection of white-owned cattle ranches, on dry, marginal land, inherently unsuited to cattle. So, more than a decade after independence, the ranchers combined twenty-four adjacent properties, totaling 1,300 square miles, into the largest private wildlife conservancy in Africa.

By 1995, the conservancy was surrounded by a double-electrified fence and restocked with indigenous wildlife, including a successful breeding program for the critically endangered black rhino. Now, most of that two-hundred-mile border fence has been ripped down and the conservancy is under acute stress. Subsistence farmers have moved onto a third of it, and poaching has soared. Generals and judges and cabinet ministers are circling the safari lodges.

Rita and her boyfriend, Spike Williamson, used to manage Hammond, one of the properties on the conservancy. Its American owners, Weldon and Kathy Schenck, had stickers printed up which said *Just Ask Spike,* because he knew the answers to all things ecological. For his birthday, Rita once bought him a CD of frog calls, and one wet night, she surreptitiously put the croaking medley on. He didn't appear to notice for a while, then raised an eyebrow at one call, and declared, "Wait a minute, *that* frog's not indigenous." He and Rita now run Ardan Safaris, specializing in designing and running bespoke wildlife trips, in Zimbabwe and elsewhere in Africa.

Tonight we are having supper under a tall cathedral of thatch, beneath a trophy buffalo head. Spike calls it Rapunzel, with its thick horns curling down like long armored bangs. Dr. Godfrey Mungwadzi and his heavily pregnant wife, Killiana, have joined us from Chiredzi town, nearby. Godfrey has dreadlocks, ankle boots, and a precisely trimmed goatee. He has treated many of the victims of political violence in this Chiredzi area, working for human-rights services such as CSU. In the elections last year, he stood as an independent candidate, and found himself on a hit list. "The actual hits were being done by guys from Angola and the Congo. I was warned to get out of the country, so we collected my daughter from Hippo Valley primary school, in case she was used as a hostage. CIO agents came to my house the next day...

"I didn't understand what I'd done wrong. I didn't understand why this country could be so much theirs, and not mine. And then I realized it was because they had the power of the gun. All of a sudden, we had become people who should be eliminated. We got killed, our friends got killed, our property was destroyed.

"The violence this time was on a much larger scale, our paupers' graves were filling up with the victims. People were killed and their bodies ferried to mortuaries in other districts. There were dozens of unclaimed bodies, unheard-of in our society—it was because people didn't know where the bodies of their relatives were, they had been moved away.

"I'd only read about PTSD, but even now I still worry I'm being followed. Or when I'm sleeping, I'm peeping through the curtains, not sure of what's going to happen. I have asylum papers in SA. I'm an HIV expert. We had a business, a way of life, kids in school.

"Now the MDC goes along with ZANU-PF. They have joined the gravy train," he sighs. Rain starts to patter lightly on the thatch, and Killiana pats her belly, big with child. "I think we'd better go," she says, "in case the river rises."

THE RAIN moves off again, grumbling thunder as it does, and we pack up ready to move on at first light. We are sleeping in thatched *rondavels* on a bend in the Mkwasine River. It's barely a river, just a trickle that meanders through a sandy bed. I fall asleep to the croaking of frogs. But just before dawn, I wake, alerted by a presence of some sort. I grab my flashlight and walk out onto the veranda. The audioscape has changed somehow; a background roar fills the air. It's not rain. I cast my beam up. It's not wind either—the trees are eerily still. It's coming from in front of me. I point the light toward the sound, and there, where the sandy beach used to be, is a rushing torrent of water, bursting its banks and lapping up the lawn toward the veranda. I lie in bed, dozing fitfully, ear cocked to the newly mighty Mkwasine, until the wood hoopoes start up at first light, with their yuck, yuck, yuck cry, which the Ndebele people call *umfazi uyahleka*—the laughing woman. Ring-necked doves and harlequin quails and red-billed hornbills join in.

After breakfast we drive to the ford across the Mkwasine. It was barely wet when we crossed it on our way in. Now the river is surging four foot high over it, and vehicles are stuck on both sides. The low-level bridge over the Turgwe river to the north is also flooded. So, for the time being, we are stranded.

We drive over to Signal Rock, a large granite *dwala* which is the one place on the whole property we can get a phone signal, and walk up it, past a stinking elephant carcass. Around us stretches the Mopani woodland. Dark clouds sit heavily upon the kopjes that circle the horizon. Spike identifies the bush around us, long-pod cassia, marulas, white syringa, wild sesamum, bird plum, squat sterculia, wing pod, knob-thorn acacia. We recline on the granite warming our backs, and look up at the birds rushing around feeding on the insects that have come out in advance of the storm. Eurasian bee-eaters, black cuckoo shrikes, go-away birds, flappet larks. Guinea fowl dizzy through the sickle bushes, and white-backed vultures sit patiently in a mopani tree. A lone marshal eagle spiraling reminds me of Roy, and we call, to find that he is still in prison.

I try to phone home. Miraculously, I get an international line. Joanna has been out buying Hugo a new winter coat. He chose a camouflage one, she says. Then he stood in the middle of his bedroom, put on the coat, and asked, "Can you see me now?"

The line cuts out and I lie there, my back warm on the granite, as the coming storm rustles the trees. The smell is of rain, but closer and more pungent is the smell of Matabele ants, of the formic acid that they exude as a defense. I think of Hugo standing solemnly in the middle of his New York bedroom, convinced that his new camouflage coat is an invisibility cloak. And I think of all the chaos around me here, the kids dying of cholera, the diamond-diggers and the gold-panners, and the army and the police and all the rest of the aged dictator's agents running around, and Roy still behind bars in a fetid jail cell, shitting into a bucket. The vultures are waiting in the mopani trees and the Matabele ants spewing their acid to ward off predators, and over in the meat room Fabian the game scout is hacking at a bloody zebra for ration meat to feed the staff.

THAT EVENING, Mugabe's birthday interview, *President R. G. Mugabe @ 85*, is broadcast on ZTV, having been heavily trailed for weeks. He is now the world's oldest national leader. First, there is a short warm-up act—a young man from the "21st February Movement" (Mugabe's birthday) tries to entice people to attend celebrations the following week in Chinhoyi, to mark "the life of our icon, President Robert Mugabe."

The interview itself takes place on the lawns of State House in the shade of a musasa tree. He's still sprightly, for eighty-five, although he uses a little dance move to disguise his difficulty with steps as he strolls into position. Once again, he is in his high-backed, thronelike armchair, his slender legs tucked back, and pressed together at the knees, in a coltish, effete manner. He wears a well-cut charcoal suit, burnt-crimson tie, striped shirt, and glazed loafers.

Mugabe peddles his imperial musings for an hour and a half straight, with only the lightest of cues from his simpering interlocutor, who smiles, fawns, nods approvingly, and even giggles appreciatively throughout. Mugabe fiddles with his gold wedding band as he drones on, and his hands flutter and join again with ecclesiastically laced fingers. It is a repetitive, circuitous performance, geriatric maundering, garnished with non sequiturs, the brain-shavings of the dictatorial dotage. And he slides further and further into the depths of his outsize chair, becoming more and more diminutive, his trouser legs riding up his shins to reveal a nasty case of swollen ankles.

He acknowledges, almost in passing, that agriculture has "underperformed" and that there had been "a ah..."—he searches for the right phrase—"a period of hunger," hunger in the way one might feel peckish before lunch, if one hadn't had a hearty breakfast!

But much of his soliloquy is reserved for his favorite parlor game, Britain-bashing. I've noticed that when he speaks of Britain, he subconsciously lapses into a magniloquent sub-Churchillian cadence—betraying his agonizing Anglophilia. "We are not an extension of Britain," he thunders now. "I will never stand for it, dead or alive, even my *ghost* will not stand for it." He is increasingly invoking the specter of his ghost, as though he is trying to extend his stranglehold on us, even after his death. "If they [the Brits] want, then we will give them the graves of their dead," he taunts.

Later, at his lavish eighty-fifth-birthday banquet in Chinhoyi, a banner across the street reads, *"Age Ain't Nothing But a Number."* A hundred cows are slaughtered for the feast. He and his family are filmed eating bulging slices of a cake weighing a hundred and eighty pounds, slathered with vanilla icing. Mugabe wears a red kerchief around his neck, like an elderly cub scout, and slumps in an olive velour sofa with Grace and the kids, while waiters in white jackets crawl on their knees to serve them.

Behind Mugabe, if you look closely, there is a familiar figure. It is Joseph Mwale. For years now there has been a warrant out for his arrest on charges of murder, yet the police claim they can't find him. And there he is, publicly standing right behind his master, licking vanilla icing off his homicidal fingers.

THAT NIGHT, still trapped by the flooding rivers, we light a fire under Rapunzel, and open the bar. David Hulme, the son of Hammond's current manager, joins us. He's in his mid-thirties, and has a hunter's license himself (and has written a book, *The Shangaan Song*, about his experiences). There's a large white bandage around his biceps. "I was bitten," he says.

"Bitten?"

"Yes. By an African. The guy was a bit *penga* [mad] and he had AIDS. So I'm on ARVs.

"It's not the first time I've been bitten by a human," he says, revealing two scars beneath his collar. "I caught a guy stealing from my car, and grabbed him, but he bit a big chunk out of my neck. We fought for ages—a big crowd gathered to watch. He came at me with a brick, so I grabbed a tire lever. And the doctor said I might be infected with AIDS after that one too, but it was back in 1994, before ARVs, so he told me to return in three months to be tested. It was three months of hell. Later, that guy was shot dead by police. He came at them with a butcher's knife."

Rita is telling us how her mother and brother are doing in their little cottage in Masvingo. "She still misses Dad. We put him in an unmarked grave, under an acacia tree out on the farm, covered it over with thorn bush. Francesca, the maid, is alone at the farmhouse now. The roof's falling in and there are black mambas in it, and swarms of bees. There are too many ghosts there now.

"Occasionally we take Mum there. She walks around the garden, picks flowers, arranges them in a vase on the table, and my sister Kate still goes there to paint. She paints the only trees left standing there, a little grove of six monkey orange trees. She calls them her 'girls,' and paints them again and again. Over the election, there were rumors that white farmers had come back from New Zealand, to our house. So the youth militia came and checked under all the beds."

We've had quite a bit to drink now, sitting there under the thatch looking out at the downpour, and laughing about how Africa resets your calculus of chaos. I tell them of a catch-up email from a childhood friend, "DB" Warren, who used to farm near Silverstream before leaving for Zululand. He reports that he's just got divorced after thirty-two years of marriage. "Kind of the cherry on the top for 2008," he goes on, "as we were attacked on the farm here and I was stabbed through both lungs...managed to kill one [of the intruders] on the bedroom floor, before making a dash for the hospital. Have to love Africa," he concludes, with amazing insouciance.

Rita reminds us of the apocryphal story about how you can tell when a missionary's "gone native," by the fly-in-the-tea test. When he's newly arrived and a fly buzzes into his tea, he fishes it out. After he's been here a while, he drinks the tea with the fly in it, and when he's gone native he grabs a passing fly and puts it in the tea, then drinks. Maybe this place turns everyone nuts in the end? Kate obsessively painting the last few trees. David saying he's been bitten by an AIDS-infected man—twice—and just taking it as commonplace. Or DB Warren mentioning casually that he killed one of his assailants before driving himself to hospital with his blood-filled lungs. Belinda telling Georgina that she's grown so used to filthy toilet seats that she doesn't even bother with them now, and has trained herself to "poo standing up."

"She has incredibly strong thighs," says Georgina. "I felt them.

"I'll tell you something I've never told anyone," she ventures, somewhat the worse for wear. "I've had sex on Rhodes's grave."

"That's sacrilegious!" squeals Rita.

"We were watched by rainbow skinks," says Georgina.

"Beach sex is overrated," says Rita. "You get sand in your guava."

THE NEXT DAY the river falls. We help clear the branches and other flotsam from the ford, and gingerly drive across, water tugging at the doors, and then we drive back up to Harare, through Zaka, up and over a rugged spine of hills, past the barracks of 4:2 Battalion, near Gutu. On the right, stretched out over a large granite *dwala*, we see tens of thousands of people lined up—it's a scene of biblical proportions. It turns out to be a CARE international food aid registration. This is the reality of Zimbabwe today. So many of its people now rely on this foreign food aid to stay alive. The local CARE officials are terrified to talk. "We don't want to say anything to jeopardize the feeding," they say. "The government can suspend our operations at any time. And then these people will starve."

AT VIC'S TAVERN in Chivhu there are cholera alert posters on the wall, next to antique farming implements, and a notice that chides: *We don't provide toilet facilities for people just loitering about.* The deserted dining room is all made up, the tables laid with white cloths, cutlery, and napkin crowns, the chair backs wearing little white linen sleeves. We order tea out on the veranda. The milk is powdered and lumpy and the tea leaves free-floating. "There is no strainer available." The waiter shrugs. I absently shoo away a pair of mating flies, buzzing around my face, and they land in Georgina's tea. "Fucking flies," she says, and takes a long, deliberate sip from the chipped cup.

thirty-two

If Ever We Should All Die,
It Will Be Forgotten Now

SPIKE AND I SIT in his truck on the dark, deserted corner of Fort and 4th Streets in Zimbabwe's second city, Bulawayo, which is experiencing one of its frequent power cuts. "Don't leave your car, it's a very dangerous part of town, even when the street lights work," Rita's brother-in-law has warned us. The back door opens and out of the night appears Max Nkandla, the man we've been waiting for. He used to be a guerrilla in Joshua Nkomo's army, ZIPRA, fighting against white rule, and saw combat twenty-eight times. He's dressed all in khaki, and though his epaulettes are empty now, at fifty-four, he still carries himself like a soldier. He's President of the Zimbabwe Liberators Peace Initiative, which represents two thousand of his former guerrilla comrades.

At independence in 1980, Max was integrated into the new Zimbabwe National Army (ZNA). As his name suggests, Nkandla is amaNdebele, and when Mugabe unleashed his Fifth Brigade in Operation Gukurahundi to attack the south in 1983, Max, by then a captain, was arrested. "The Military Police took me and accused me that I had an arms cache somewhere. I was put in leg-irons and handcuffs. Five days after my arrest, I heard from a fellow prisoner what had happened to my father—that he had been shot, executed.

"He was a primary school teacher, and the Vice-Chairman of ZAPU for his district, and when the soldiers searched his home they found a photo he had by his bed of me in my camouflage uniform— and they accused him, saying I was a dissident, and asking, 'Where's your son?' And he tried to tell them I was in the ZNA.

"He was forced to attend a rally, and at the rally the soldiers took him and three of the other elders, and they shot them, in front of everyone, the whole village—about two hundred people. They were seated and just shot.

"The community buried him, near his cattle pens, just outside our family kraal. My sister, Elizabeth, now forty-seven, witnessed his murder. She still cries about it, even today."

WE SET OFF, Max, Spike, Georgina, and me, early the next morning, through the wide city streets lined with flame trees and silver oak, and tree-wisteria, laden with purple blossom, past the Esoteric Beauty Salon and the Scoff Box, the Heads 'n' Hooves Butchery, and, above a petrol station, the Underground Cabin Company, a coffin shop with its caskets displayed prominently in the window, and headstone samples around the corner. One suggested epitaph: *YOU LEFT A   GAP THAT NO-ONE CAN FILL.* We drive southeast on the Matopos road, past the faux-Tudor Churchill Arms Hotel and its Inglenook Restaurant, and the Musketeers Lodge, and a sign welcoming us to Matabeleland South. Three inches of rain have just fallen and it is uncharacteristically green. Baboons scamper away into the tall blond grass; a convoy of Lutheran Aid trucks pass by. And in a clearing, ZANU officials, judging by their banners, are holding an open-air meeting. But this area is an almost completely ZANU-free zone—for one overwhelming reason.

Even though the Matabeleland massacres were perpetrated twenty-five years ago, they still loom large to the people here—an unrequited tragedy that shattered their society, and festers at the heart of everything. Roy Bennett reckons that what happened in Matabeleland remains Mugabe's biggest motive for holding on to power: he fears that if he leaves office he will become victim to what the Shona call *kudzorera pamavambo*—retributive justice, the real blood-revenge, the kind that doesn't need the Hague to happen.

Mugabe used a small and sputtering "dissident" problem, some of which is suspected of having been staged, as a pretext to wipe out the entire leadership of Joshua Nkomo's ZAPU party. This was to the Ndebele people what the Katyn massacre was to the Polish, and the casualties were similar, around twenty thousand civilians, although out of a much smaller population (two million) than Poland's (thirty million).

"It's not easy to give it [the massacre] a name because it was so distressing," says Max. "And even during the last elections, some of the original victims were visited again and harassed, so they are still scared to talk."

We pass through the town of Kezi, and on through the village of Maphisa, where the road turns to dirt. In spite of the rain, the land here is thin and tired. "Nothing is developed in this area," says Max looking around, disgusted. "Mugabe just vandalized it, and sent all the money to his own region—not to ours. The ones between eighteen and forty, they all fled this area to South Africa to work. They are the ones who are helping us—sending money back—they are the only reason we survive."

We turn off after a few miles and head along a track made by carts pulled by dainty Jerusalem donkeys with gray crosses along their backs, until we reach the kraal of the local MDC councillor. Chickens scatter, clucking in alarm, and small children dart indoors and return with an old lady in a frilly green-and-white gingham apron, a floral headscarf, bare feet, and a pronounced limp. She seats us on small wooden stools and sits herself on the bare beaten earth. Only then does the greeting ritual begin.

"*Salibonani*" ["Hello"], Max says.

"*Salibonani*" ["Hello"], she says.

"*Unjani?*" ["How are you?"], asks Max.

"Ah, *mbijana*" ["just a little"], she replies, which is what people here say now, instead of the traditional *ngisaphila* ["I am well"]. They haven't felt well for twenty-five years.

Summoned by the kids, a group of men return from the fields, including her husband, Elmon Dube, seventy-six. "I am the head of this kraal," he says, smoothing his dirty Billabong T-shirt, a hand-me-down from some Western charity drive.

Like many here, he is still nervous talking about Gukurahundi. "I walked to Bulawayo to escape during that time," he says. "My wife was assaulted by those Gukurahundi, and even up to today, she is crippled. She was beaten on the hips. They told her to lie down, then they whipped her with sjamboks. Most of the women around here were beaten at their kraals by those ones with the red berets. They were Shonas. And they assaulted the men here too—seventy strikes per man, hitting us with logs."

"The soldiers accused us of harboring dissidents," says Stephen Nkomo. "They had someone in their vehicle, who we couldn't see, who identified us—those he identified were taken away and we never saw them again. So many were killed—they just never came back. No one has asked about this, even until today. No one spoke to us about it. The soldiers' intent was to shorten the number of Ndebele-speaking people as a tribe."

"Since my wife is crippled for life," says Elmon, "an apology is not enough—they must pay for what they did. There should be a trial and compensation."

"I'm not willing just to forgive," says Joshua Moyo, defiantly. "There must be some sort of punishment against the perpetrators."

Daniel Moyo, sixty-eight, is the MDC-M local councillor. He shrugs off the division into two wings of the MDC, one headed by Mutambara, which is predominantly southern, and that headed by Tsvangirai. "It doesn't matter," he says. "We are hunting the same animal."

He pauses while the old lady in the gingham apron approaches with a watermelon. She expertly cleaves it with a machete, and offers the slices to us.

"Who should be punished for Gukurahundi?" he continues. "The perpetrators had a leader, who was supposed to control them. The one who was leading—who was that? It was Mugabe, and his generals, especially Perence Shiri. There is a pattern to this, you know. They still do it. It's the same government."

Max says, "You know, we are hearing about Charles Taylor being taken to the ICC—why not this bastard, Mugabe?"

"The soldiers beat me for an hour," says Mlaga Maposa, who works at the local irrigation co-op. "Even now, this part of me"—he gingerly touches his lower back—"it hurts when it becomes cold.

"My uncle, a councillor, was killed. We never saw the body. We think he was thrown into Antelope mine. And Nkosi Dube, my cousin who was a headmaster, he was also taken. And we never even saw his body either. Sampson Ncube, a teacher—he also disappeared. All senior ZAPU members were in danger. The strategy was to kill ZAPU—to break it totally. The only men who survived were those who fled to town.

"If ever we should all die, it will be forgotten now. We were left—but many were killed. I am still so angry today about it."

Isabel Ngwenya, who has a goiter on her neck from iodine deficiency, was heading for the Tachani River to fetch water with two other women when they were stopped by Shona-speaking soldiers in red berets, who accused them of "going to meet dissidents." "We denied it. They said, 'Today you will tell the truth.' They made us to lie down with our arms stretched out in front of us, and then they beat us. We were not allowed to put our arms in the way to protect ourselves from the sticks. One of the women was seven months pregnant. But there was no time for reasoning with them. I was too scared to go to hospital afterward, and I still limp even today."

"What can be done, after all this time?" I wonder.

"A human needs a memorial," she says. "We need to do that." And after a moment's thought, she continues. "You know, we have a word in siNdebele, *cithumuzi*, it means 'to destroy a family, a

people, a nation.' That is what has happened to us—*cithumuzi*."
The word is as close as you can get in siNdebele to genocide.

THE MAIN torture base was a place called Bhalaghwe (also spelled
Belaghwe), near Maphisa town. In siNdebele, Bhalaghwe means "a
wide rock." It still strikes fear in my heart. Above it rises Zaman-
yoni Hill—"The Hill of Birds." *Nyoni,* a bird—the word Shiri
used to sign in at La Rochelle. I remember crawling up to the top of
the hill and looking down at the infernal scene below.

Thompson, who's now fifty-four, and still too afraid to use his
surname, was working at a local bakery when the army picked him
up and brought him here. "They blindfolded me and beat me with
sticks. There were hundreds of others imprisoned here too. I was
kept prisoner for a month—and they beat me nearly every day. At
the end my mother came here to the camp, and she pleaded with
the CIOs to release me."

"Did she pay some money?"

He looks down. "I don't know. Maybe. Yes."

There's almost nothing left of Bhalagwe today. I have an old
photo of it which I am using to navigate around the ruins, but
Thompson still knows the layout by heart. "This is where the soldiers were keeping their lugagges," he says, pointing at the only
intact brick walls on the site.

As we talk, a tiny brindle kitten comes bounding out of the
bush, and leaps straight up into Georgina's arms. She walks around
the torture site with it purring there.

"Three years ago, the community decided to gather the bones
of the victims, the bones from Antelope mine and elsewhere, and
put them in a mass grave," says Thompson. "We collected money
and made these graves by ourselves." He shows me two improvised
graves in a small clearing. They have low cement walls, cheaply
built, and already subsiding. Into the cement of each grave, when it
was still wet, they have traced the words *MASS GRAVE.* That's it.
Nothing else. They are still afraid to write more, to name the

perpetrators or even the victims, to properly memorialize their dead. Twenty-five years on, and still the fear has them in its grip.

As WE GET ready to leave, Georgina announces that she wants to keep the kitten. But of course she can't. We walk up and down looking for its mother, calling for its siblings. But the nearby kraals are deserted, of both people and animals. And eventually we have to leave it at the gate of an empty kraal, the closest one to where it found us, hoping that this might be its home. As we start to drive away, the kitten totters down the dirt road after us, a furry ball of khaki with irregular black spots, and Georgina bursts into tears.

"Over the *kitten?* Really?" I ask, gesturing around the ruins of the torture base and the mass graves. "With all of this?"

"No," she sniffs. "It's not just the kitten. It's everyone here. They've all been abandoned. No one gives a fuck about what's happened to them, they're completely alone."

And I realize that she's right. The Ndebele have been stranded by history. A remnant people, deserted in the land they had once conquered. In that respect, I suppose, they are similar to the remaining whites.

As we round the last bend, I look in the mirror, and the kitten is still there, bobbing up and down between the tall grass-tufted median and the overhanging thorn trees, and sprayed with our dust plumes now, but still vainly trying to follow us.

thirty-three

The Ordeal Tree

Max Nkandla is subdued on our return to Bulawayo. Hearing all the recollections of the massacres seems to have triggered in him simultaneous feelings of anger and impotence. These days he makes a living driving a taxi. But he spends most of his time trying to help orphans. Zimbabwe now leads the world in number of orphans per capita—produced by AIDS, poverty, health-care collapse, and a repressive ruler, indifferent to the plight of his people. Max and his wife, Sukoluhle, a pre-school teacher, used to board six orphans in their small house in Entumbane township. That was before Sukoluhle left home. "She now has to work as a maid servant in Johannesburg," says Max, grimly, cracking his knuckles.

The irony is left unremarked. That he fought in a liberation war against white rule only to find that all these years later his wife must still clean the white man's toilet, that the flower of amaNdebele nation is reduced to servitude. Their two younger daughters, sixteen and fourteen, live here with Max. "The girls miss their mother so much," he sighs. "This is her second year of doing it. She would love to come back, and I would love her to, but we really can't survive." His widowed sister, Elizabeth, the one who watched their father being shot in the head in front of the entire village, works as a maid in Cape Town. "She used to come back home for two weeks, every December," he says. "But last year she didn't come back."

Max still helps hundreds of orphans; he wants me to visit one of several informal orphanages he supports. House number E299 is simply another in the endless rows of box houses in Dube township, below the giant cooling towers of the city's moribund power station. Sipho Mhlanga cares for forty-two AIDS orphans here. She calls her home Csingcino Nkosi, "With God's Guidance." Divorced with five grown kids, she started taking in orphans in 2006, "because the country was getting poorer and poorer, and children were being lost, becoming street kids, scattered all over. I want to occupy them and make sure all of them go to school," she explains, sitting in her lime-green kitchen beneath a poster that reads, *I am single but not desperate.*

After we have given Sipho the bags of maize meal and cooking oil we brought, the orphans arrange themselves in size-calibrated rows for a farewell song. "My home, my home, my home," they sing, "is far, far away."

The kids are in the same age range as my own, dressed in eclectic Western hand-me-downs. One little girl, Thandiwe, wears a neon-pink T-shirt with the word *heiress* picked out in silver sequins. From a distance, she has an ever-present, beatific smile, but every time Georgina raises her camera, Thandiwe covers her face with her hand. Only when I get closer do I see that Thandiwe's smile is a deformity; the flesh of her lips is pared back off her teeth in a fixed rictus. And her eyes are not smiling at all—they glisten with shame.

Now THAT Dominic, Georgina's English boyfriend, has joined her, for his first visit to Africa north of the Limpopo, she wants him to see the wildlife, to show that this place, for all its tragedy, can still be beautiful too. So the next morning we drive northwest from Bulawayo on the Victoria Falls road. Rita sits in the back reconciling her check book. She's having problems fitting in the zeros. The last check she paid in Zimbabwe dollars was her monthly electricity bill—$865 trillion. Georgina is tapping at her netbook, which is covered in leopard-print laminate and coordinates with her blouse. "It's my *Out of Africa* look," she says. "I'm wearing it in honor of Dominic."

The first roadblock is on the outskirts of the city. Spike checks we're belted in. He and Rita only pretend to be. "I once got out of wearing my seat belt at a roadblock," says Rita, "by telling them my *amazambane* were too big." She laughs as she palms her generous bust.

The road soon empties of traffic, except for bony livestock, which emerge without warning from the head-high elephant grass. This used to be commercial ranching and forestry land, but most ranches here have been jambanja'd, and the Gwaai Valley conservancy too. The roadside is punctuated now with freshly fashioned, higgledy huts of red mud, and tiny plots of wilting maize. But the new settlers tend only to colonize a narrow strip on either side of the main road, seldom venturing into the interior. From time to time, we see government-issued tractors lurching along, festooned with passengers. War vet company cars, Rita calls them.

There was some spirited opposition here to the land takeovers, Spike says, smiling—notably the Gwaai Valley Resistance, the GVR, which consisted of several young white farmers who entrenched themselves in some sort of bunker, with a large supply of beer, vowing that they would never be evicted. But when the beer ran out, their tenacity drained with it and they re-emerged.

Four and a half hours up the Falls road, we reach the Gwaai River. On its southern bank is the Gwaai River Hotel. I remember it as a gracious thatched building, resting on pillars of smooth round river stones, run by a Jewish couple, the Broombergs. There was an Indian-style punkah flap in the dining room, and in season, fireflies in jars replaced candles on the tables. Semi-tame zebra drank from the swimming pool. Now the place is a charred ruin; the river stone pillars stand alone, watch towers to the destruction around them.

We turn left here into Hwange Wildlife Reserve, the flagship of

Zimbabwe's game parks and, at the size of Wales, its largest. Spike grew up here, at Main Camp. He and his three rumbunctious brothers were called the Demolition Squad. His father, Basil, was an elephant ecologist who died at forty-one from bladder cancer. As we pull in, Spike points to the sign outside the pub, the Waterbuck's Head. "My father was famous for being able to piss over the top of that sign," he says. No mean feat, given that it's eye height.

We just have time to take Dominic to the Nymandlovu game pan for the sunset congregation of thirsty animals. From a distance, we see that the viewing platform is already full of tourists, though oddly there is no sign of their vehicle. They seem to be jumping up and down, dancing perhaps, but we hear no music. As we approach, we see that they are actually baboons, sitting on the chairs, scampering up and down the steps, dangling from the rafters, copulating and grooming one another on the tables. And they have pissed and crapped everywhere.

They reluctantly lope off, barking and shrieking resentfully, and we sip our sundowners up there, trying to ignore the reek. The last time Rita was here, the Bulawayo Symphony Orchestra was playing a benefit under a full moon, in aid of hyena research. As they played, a huge elephant herd came down to drink at the pan. "They didn't seem to mind the music," says Rita, "except the flute solo, when that started they were a bit freaked out."

We are the only people staying at Main Camp. These government-owned lodges used to provide a tidy, utilitarian, low-priced alternative to the elite safari market, whose luxury camps are out of reach to most locals. The chalets are still scrupulously clean, if threadbare now, but the bar and restaurant are derelict, with broken windows and thatch shedding in great moldy clumps. In fact, little that requires capital investment or actual resources has been kept up. There is only one working light bulb in our section, and Lameck, the camp attendant, moves it around. He says he hasn't been paid for three months. His khaki uniform is disintegrating. His shoes are antique boats, bound together with twine, the heels steeply sloping, from years of supinating.

In the morning, there is no water, so Lameck insists I trek across to the other side of the camp where there is a working shower, with hot water, he promises, from the fire he has stoked up in a donkey boiler. He turns on the tap and we both hold our hands under the stream of cold water. "It'll get hot," promises Lameck, and we solemnly continue to feel the cold water. "I work here since 1971," he says. "It was better before. Now it is too bad. This government is useless." Still, the water remains icy. "It will come," says Lameck, but I can see that he is starting to lose faith now. "It's fine, really," I say. "I'll just have a cold shower." He lowers his head in defeat and withdraws.

I splash myself with icy water and step out of the stream to soap. And finally, just as I'm finishing, the water does turn warm, and then actually hot. Lameck has triumphed after all. On our way back across the camp, he dances a little victory jig.

Like so much else in this blighted country, the National Parks Department is hanging on by its fingernails. When rangers aren't paid enough, or indeed at all, they help themselves to the wildlife they are sworn to protect. Hwange Reserve is nicknamed National Parks Department's pantry. But the real picture is more nuanced. There are many here doing their best under terribly straitened circumstances, those with a memory of institutional integrity, and pride in their job, even as they struggle to survive and feed their families.

THE NEXT DAY we drive slowly through the reserve, through fields of yellow hibiscus, while Spike answers Dominic's questions about the animals we see. The cory bustard is the heaviest flying bird in the world, weighing in at over forty pounds, and the male's call is like the throb of an African drum. The black-and-white pattern on zebra helps them to blend in with one another and confuses their predators trying to single out a quarry. A spur-wing goose is really a duck. The difference? Among other things, two more vertebrae. The sun-strobing shoals of butterflies congregate on mounds of elephant dung because elephants' digestion is so inefficient that their dung is rich with nutrients. The birds that remind Dominic of pterodactyls are ground hornbills. The giraffes that loom at angles over the *terminalia* brush, like cranes over a harbor, were thought by the ancient Greeks to be a cross between a camel and a leopard, hence their scientific name: *camelopardalis*. An impala doe can reabsorb her fetus during the first three months in a drought, or extend gestation from six and a half to nine months after that, if necessary.

The ordeal tree, *oppositifolia*, under which a trio of tawny lion are napping, is highly poisonous. The San use it on the tips of their arrows. In the old days, if you were accused of witchcraft, you were forced to drink a potion made from it. If you died, you were innocent.

We talk about what to do if we are injured out here in the bush. To stop a wound becoming septic, honey works, says Spike. Sugar and salt too. Termites can be used as sutures. You pinch the wound closed and make the termite nip onto it with its mighty mandibles, then break off its body, and repeat, along the wound. But none of us has actually seen it done.

THAT NIGHT we stay at the Hide, one of the luxury private lodges. Again, we are the only guests. On the deck, over drinks before supper, Georgina and Dominic page through a coffee-table book entitled *Zimbabwe—Africa's Paradise,* which displays the country at its post-independence zenith. In the section on Chimanimani, there's a double-page vista of a bountiful coffee plantation, perfectly aligned ranks of coffee bushes with the mountains shimmering behind them. The picture is of Charleswood, whose ruined coffee fields are now destroyed and whose lodge is burned down.

We have just heard that the Mutare magistrate, Livingstone Chipadza, ordered Bennett to be freed on bail, but a senior prison officer refused to carry out the court's instructions. Now the magistrate himself, the one with thick glasses and owlish eyes, has been arrested "for exceeding his powers." His colleagues in Mutare have gone on strike. Bennett remains in prison.

At supper, the black rangers, hosted by Daffwell Marumahoko, the acting manager, vent their fury at Mugabe's policies, for destroying the tourist industry. Then talk turns, as it always seems to in wildlife reserves, to animal attacks. The American girl who was taken by a crocodile on Lake Kariba. Her parents came and cast red rose petals upon the water at the site of the attack, and as they sailed away, the guide turned back and saw an eerie sight, crocs' eyes emerging through the floating carpet of petals. Leopards always feature prominently in these recitations, because they have adapted most successfully to the proximity of man. Spike's brother was scalped by a leopard. Daffy's aunt was attacked by one. She was saved by a village dog, which bravely nipped at it. "Ah, ah, she really loved that dog," he says. The friends who returned one evening to find a leopard in their bedroom, trying to scoop their Jack Russell from under their bed where it was cowering, just beyond reach.

After supper, the guides slip away to listen to *Studio 7*, a nightly broadcast Voice of America transmits about Zimbabwe. They return looking grim. "Terrible news," says Daffy. "Morgan and his wife Susan have been in a car accident. Their vehicle has collided with a truck." With the long history of "car accident" assassinations in this country, foul play is almost immediately suspected. We troop to the office and huddle around the radio, but details are scarce. Then one of the guides manages to get online. Susan Tsvangirai is now dead, he says, and Morgan is in the Avenues Clinic, where so many of his tortured supporters ended up. We also read that Mugabe and his wife, Grace, had rushed to his hospital bedside and stayed there for nearly an hour. That Grace wept when she saw him. "She was probably weeping to see that he was still alive," says one of the guides.

By the time we drive up to Victoria Falls the next day, to fly from there back to Harare, Morgan has been moved to Botswana to "recuperate," but obviously for his own safety.

thirty-four

Dynamics of Distress

W HEN SOMEONE DIES in Zimbabwe, you must go to their house for a mourning vigil, *kubatamaoko,* to hold the hands of their family. We park half a mile away from the Tsvangirai house, unable to get closer due to the crush of cars. As we walk through the dark, we hear the pulse of the funeral drums. At the gate, MDC security personnel are frisking a group of women in red-and-white Methodist Church uniforms. They continue singing, *"Tichasangana kudenga, neropa raJesu,"* to the tune of "Auld Lang Syne." "We will meet again in heaven, through the blood of Jesus."

The garden has been colonized by tents and canopies. Morgan's red battle bus, from the election tour he was forced to abandon, is parked in the driveway. On its side, the outsize image of his face grins at us. Smoke drifts over from large open cooking fires, which are bubbling giant black cauldrons of *sadza* and beans. Lynette Kore-Karenyi, the MP who took us to the diamond fields, hails us, and escorts us to a line of people waiting to sign the condolence book in Morgan's office, out at the back. "It's ironic," says Georgina, who knew Susan quite well, and had written speeches for her. "She supports him through his treason trial, and at least four assassination attempts, and several beatings—and now she's the one who's killed first."

When our turn comes and we are ushered into the darkened room, we are surprised to see that it's not a condolence book at all, but Morgan himself, back from Botswana, his head swollen and bruised from the crash. "Thank you for coming," he says, rising gingerly from his chair. Georgina is close to tears, and he envelops her in a hug. "What can we do?" he sighs. "Nothing. There is nothing to be done." I shake his hand, and it turns into a bear hug. His breathing is ragged with repressed sobs. He is a man still in shock. For now he refers to Susan's death as "the Accident," at least until the serious business of the burial is conducted.

We know her body has arrived when the ululating and drumming swell in a crescendo. The coffin is placed on a table in the sitting room and mourners rush to the French windows for a glimpse of it.

All the MDC hierarchy is here, from both wings. David Coltart, the new Minister of Education; Giles Mutsekwa, the Minister of Home Affairs, battling vainly to control the police force. Even some of Mugabe's men are present. Georgina points out ZANU-PF's Herbert Murerwa, the new Minister of Land Resettlement, who now presides over the farm chaos. His presence brings to mind an old Shona saying, *Moyochena ndowei bere kugarira munhu akafa?* "What kindness is it for a hyena to mount guard over a dead man?" Before we can slide away, someone presents us to him. He appraises us coolly. "I hear what you say, and I see what you do," he says, and moves off. Neither of us can decide if this is an olive branch or a threat.

That night we are followed again. And again, it continues for miles. Is it the CIO, or just an opportunistic hijacker? I've no idea; I just concentrate on driving fast, looping this way and back, through the dark, while Georgina calls ahead to the people we are visiting for supper. As we arrive, the guard pulls the security gate open, and slams it closed behind us. He is wearing a pith helmet.

* * *

AFTER A LONG absence, Georgina must get back to Xanthe and Mum in London. She and Dominic are scheduled to leave the next day. She jokes that she knows it's time to leave when she starts asking for the "bull" instead of the bill, and "yes" becomes "yis," as her accent creeps back to its Zimbabwean default.

We spend their last evening at the residence of Andrew Pocock. Jim McGee is here too, and Albrecht Conze, the German ambassador who gave Roy sanctuary before his arrest. The unholy trinity is complete. All of them are having to advise their governments whether to lift the personal sanctions on Mugabe and his inner circle of two hundred henchmen, now that the "inclusive government" has been established. Tactically, it's a tough diplomatic call. Mugabe says that he won't make the further concessions required of him until the sanctions are dropped. Keeping them in place gives him a pretext for blocking reforms, but dropping them prematurely undermines his motivation for further reform.

Jim McGee is recalling his last Tex-Mex party, to celebrate Cinco de Mayo. His staff had invited Gideon Gono, Mugabe's personal banker, as a formality, and were amazed when he showed up.

"Was he the piñata?" I ask.

"We forced him to wear a sombrero and do the Mexican hat dance," says Jim. "But he said he hadn't had so much fun in years."

Andrew Pocock looks a bit green at the memory.

"Andrew asked to be airbrushed out of the photo," says Jim.

Albrecht Conze says that he felt nauseous, and kept washing his hands afterward. Later, he tells Georgina that he's had postings all over the world, but this is the only place he's felt tempted to put down roots. For the first time in his life, he finds himself wanting to get a puppy, a horse. "That's what this place does to you," she tells him. "It makes you want to belong."

SUSAN'S FUNERAL is held on the hot afternoon of Wednesday 11 March, at the Tsvangirais' home village of Humanikwa in rural Buhera, a hundred and fifty miles southeast of Harare. Most of the ambassadors are content with attending the official service at the Harare Methodist Church, or the stadium event. But Jim McGee feels that the rural schlep is the real gesture. "I really want to do this," he says. But he has thrown his back and is in agony. He winces into his office chair as his health officer arrives armed with pain-killers, Fexidon, and super-strength ibuprofen. McGee palms them.

While we wait for the pills to kick in, he talks about the irony that the truck which hit Morgan's vehicle (the middle one of a convoy of three) was actually a USAID truck coming back from a supply run. But it was operated by local licencees, says McGee, not by the U.S. government. This hasn't stopped Jonathan Moyo, Mugabe's once and future Goebbels, from suggesting that Susan's death was an attempt by the Americans to get rid of Morgan, for supporting the GNU.

The *Herald* is also suggesting that white farmers must be involved in the conspiracy, because one of their members had been arrested trying to film the accident scene. That, and the highly suspicious fact that the company which owned the truck had an office in the same building as the Commercial Farmers' Union (CFU).

Closely observed by his office manager, Lori Enders, and Glenn Warren, his chief political officer, McGee slowly rises to his feet, and exhales. "I'm going to do it," he announces, and begins a stately descent of the embassy stairs to the waiting Land Cruiser. The armored BMW can't get there and back on one tank.

We are just nosing through broken traffic lights when a pair of police motorbike outriders with sirens ablaze go speeding by, then another pair. Around us, cars are reversing to get well out of the way. This can only mean one thing. The President is imminent. Two pairs of police cars follow, and a truck bristling with soldiers. Then a school of black limos, going two abreast, taking up *both* sides of the road—and somewhere within the decoy cars, the gerontocrat-in-chief swaddled in his plush leather cradle—and finally an ambulance, followed by more troop carriers, their central benches crammed with AK-wielding soldiers in motorbike helmets. They yowl past, north, toward his residence. "Christ," says McGee, "even

Obama hasn't got anything like that, and he's leader of the free world."

AT THE 84KM PEG, by the sign to Ngezi, we pass the accident site. Black-rubber skid marks veer off the road and red fragments of rear lights litter the verge. We look at it in silence. At Chivhu—opposite Vic's Tavern—we turn left to Buhera. There are dozens of other vehicles going to the funeral. From late-model Mercs and BMWs to pick-ups, trucks, buses, most of them have posters of *"Amai* [mother] *Susan Tsvangirai—mother of our struggle"* taped to them, and from their rear-view mirrors flutter strips of red cloth, the sign of the funeral mourner. The passengers make the open-handed MDC gesture at us.

As we approach Buhera, the countryside opens up, with undulating plains sloping east to a low range of hills. We join the convoy of vehicles jostling to get into the funeral. There are hundreds of vehicles—a whole soccer field is filled with buses. *Parking for Terminal 4—Heathrow—Park and Fly* is emblazoned on the side of one bus.

Morgan's kraal, Humanikwa, is spread out, several brick buildings with corrugated roofs among the neatly thatched huts surrounded by banana groves and maize fields. A satellite dish and a security fence distinguish it from its neighbors.

We park at some distance to the white marquee of the funeral, and an MDC security official leads McGee through an apparently impenetrable crush of mourners. "Move aside, move aside," shouts the official, and the crowd turns in annoyance, but when they recognize the U.S. ambassador they start chanting, "Ma-Geee! Ma-Geee!" They cheer, and whistle and salute, and miraculously part to allow his passage, reaching out to shake his hand as he goes by. He is right to have made this pilgrimage.

There are more than ten thousand people packed into the gravesite. Some of them wear black T-shirts with slogans reading *"Free Roy and other political hostages."* The Chief Justice is due to announce today whether Bennett can come out of prison on bail.

Others read: "*You have the right to hold different opinions,*" and "*Our Heroine, rock, idol, mother.*"

We file past the open coffin. Susan's face is smooth, serene, waxy, in a white-cotton church beret, red blouse, white daisy pinned over her heart. Her head rests on an ivory satin pillow. Then the coffin is closed and hoisted on the shoulders of the women of her congregation. Morgan throws a single red rose onto the casket.

AT THE OFFICES OF CSU, back in Harare, the staff are bracing themselves for more violence. A white board on an easel identifies "Nine Areas Where Violence Has Started." Dr. Frances Lovemore says that ten MDC villages have been burned down by Mugabe's youth militia, the day before the funeral. And in Zimunya they petrol-bombed the house of an MDC security guy, and his kid was badly burned.

Any return to normality threatens Mugabe's power, she explains. Improvement in conditions is associated with the MDC coming into government. If it continues, Mugabe and ZANU are undermined. So they will likely try to destabilize things.

Together Lovemore and her colleague Zachariah Godi paint the bleakest picture yet of where we are in this tussle to unseat the dictatorship. The continued incarceration of political prisoners shows where the real power lies. "You know," says Lovemore, "Morgan Tsvangirai looked across the table from me and said, 'I will not be sworn in unless the political prisoners are released.' He looked across the table at me and said that. So, the week before the inauguration we were all expecting them to be released. The deputy head of prisons told me that they had been expecting it, but then, he said, 'We got an order that no, they would stay behind bars.' And at that point, we realized that JOC is still in control. That nothing had really changed. And still, that Friday, Morgan went ahead with his marriage vows to Mugabe."

Who is really in control of ZANU-PF now?

"Mugabe," they both say at once. But he has taken a step back to allow Mnangagwa and others to deal with the main threats they face at the next elections, which come from Morgan himself, and Roy Bennett, who is a key mobilizer. Mnangagwa very much wants to be the next President. Mugabe will give Mnangagwa his head — he plays with his ego — and allow him to do his dirty work, until he becomes too much of a threat and later he'll be dealt with.

"ZANU-PF won't give up," says Godi. "It's not wired that way. They are already gearing up toward the next election, on their own terms. Mugabe's not like other African dictators. He's well educated, capable of planning. Every Friday he buses in his youth militia and war vets for strategy briefings at Jongwe House. Mugabe was there all day yesterday.

"He has a think-tank that meets every day in one of their Borrowdale houses. They analyze, consider options, role-play. And they keep MDC off balance, reactive." The GNU can be suspended at any point by one of the parties leaving it, Godi reminds me. Failing that, the constitutional process will run its course, leading to a referendum on a new constitution, followed by elections.

Mugabe has a number of ways of pulling the plug on the opposition, at a moment of his choosing. If he feels his power slipping away, he can invent an insurgency or other national-security threat and declare a state of emergency, taking back power to deal with it. "Two months ago," he says, "CSU was suddenly besieged by traps; calls from people saying that they were under extreme threat and had been given our numbers by British soldiers, who told them to ask us for protection. We traced it back to Charlie Ten [CIO]. We had to close our office for three weeks, after they arrived with sixteen police officers to question us about the detainees."

Another way to trigger a state of emergency would be a bogus attempted military coup.

"You know I wake up every morning with a panic attack about what might happen," says Lovemore. "Fridays are always the worst, as that's often when they act. Last Friday I had just arrived from a trip to Johannesburg when I got the call about Susan and was asked to deal with the air evacuation. We, here at CSU, we knew what might happen. The MDC youth were very worked up, they were running through town in large groups and we were concerned that the whole thing might just blow. Mugabe has been targeting the MDC security guys. Chris Dhlamini, head of MDC security, and ex-Charlie Ten, in Avenues Clinic under prison guard, until he goes back to Chikurubi, was horribly tortured. He was beaten then hung by the feet from a tree and repeatedly dunked headfirst into a drum of water."

When I ask about conducting follow-up trips to see some of the torture victims, they both ask me not to. "We have suspended our own follow-up trips," she says. "We did one, in Zaka, and the people involved are now under bad threat. We were trying to follow up on medical cases, see how they were faring, also to look for ones we might have missed. In just one day in Zaka, we discovered another eighty serious medical cases of beating and torture, some of them ZANU-PF members beaten by their own colleagues for not showing enough loyalty.

"We've been writing a medical plan for a disaster scenario," says Lovemore. "But we don't know how or where or when it'll happen. Will it involve the army or the police or South African–based hot bloods from MDC? We sit here like scared rabbits. We don't know how this will all end, but one thing's for sure, it won't be a hand shake. Mugabe still has his freelance killers. And there's a lot of fear of how they will be unleashed. There are so many danger points. ZANU-PF has its own dynamics of distress. The final scenario could be awful.

"I fear we haven't seen the darkest days yet."

thirty-five

The Cutter-of-Clouds

I T W A S Dostoevsky who said that you could tell the degree of civilization in a society by entering its prisons. Yet another calculus by which to measure the depths of depravity of Robert Mugabe's Zimbabwe. Like so many who come out of jails here, Roy Bennett is filled with anger at the conditions inside, and the prisoners "lost" in the system. It completely eclipses any anger he has at his own predicament.

Mutare Remand Prison, in fact any remand prison, is better than the other jails, as at least you're allowed to receive food from the outside, which wasn't the case when Roy was in Chikurubi, when he only got to see Heather every two weeks for fifteen minutes—through bars—and she wasn't allowed to bring him food. But most prisoners don't have family support: their families are too poor to help, or they don't know where they are. Those ones, says Roy, have to survive on prison rations alone, which have been cut from three meals a day to only one—consisting of a modest sliver of *sadza,* scooped from the drum using the plate itself, with water and salt.

You can tell how long people have been in by their stages of physical deterioration, he says. Most suffer from pellagra—a severe vitamin B3 deficiency that was common in Soviet labor camps. The symptoms are awful: alopecia, aversion to sunlight, aggression, insomnia, diarrhea, and terrible skin lesions—it used to be called Asturian leprosy. Many of the inmates are already suffering from untreated AIDS, and its opportunistic diseases, TB, malaria, pneumonia. Without outside help, the average inmate is dead within a year. In the four weeks that Roy was in Mutare Remand Prison, five prisoners died, and it took days for their bodies to be removed from the cells.

The death rate across the entire prison system is appalling. Khami Prison in Bulawayo has forty-eight deaths a month on average, and there are more than fifty a month at Chikurubi—seven hundred and twenty in the last year. Rats and lice infest the place, and the makeshift mortuary, the old TB ward, is next to the kitchen. The noses and eyes and lips of the corpses are routinely gnawed off by rats, before they are given anonymous paupers' burials in mass graves. This appalling deterioration of what used to be a respectable prison system, which fed itself from productive prison farms, has happened during the watch of Major-General (retd.) Paradzai Zimondi, head of prisons since 1999, and a hard-line Mugabe supporter.

Recent photos smuggled out by sympathetic warders show dull-eyed, rib-racked prisoners who would look at home in Auschwitz portraits. With Zimondi's help, Mugabe has achieved his own gulag.

"Mutare Remand," says Roy, "is designed to hold a maximum of a hundred and fifty prisoners. When I was there, there were three hundred and sixty. Cells are packed so tight that, at night, when one turns, all must. Fifteen were foreign, including a South African who'd had his arm broken during arrest, six months earlier, and never had it treated." On Roy's release he contacted the South African embassy, and they came and took their national away.

"I was classified as a Category D, who are dangerous prisoners and have no privileges at all. Every night we were strip-searched, and made to sleep naked in our cell. You have to strip and then stand naked and jump, kicking one leg out at a time and clapping," to show you have nothing concealed up you. He gets off his bar stool and demonstrates. "It was humiliating, man!"

Roy's friend Kurt pours him another Scotch. "This is what you were drinking the night before you were arrested," he says. He and his wife, Laura, are throwing Roy a small dinner to celebrate his release on bail, but the power is out, so we are sitting in candlelight, while a thunderstorm rages outside.

EVEN IN THIS appalling prison demi-monde, Bennett was protected by those around him. "The other prisoners in my cell—the D-category prisoners—were in for murder, armed robbery, rape. But they were all helluva nice to me. They looked after me—laid my blanket out for me, gave me extra room. Every morning our prison clothes were returned, scrunched up in a ball, but mine were ironed. I had a water bottle of treated water by the top of my sleeping blanket, and every time I took a sip, they topped it up. They were amazing."

And when four soldiers tried to infiltrate Roy's cell, allegedly as prisoners, his cellmates chased them away, and warned him to be careful, that they suspected they weren't really prisoners, but were from military intelligence. They spent all day on the outside and just came in at night—but they never got near Roy.

I ask Roy about Mike Hitschmann, who is supposed to be the principal witness in the terrorism case against him.

"Ol' Mike Hitschmann was so badly tortured he can't control his bladder now," says Roy. "They kicked him repeatedly in the balls. Burned him with cigarettes on the anus. For his first eighteen months he was made to sleep in leg irons and handcuffs—to *sleep* in them. But man, he's one tough individual. I was in the cell he'd been in, and he'd written on the wall *MPH Hitschmann — Who Dares Wins* [the motto of the British SAS]. He can speak fluent Portuguese too, and he virtually runs that prison now.

"I used to tell him funny stories, to cheer him up. Like the one about our mate who ran a coffin business and lay down in one of his coffins, after covering himself with tomato sauce, and told his mate to take him back to the farm, open the coffin and tell the night-watchman he'd had an accident. The watchman went rushing to wake up George, the solemn farm manager, who came over in his dressing gown and peered, appalled, at his dead assistant, who then sat up, threw open his arms and said in a zombied voice, 'Heee-llo, George.' And none of the farm workers wanted to go near him for a while as they suspected he really might be a *mudzimu*, a zombie.

"Hitch was almost crying with laughter. 'God,' he said. 'That's the first time I've laughed in three years.'"

I tell Roy that I have just visited Charleswood. "How is it?" he asks sadly. "Is it all destroyed?" I describe the state of Mawenje Lodge, how just some walls and the stone chimney breast still stand, and foliage now grows out of it and a forest has grown up around it.

"Have the guest lodges been looted?" he asks. "Have all the door and window frames gone, are vets living in them?"

"No," I tell him, "they're still intact, their thatch is still on, and no one's living in them now. But they have been. They had cooking fires on the floor, and the walls are full of graffiti abusing you." He grins. "And pictures of you in manacles."

"You know the guy who burned down my house, Chamunorwa Muusha — a war vet — was inside Mutare Remand Prison, starting a six-year sentence for rape," says Roy. "He abducted three of my woman employees and raped them for three days." I nod. I have seen in a Human Rights Watch report that Muusha bound their necks with leather leashes, and tethered them to a tree, like goats.

"And Muusha also tied several of my guys by the balls with wire and led them around the farm like that, and used a red-hot spear blade to brand the mark of an X into their backs for voting the wrong way, for voting for MDC. And he speared my cattle and burned some of them to death too. When he heard I was in the same prison as him, he shat himself. I used to send him bloodcurdling messages through other prisoners that I was going to 'get' him."

One prison experience has amazed Roy more than any other. He speaks of it with a reverence that can only be described as religious, and it shows you just how far up-river he has sailed on his journey of cultural transformation. "There's an old spirit medium called ambuya Makopa," he says. "She's the most important medium in all of the Ndau people, in Zimbabwe *and* Mozambique, she's the medium to the Ndau chiefs. She speaks very, very deep chiNdau — even I battle to understand it. She lives up in the hills of Ngaona, past Gwendingwe, and has huge authority. In the last elections, she sent down an edict that there would be no violence in her area — woe betide anyone who transgressed — and there was none.

"When I first arrived in the district, I went to see her to introduce myself, and I took a bag of maize, and some ginger, she *loves* ginger, eats it like candy. She told me that Robert Mugabe went to see her during the war [with Emmerson Mnangagwa] and asked her for her blessing. 'They took our kids,' she said to me, 'and then they never came back to say thank you, or to tell me that the war had ended.'"

I have read about ambuya Makopa, how she's the vessel through whom the whole Mutema chieftaincy is channeled. The Mutema chiefs believe that they are the bringers of rain — their name means "the cutter-of-clouds" — and they have a special ceremonial sword for the purpose. And she is the royal ancestral spirit medium.

"She brought this little bottle of 'sacred snuff' to me while I was in prison," says Roy. "It was delivered by a guard who gave me her instructions on how to use it, told me I had to break it and rub it on my face, feet, and hands and put the rest back in the bottle and return it to him to give back to her. You should have seen the other prisoners, when it was delivered — their eyes were like saucers.

"And when I got out, she was there, at the prison gates. She came to me and said, 'My child,' and she began to weep. I didn't know what to say. It was such an *incredible* honor. She never normally leaves her home. The prison warders were all gob-smacked. They were convinced that she'd sprung me out of there. Then she presented me with this old ebony chief's stick. It's a beautiful stick. You flick a little iron latch, and a sword pulls out of it. It's in the car, I'll go and get it." Roy disappears into the rain outside.

"Roy has a fetish about sharpening knives," says Laura. "When he's stressed he sits and sharpens knives."

Roy bounds back in, soaked, with the chief's stick—it is artfully made, obviously antique; its round head is smooth and burnished, and intricate metal strips are inlaid down its elegantly tapered shaft. He flicks the latch and slides out a sword. "Look," he says, fingering its sharp blade respectfully, "it's even got a blood channel to stop suction, and give it an easy entry and exit. I'm going to use it as my side arm from now on." For a moment, he reminds me of Peta Hall, carrying her quartz stone with her everywhere, because it has been blessed by the *nganga*, and sprinkling rock salt before crossing unknown thresholds.

And sitting there, seeing Roy so excited about this little old lady who had visited him in prison, an old lady that few outsiders would give a second glance, made me wonder. After all, ambuya Makopa, the ancestral spiritual leader of the Ndau people, chose to come down from her mountain in an attempt to secure the freedom of Roy Bennett, and calls him "my child." No wonder Mugabe is so afraid of Roy.

"Why was I arrested in the first place?" he asks now. "This thing comes from Mugabe personally. He's convinced that I want to assassinate him. It's ridiculous. He's put war vets in the top three positions of each branch of the security forces in each province. He has no other support now."

When Roy arrived back in Harare from prison, having gone via Susan's freshly filled grave, he walked through Unity Square Park, between appointments, and he was mobbed by well-wishers. And when he went to check in at Harare Central Police Station, as required by his bail conditions, he got lost nearby and went down a little one-way street, the wrong way. It was full of taxi drivers all honking in irritation that he was blocking the road. So Roy rolled down his window and said, in Shona, "Hey, guys, sorry, we're lost, man." They immediately recognized him, and a great cheer went up. Then they all insisted on waiting outside the police station to make sure Roy was let out again, and providing him an impromptu honor guard.

thirty-six

Bullets to Be Paid For

THE SPEAKER'S GALLERY in the House of Assembly is so full that at first all I can see is the notice in front of me, which reads *Do not: smoke, converse, sleep, applaud, knit, take notes, eat or drink.* Then there is a shift of bodies and my view opens up. Below is an extraordinary scene, an almost perfectly preserved colonial debating chamber, a mini-Westminster. Hardwood benches padded in the same shade of apple-green leather face one another across a room that has a high, ribbed ceiling held up by a pair of plain Doric columns at either end.

Hardbound Hansards line the room, and on a wall above the legislators' heads this African parliament has a stuffed leopard crouching on a fake rock ledge, gazing across at two mounted kudu heads, which look back, glassily perturbed. The Speaker, Lovemore Moyo MP, the first opposition one ever, sits on a mahogany throne, beneath an arch of intricately carved elephant tusks. Behind him stands the sergeant-at-arms, severe in countenance, attired in white tie and tails.

In their behavior too, the local MPs channel their unruly British counterparts. The debates are in English—still the official language—and there is boisterous back-chat and banter, some in Shona, with cries of *Nyarara! Nyarara!* ["Shut up!"] when a member bores. And there is much giggling and talking, notwithstanding the Speaker's periodic cries of "Order. Order! Order in the House!"

This current term of parliament got off to a controversial start when MDC MPs threatened to boycott Mugabe's opening session in protest at his bloody campaign, which forced Tsvangirai to pull out of the presidential contest. They eventually attended (since they had a majority), but refused to stand when Mugabe entered the chamber, and loudly sang opposition songs, and jeered him while he tried to speak. He was trembling with rage by the end of it.

In front of the Speaker is the shimmering golden mace—his symbol of office, which he lifts down now, to show that parliament is in session. The trappings of a British-style democracy may have been retained, but this country has effectively been a one-party state for many years, since the days of Ian Smith and his Rhodesia Front. Mugabe passes the bulk of his contentious laws by emergency decree. Yet there is still something about this pomp and circumstance that clearly appeals to the elderly autocrat, a faint echo of constitutional propriety.

Today is Wednesday 18 March 2009, and Tendai Biti, the newly appointed Minister of Finance, is presenting his first budget—trying to roll back the utter shambles he has inherited. Afterward I am to meet him to hear how he's been faring as one of the most senior goats in the leopard's lair.

As Biti winds up his presentation, I become aware of a figure looming disapprovingly over me. It is the sergeant-at-arms. "It has come to my attention that you have been taking notes," he declares. I draw breath to argue, though it's true I made what I thought were a couple of surreptitious jottings, but he looks me up and down and adds, scandalized, "Are those *jeans?*"

"Not really," I say. "They're a sort of dark green moleskin that aren't jeans as such." He cocks his head to the exit.

"I am ejecting you," he says, and turns on his heel, leaving it to his underling to carry out the diktat.

I think better of making the point that there seems something particularly preposterous about an over-fussy parliamentary dress code in a country where voters and opposition candidates are bludgeoned into submission.

As the clerk escorts me down to the visitors' lounge, he apologizes. "Some of the rules here are a bit stiff," he concedes. "Mind you, none of them are new." It's true, all these fusty and contradictory rules are inherited from the old ways, the old days, the white days.

But not all is the same. The pantheon of dead Zimbabwean heroes that lines the corridors I am led down is certainly different. White pioneers have been jettisoned in favor of liberation fighters and ZANU elite. The only live person, at least for now, memorialized here is Mugabe himself. Next to his portrait is a large framed oil painting entitled *The opening of the parliament of Southern Rhodesia. 30 May 1924*. There is not a single black face among them, and they are backed by jaunty bunting in the colors of the Union Jack.

The clerk walks me past open offices where desultory secretaries play at solitaire on their screens, and down a hardwood staircase, whose balustrades end with a pair of elephant-tusk finials.

The clerk leaves me in the visitors' lounge, where I will wait for Tendai. It is a musty, threadbare place, cruelly lit by a flickering neon tube. Mugabe's image appears again on the wall here too, in youthful iteration—it seems that every room in this parliament must play host to his glowering eminence. Above the fireplace is a large ornately gilt-framed photograph of the entire parliament, including senators, fanned around Her Majesty the Queen, to commemorate her visit here, for the Commonwealth Heads of Government meeting, in October 1991. The Duke of Edinburgh rubs shoulders with Emmerson Mnangagwa, the man who, as the head of the CIO, helped mastermind the Matabeleland massacres a few years earlier.

Tendai finally ducks in and we arrange to meet in his office at the Ministry of Finance.

Someone tries to rob me as I return to my car. It's a double act. One young man approaches, saying he has been "guarding" my car and that he scared off a guy trying to loosen and steal one of my wheels. He cocks his head to one side, expectantly, wanting a reward for securing the car. I give him a U.S. dollar as I point the fob at the car and press the button—which opens all doors. I get in, throw my backpack down in the passenger-side footwell, and as I do, I notice the front passenger door is opening, and through the crack a hand is reaching in to grab my backpack. I reach over and pull the door sharply and there is a squawk from the crouching intruder. He pulls his arm out and canters away down the pavement, while my vigilante parking "guard" halfheartedly pursues him for a few paces, and shouts, *"Musatanyoko!"* which means "You devil." "Bad people here," he says to me, clucking sympathetically.

I'm a bit shaken by the incident, but then I think—if it had happened in South Africa my brains might now be spread across the inside of the windscreen. Later, when I'm waiting to turn into Fourth Street, I see the two of them, my vigilante and *musatanyoko,* strolling companionably, chatting together, across Africa Unity Square. *Musatanyoko* is favoring his good hand. I roll down my window and hail them, and when they look over and recognize me, I lift my arms and bump the insides of my wrists together to mime handcuffing. They both wave, and laugh, and jog slowly away.

TENDAI BITI flops down onto the claret chesterfield, in his large south-facing office. He looks exhausted.

"There's no money, no resources—it's a disaster. You are hustling all the time, that's what I'm reduced to, I'm just a hustler. It's worse than I expected—seeing it from the inside at last. The extent of the dilapidation of the economy.

"I've gone through round one—the policy framework and budget. But it's a never-ending catalog of fire-fighting." Doctors and nurses and teachers and soldiers and policemen to pay, power to restore, water to be rehabilitated. "It's a sewage pool the size of Lake Kariba, and I'm supposed to try to clean it up with a mop."

The in-tray on his large wooden desk towers with folders. The electric wall clock doesn't work here either. The second hand just wavers back and forth, without making any progress. On another wall hangs a gold-framed organogram of the Ministry of Finance. At the top of it now sits Tendai Biti, who, until a few weeks ago, had a treason charge hanging over his head.

"What I've come to understand is that Mugabe had no choice but to be in bed with us. It's a self-defeating move for him, but the problems are just too great. The majority of his party realize the game is up. If there were elections tomorrow, they'd be wiped out. But there are others in the party with a junta mentality, who think they can continue reproducing themselves. Mugabe is a prisoner of the junta forces—they worry he has sold out—that he is just trying to secure his own future and that of his family—and left them to hang. I don't think he can persuade them.

"It's an experience, I tell you, we are on a knife-edge. Clearly, there's a huge chunk of people in ZANU who want this thing to collapse. They *want* us to fail. They have laid a trap to destroy the GNU, which makes it all the more desperate that we succeed. There is this strong cabal that doesn't want this thing to work—who are hugely irritated by our very presence, and want us out. Those are the ones we are in a war against, the ones who are against democratization. If we give in, we are allowing them to win. Our credibility as a party, and as individuals, is at stake. We just have to deliver."

Does he regret going in to it now?

"Regret doesn't arise because I was forced into this thing. I'm not here voluntarily. But now I have to do the job to the best of my ability and sacrifice my own opinions.

"You have to bear in mind the pressure put on Morgan by SADC. His options for maneuver were very limited. SADC used Mafia-style pressure—they told him he was totally on his own if he didn't succumb. History is irony—here I am leading the GNU that I opposed. Also—I am thrust into the position of Chancellor of the

Exchequer—all the problems are mine, directly. There's a madness to this irony, it's very cruel.

"I won't sulk now that I'm in, I'll do my best. But I refuse to hide my opposition to going in, in the first place. One of the problems I faced, as an individual, was the labels and conspiracies that were leveled against me. I'm suing the *Herald*—they ran daily—every single day, from end of December to end of January—an article or cartoon vilifying me, because they'd identified me as the sore point, the resistance to this GNU government.

"The party said to me, you can't run away when we need you. My only basis of saying no was to have left the country to start a new, separate life. I wanted to go to Harvard Law School to study for a JD [a doctorate]. On 4th January, we agreed not to go in. Then there was the SADC summit on 27/28th Jan. And our national executive council met, and had a furious debate, but ultimately we went in by consensus.

"Donor finance is the key to whether this thing works. There is so much that I don't control. You get donors like Britain and America that wanted Mugabe's head. And there could be no solution as long as he is in the picture. That didn't happen.

"The problem with personalizing the struggle is—what if the person never *goes?* The people are suffering in the meantime. What's the higher ideal—the anti-Mugabe mantra, or attempting to make a difference to the people of Zimbabwe?

"We are in a war situation. We are trying to get rid of something and that thing will fight back. I feel amazement and shock at why Mugabe wants to do such a crazy thing for all these years. This guy must be abnormal to want to stay in power so much."

How is Biti bearing up?

"You know opposition politics is much easier—you can remain true to your feelings—you don't have to censor yourself, you are not stifled. You don't have that sense that everything you do is being watched. I hardly use this office—I feel that there are eyes on me here.

"My budget is a vote of no confidence in what they've done.

Nearly halving their annual-revenue estimate, for example. The junta elements — Mnangagwa et al. — weren't in parliament for it.

"There's been a terrible brain drain from this country," but for the time being he's relying on the present staff. "They're excited by the new direction, supportive to my face, but I don't know what happens when my back is turned."

The first battle he faces is to wrestle back power from Gideon Gono at the Reserve Bank, who has, as Mugabe's close confidant, become the country's financial supremo, sidelining the Ministry of Finance. One of the first things Biti wants is a full audit of the Reserve Bank — but that would shine a light on the extent and details of the Mugabe government's corruption, and is being vehemently resisted.

The phone rings. It's his mother, who's just returned to the country — all his siblings are in Australia; his wife, an IT manager, is packing up their house in Johannesburg. He rests his shaved head in his hand. "Oh, I'm so tired," he says to his mother.

What would make him leave?

"If they interfere with my job — I'd leave. Or if we get to the stage where we are not allowed to make a difference — in democratizing, in the constitution, in the media — we will pull out. But we are very elastic. What's so evident is that the battles we've fought in the streets are now being fought in cabinet, in the corridors of power — the arena has changed. It's tough — it's war. We battle every day. It takes a lot to wrestle real power from the state — which is our central objective.

"These guys have a lot to answer for. And it's certainly debatable if we're doing the right thing to go in and sanitize it all for them." He tells me, for example, that one of the bills in his in-tray is for ammunition. "Literally, there are *bullets* to be paid for," he says.

Here is Tendai, trying to scrounge the money to pay for the bullets that were used against his own supporters in the last elections. It reminds me of Mengistu's awful "wasted bullet tax," where the family of the person executed was forced to pay for the cost of the killing.

When I ask him how he feels about his own security he says he simply can't allow himself to worry about it. "Once you do that you'll never engage against the dictatorship. You can't allow yourself to think about it. They can take me out in a second if they want—we are very exposed.

"If I had remained here, but not participated in the new government, they would have imprisoned me again. Only in December did they indicate that they might drop the treason charges against me. But in January they still hadn't—the prosecutor went on record to say that he was going to 'fix' me.

"Prison was a disaster for me," he admits candidly. (He was held in Chikurubi Maximum Security Prison for three weeks before being bailed.) "You sleep on the floor. The sock became for me the symbol of freedom, because they take your socks away from you in jail. That and a clean toilet, which is the symbol of ultimate freedom. The toilet was so full in our cell that you couldn't even urinate in it. There were five people in a cell meant for one. It's abuse. There were no blankets even though it was winter. My wife brought me food every day, but you have to share it. The others are so desperate they will sit around you begging for scraps, they will eat your orange peels. The place is not fit for pigs, never mind humans.

"On Sundays, they have a thing called 'search warrant.' Everyone has to come out of the cells and they make you strip and parade past the guards. It's supposed to be so they can check for contraband, but actually, it's just to humiliate you.

"In the new Zimbabwe, we will shut down that prison. We will erase it. People die there. The mortuary in Harare Remand Prison is designed for twenty-five bodies—it usually contains at least eighty. When the power goes, as it so often does, the body fluids from the rotting corpses melt under the door and into the corridor. The stink is indescribable. Bodies are brought there from the other Harare prisons by truck, and they throw them off the trucks like bags of maize.

"And now," says Tendai, "there's no food—the prisoners haven't been fed for the last two days. So tomorrow I'm going there to see for myself, and see if I can find some emergency funding to buy food for prisoners."

THE MINISTRY OF Education is in Ambassador House, an eighteen-story building next to the Defense Ministry, where Mnangagwa and his JOC masterminded the election violence, and across the road from the Anglican cathedral, where self-styled Bishop Kunonga attacked the real Bishop Bakare with his crozier. I wait for the elevator in the gloomy lobby, lit only by a single low-wattage bulb. On the walls are the tattered remnants of the ministry's glory days in the 1980s, when universal free education was a real goal, and volunteer teachers were pouring in from around the world to help. When Zimbabwe established an astonishing 92 percent literacy rate, the highest on this continent.

Ministry staffers, some in heels, some in business suits, wait with me for the one elevator that we can hear clattering somewhere above. The other two are defunct, and this one only recently repaired, they tell me. Most of them carry buckets of water, some balanced on coils of cloth upon their heads. There hasn't been running water here for years, they say, so they need the water to flush the toilets. When the elevator fails to appear, we climb the stairs, and at each stairwell, where the toilets are sited, there is a terrible stench.

David Coltart, the new minister (a member of MDC-M), bounds in, late from the airport—he commutes weekly from his home in Bulawayo.

"Congratulations on your appointment," I say.

"I'm not convinced that's the right word," says David, his self-acknowledged pathological optimism in danger of being overwhelmed. "I knew things would be bad at the Ministry of Education, but still I was unready for how shockingly decayed it was. Of the fifteen vehicles available to head office to visit the schools across the country, only two work. We have no Internet connection. None of the rural schools is operating. (In fact, many were used as torture bases.) Most of those in high-density suburbs are also closed.

Ninety-five percent of our teachers are on strike. We have ninety-four thousand of them on our books, but there are nowhere near that number, in reality. We have no computerized database. So, for example, no one can even tell me exactly how many schools we have!"

His first order of business is to get the teachers back to work. "There were terrible priorities here—I mean people are walking up the stairs with water buckets on their heads, and yet as soon as I arrived the transport officer was here saying to me, 'Quick, you must come now as your new white Mercedes is waiting to be collected.' And then I looked into the water situation here and found that it'll only take a few thousand dollars to fix the pump."

The Government of National Unity, he says, was "the only viable, non-violent option left to us. I'm under no illusions, it's very fragile—the hawks are doing their utmost to disrupt it, unsurprisingly."

LIKE EDUCATION, the health system, once my mother's pride and joy, lies shattered. Trish McKenzie, who was once the matron in charge of training Zimbabwe's world-class cadre of nurses, walks me into the flagship three-hundred-bed hospital, Parirenyatwa. The staff clinic, where Mum worked before her retirement, is as I remember, but more tattered. The Alpine scenes from one of Mum's old calendars that she tore out and taped to the wall "to cheer the place up" are still there. But the hospital is without water. A sign at the toilet over a bucket says "after using please pour water." Trolleys sit in the stained linoleum corridors with plastic water jugs for patients. Clusters of worn gurneys gather in corners, and rubbish too. Urine oozes from one. The drug stores are empty, as are the linen cupboards.

"Our standards have fallen very low," says the hospital's chief of nursing, Matron Ann Marufu. "I'm not exaggerating. Very low." I decide not to ask about the bodies that Henry Chimbiri had seen being thrown from an upper floor. Marufu is Grace Mugabe's aunt. She is also English-trained, and fiercely proud of it. "We lost it when we changed from the English system in 1980. It was better before," she says sternly.

The pediatric ward is heartbreaking. Torn stickers of Disney characters line the glass wall-divider. Lying listlessly in their cots are kids with severe burns, kids with drips attached to their arms, kids with AIDS, malaria, cholera. Some have family in attendance, but there are no nurses to be seen. In the corridor, a little girl with a bandaged head and an eye patch disconsolately kicks a deflated football to a small boy with broken arms.

Casualty is chaotic. A young girl sits with a bloody plaster across her mouth, like a gag. Her mother is dabbing at it with an old mutton cloth. No nurses are in sight.

We find them clustered around a notice board, peering at a memo saying that the Crown Agents will now pay them $100 a month, in U.S. dollars. That's why they have dribbled back to work now, after a lengthy strike. Nurses here are bonded for three years after training—and then they usually scarper into the diaspora, helping to run British NHS hospitals, for example. Zimbabwe pays to train nurses and then exports them to the developed world. It's crazy. In a double blow, insulting both the venerable British broadcaster and refugees from his own ruinous rule, Mugabe taunted such fleeing health workers, calling them the BBC. "British Bum Cleaners," he explained, giggling.

thirty-seven

Behind the Blindfold

THERE'S A MOTTO on the old Salisbury coat of arms, which still stands beneath the lion's mouth gutter spout at the entrance of Harare City Hall: *Discrimine Salus.* We used to joke that it meant "In Discrimination Is Safety," a declaration of the racial segregation this city practiced for decades. It actually means "Safety in Danger." Salisbury was originally Fort Salisbury, built by white pioneers around a defensible kopje. In the lobby stands the carved granite capstone of the original town hall. Its inscription tells us that it was laid "*on Occupation Day, 12th of September 1902.*" Back then, the word "occupation" didn't have quite the same connotation.

The terracotta-roofed building surrounds a Mediterranean-style courtyard with high arches and white walls, and in one corner, emerging from a quartet of potted palms as though from a bedraggled jungle, stands a crudely fashioned duo of his 'n' hers guerrilla statues, Kalashnikovs at the ready. The lady insurgent, her mouth agape in battle cry, wears her beret perched on the very back of her head. Her male colleague wears a long peaked baseball cap, and staggers slightly under the weight of his bullet-heavy backpack. A municipal cleaning woman in a white coat sweeps impassively around them.

The walls of the corridors inside are lined with gold-framed oils presented by old white mayors, mostly of bucolic English scenes. I am asked to wait in room 103. The sign on the door says it is the "Mayoress's Parlor and Lady Councillors' Retiring Room," and it is furnished with floral armchairs, a divan, and a dressing table.

Much Musunda will see me now. The poster on his office wall proclaims: *A man who wants to lead the orchestra must turn his back on the crowd.* He's a prominent commercial lawyer, and an old friend. He tells of his efforts to restore the city's water supply, fend off cholera, and fill in the pox of potholes—all with no budget. Musunda has agreed to stand in as acting mayor (without salary) while the man originally voted to the job, Emmanuel Chiroto, serves as his deputy.

"The idea," says Much, "is that I guide and mentor Emmanuel. He usually sits in on all my meetings. My aim is that within my five-year term, by year three, I hope, he will take over as mayor himself."

Emmanuel Chiroto sits in an office next door, under—as the law requires in every office—a scowling portrait of *"His Excellency, the President of the Republic of Zimbabwe, Comrade Robert Gabriel Mugabe."* A poster promotes *Harare—Sunshine City.* His clock has stopped at 11:45. A small, intense man, in a purple shirt and dark suit, he has an open, troubled face.

Chiroto used to live with his wife, Abigail, twenty-seven, and their four-year-old son, Ashley, in Hatcliffe, a working-class township twelve miles out along the Borrowdale Road, from which he ran a little textile business—screen-printing logos on T-shirts, mostly. Abigail sold eggs and freeze-its (frozen drinks), and was training to be a tailor.

In the last elections, he stood as a city councillor. "There were warnings about my security," he says, "but I didn't take them seriously, I thought it was just rumors. I was such a small fish—why would they want to kill me? After I won the ward in Hatcliffe, MDC youth said that they'd heard more death threats against me, so they'd decided to send a group of seven youths to guard my place. And, just to be safe, I told my wife to go and stay at her mum's place in Chitungwiza."

In Zimbabwean cities, the mayor is voted in by the other city councillors. The MDC had won forty-five out of forty-six seats in Harare. That's how hated Mugabe is here. Three days before the mayoral election, some of the councillors suggested Emmanuel put his name forward.

"I asked my wife, and she said, 'Why don't you go for it.' So, I agreed, though I didn't actively campaign." He even missed the caucus meeting itself, because he was in Epworth, a slum east of the city, collecting some MDC women who had been badly beaten. "When I came back from Epworth, they told me, 'Congratulations, you have been elected mayor!'

"I was happy, honestly. I phoned my wife and said, 'I'm now the Mayor of Harare!' She said, 'I won't congratulate you on the phone, I'm coming to do it in person.'"

They met in town and drove out to Hatcliffe together, where he dropped her at home and went to park his pick-up truck. As he walked back from parking the car, he got a call. "One of our guys — Jairos Karasa, our ward chairman — had been attacked by Mugabe's militia at their torture base in Hatcliffe — they had three there — and he was being carried back in a wheelbarrow. So I turned back, got my car, and went to collect him. I phoned my wife and told her I was taking Jairos to hospital, so I'd be late . . .

"When I found Jairos, he was in agony, he couldn't stand or sit, he had been beaten so badly, he was covered in mud, water, and blood. I took him to Avenues Clinic. While I was there, I got a call from an MDC guy out in Hatcliffe saying that my house was on fire. The first thing I said was, 'Where is my family — are they safe?' But no one knew what had become of my wife and my little boy."

Emmanuel took refuge at the closest foreign mission, the Namibian embassy, getting in by fibbing that he was meeting some-one there. Then he alerted the African Observer Mission, and returned with them to his house.

"The fire was out by then, and a large crowd had gathered outside. No one knew where my family was. I went straight into our bedroom, but there were no burnt bodies in there. And then I knew they had been taken. We heard the approaching chanting of a big column of Mugabe's youth militia, so we left the area."

One of the youths who had been trying to guard his house told him what had happened. At 7 p.m., just as they were listening to Voice of America's *Studio 7* program on Zimbabwe, three twin-cabs without license plates arrived. A group of men ran out, some of them in army fatigues, armed with AK-47s; there were party youth too, brandishing machetes.

"No one knows exactly how many, my maid counted at least nine. She was in the garden filling a bucket of water when they came—they asked her where I was, and before she could even answer they smashed down the front and back doors. She heard three loud bangs and looked back to see the whole house on fire. Then she heard the doors of the twin-cabs slamming shut and heard them drive away, very fast.

"An MDC guard said that they carried both my wife and young son out of the house, that my wife was struggling and screaming. It's one of those things I don't want to know about in any more detail."

Emmanuel got the election observers to drop him off in town, at his nephew's flat. But the CIO were waiting for him there, "so we had to run for our lives and jump over wall after wall, from house to house, until we lost them."

He called a friend, who took him to a safe house. "I had to disguise myself in a huge hat and funny jacket and lie on the floor of the car. So I didn't even know where the house was, it was safer that way."

In the meantime, his brother had gone to Borrowdale police station. "As soon as he arrived there, a black twin-cab pulled over at the gate and dropped off my kid. He came running across to my brother, saying, 'Daddy's car, Daddy's car,' which he recognized. My sister went over to the black twin-cab—there were two huge guys in the front with sunglasses, and in the back a policewoman in uniform, she was a sergeant. My sister said, 'Where is his mother, tell me where is his mother?' But they drove off. Ashley said, 'Let's go and get Mummy, she's in the bush. The soldiers left her there.'

"Later I asked my brother to go to Parirenyatwa Hospital, to see if there were any unidentified bodies there. And he found my wife in the morgue there, her body was swollen and battered.

"It took us a week to do her burial. We were waiting for the pathologist to ascertain her cause of death, there's only one left here, and he was away. Then my father-in-law demanded four head of cattle before he would allow her to be buried." Abigail's father was a war vet, an avid supporter of Mugabe, who disapproved so much of her marriage to an opposition activist that he divorced his wife, Abigail's mother, over it. Now, "He said that her death was my fault, because I had opposed Mugabe, I was the cause of it, and I should pay him compensation."

Mugabe's youth militia came and threw stones at the mourners who had come to pay condolences — *kubata maoka*. "We called the police and they had to fire shots in the air. But then they arrested four mourners, and none of the ZANU-PF youth. So we had to move the funeral to Chitungwiza."

But Emmanuel went neither to the funeral nor to the burial at Warren Hills. "Everyone said I had to stay in hiding as it was too dangerous for me to come out. They said to me, 'You must stay alive to look after your kid, that is the most important thing.' I really wanted to see my wife before she was buried. But they all said no. The burial itself was very tense, because there were CIO agents mingling in with the mourners, looking for me.

"Later, Morgan, our President, phoned to see if I wanted to continue as Mayor, if I felt I could manage, after what had happened. I said, 'My wife has died while we were fighting this election, so I must continue.'"

ON SUNDAY MORNING, I meet Emmanuel out at Hatcliffe. He is something of a folk hero here, lobbying to replace a burnt-out transformer that left residents without electricity for four months. "And we got twenty boreholes done. Fifteen of them came on-line just last week. Hatcliffe has had no mains water for two years. Seven thousand households, thirty-five thousand people living here—and no water!"

His house is at the entrance of the township, close to the police post. He surveys the ruin and inventories all he has lost. "My home is totally destroyed, and my business, everything I worked for all my life, my wife is dead. Now I live in a loaned council house, and I have to do everything on my own. I have no assistance from anyone to rebuild."

There in the small, wild garden that Emmanuel admits he hasn't set foot in since the attack, I find the burnt hulk of their sofa, and in the overgrown weeds of their front lawn, a charred Zimbabwe passport. I open it to see that it is Abigail's; her burnt photo smiles back at me, charred at the edges. Nearby are Ashley's tiny sneakers, and Abigail's flip-flops, both charred too. All the detritus of a normal urban life—the melted black plastic TV remote, an empty tub of I Can't Believe It's Not Butter.

Emmanuel walks around the burnt walls. "I don't think I can ever live here again," he says, "but I wanted to turn it into a home for displaced kids—in commemoration of my wife, of her efforts to fight for real independence. Susan Tsvangirai was going to assist—but she's dead too now. There was an anonymous donor from Alabama, but he's disappeared.

"You know, during the attack everyone ran, but Abigail went back to find Ashley and that's when they grabbed her...It should have been me," he says sadly.

His Nokia rings, and the screen lights up to show a photo of Abigail on their wedding day. She's dressed in an exuberant froth of white taffeta with a diamanté tiara perched on her head, smiling, excited. Into her image, he has a short, urgent conversation. When he hangs up, he is tense. "I've just been informed that Mugabe's militia have reopened up a base here today. I need to find out how many there are and where they're coming from. We should probably leave."

I ask if I can look at Abigail's screen photo, and Emmanuel holds the phone up to show me. "This is my lovely wife," he says simply. "And they killed her."

Ashley emerges from the pick-up parked outside, bored of waiting on his own. He is in his church clothes, a wine-dark corduroy jacket with gleaming bronze buttons, jeans, trainers, and green-and-yellow banded socks. There is a somber, unsmiling quality about him, as though his childishness has been extinguished early. "I don't like bringing Ashley here," Emmanuel says. "It affects him badly." The little boy looks solemnly at the house, and then turns away.

"In the early days," says his dad, "Ashley used to say, 'We were taken by soldiers. We left Mummy there in the bush.' Over and over, he begged me, 'Let's go back and get her.' He didn't want to see twin-cabs, they frightened him, and he would cry. He didn't want to see men in army or police uniforms, or hear men raising their voices. I think they must have shouted at his mother and it reminded him of that. He would get a belt and tie it around his eyes, to blindfold himself, and he would say, 'This is what Mummy was like.' He thinks if he blindfolds himself, that maybe he can see her again…"

I MEET UP LATER with the Beatties for lunch at friends of theirs, Mike and Roxy Laing, who run horse stables close to Hatcliffe, in Teviotdale. Also at the lunch is a group of displaced farmers.

A microlight buzzes overhead, low, very low indeed, and wiggles its wings, the pilot, a friend of theirs, hanging out, waving. Mike's a pilot too. He shows me the plane he's building in his garage—it seems every white man in this country is trying to construct a flying machine.

The farmers here tell air-crash stories the way the game rangers tell animal-attack ones. Mike has had several himself. He crashed his microlight into the Zambezi, just below Victoria Falls. "The tail wind in the gorge was too strong, and the propellor couldn't get purchase, and we went down. I had a passenger, and as we were ditching, she tells me she can't swim! We hit the water, and I got her out. She was bleeding and I was trying to pull her against the current to get her to the bank, but my flying suit was sodden and heavy. We only just made it."

A friend of his refused to wear a seat belt in his little plane, and one day when he'd had a few to drink he flew too low over their maize field, clipped the stalks, flipped the plane, and fell out. "He lost a couple of fingers and injured his head. Our grooms carried him to the road, and stood in the middle to stop vehicles to get him a lift to hospital."

Every single one of the farmers here today has been jambanja'd. Peter Martin says he still flies over his old farm. "The infrastructure's completely shot. No electricity now, grain silos filled with water. From the air, all you see across the whole district now is roofless buildings — the whole place has just been stripped, looted."

"When I last flew over my farm," Solly Ferreira says, "they had burned all my citrus trees down. Most of the three hundred workers came from Mozambique, and they went back there after the farm was jambanja'd. Shame, they send over one of their number every few months to see if the farm is back on stream yet. But it never is…"

FROM WHERE WE sit on the lawn, there is an astonishing view over the Mazowe Mountains, fold after fold of them; I count ten distinct silhouettes in diminishing shades of blue. In this view nestles the lake where I rowed, at school, and above it, the hilltop mansion of the millionaire John Bredenkamp, once the biggest private tobacco merchant in the world, before he fell from Mugabe's favor. The Laings are telling a story about Bredenkamp's attempt to add a giraffe to the stock of wildlife on his property. The giraffe had to travel in a horsebox with the roof cut off, its head poking through the top, its eyes blindfolded. On the very last leg of the long journey, just as it was nearing its destination, it was decapitated by a low-hanging power line.

I tell them I've been in Hatcliffe, with Emmanuel Chiroto.

"Oh," says Mike, "we found his wife's body at the bottom of our property, over there, in the thick bush," and he points into the view where the sun is now nudging the ranks of the Mazowe Mountains. "The kids chopping down trees for firewood found the body. She was a mess, man. She'd been burned." He takes a swig of his Zambezi. "It's quite close to the Pomona army barracks," he says, and leaves the implication hanging.

And I sit there, thinking of Abigail in her taffeta wedding dress, memorialized on Emmanuel's Nokia. Of her being bundled, screaming, into the unmarked twin-cab by Mugabe's hit squad. Of her corpse, blindfolded, beaten, and burned, lying in this stunning Mazowe Mountain view. I think of her little boy, Ashley, who blindfolds himself, even now, in the hope of seeing his mother again.

thirty-eight

Delicious

AT THE SOUTHERN END of Borrowdale Village shopping
center is a café called Delicious. It's one of the few places here
to offer a wireless connection, and the tables are peopled with
laptop-tappers, tending their email. The owner walks among them,
resolving connection hassles, his baby daughter on his hip. On the
walls hangs work copied from the Scottish painter Jack Vettriano.
They are film-noir scenes of white people in evening dress, dancing
or dining on what looks like a rain-lashed deck, with servants brandishing umbrellas over them, serving them flutes of champagne,
even while the storm rages around them. The scenes have a fin de
siècle feel to them. In Delicious, you get a revealing glimpse into the
minds of the strange selection of whites who've somehow survived
the end of their era.

"It's the best cappuccino in town," declares Ed Byrne, who used
to be a cameraman. Georgina once worked as his producer, and had
to lie under the camera puffing on five cigarettes simultaneously,
in place of a smoke-effect machine. Since then, Ed's dabbled in

prospecting, mining, well-drilling, trading. He rues that I have already pegged him for a latté-liberal, who bemoans the repression, violence, cholera, AIDS, starvation, and hyperinflation, while licking cinnamon-speckled foam from his lip.

Today Ken Schofield is here. He's Amanda von Pezold's brother, and runs a timber outfit in Chimanimani with Heinrich. The last time he was down there, he says, was to inspect their newly acquired lumber "skidder," when who should appear but Joseph Mwale. Call me *sabuku*, "headman," Mwale said, and after appraising the large yellow machine, asked what it cost. $350k, said Ken. Mwale whistled, and shook his head. Why are you still investing in Zimbabwe, he wanted to know. Because in ten years you'll be gone and I'll still be here, replied Ken. Mwale just looked at the machine some more, and then walked away. Later on, says Ken, Mwale went to the lumber manager to inquire about getting a job there. Work skills: beating, torture, a spot of arson and murder. A chilling résumé.

I see a familiar figure in the corner of Delicious. Bull-necked, white-haired now, he is reading an article in the *Zimbabwean* about Matthew Mufiri, who is claiming to be Mugabe's pilot, and now wants asylum in the UK as he fears the President will kill him if he comes back.

"Paddy?"

His face cracks in a grin, like theater curtains going up. John "Paddy" Crean is an old friend from the 1980s, when Zimbabwe was the brave new world and we were caught up in a whirl of parties, living and drinking hard. So hard that Paddy realized he was an alcoholic one day when he drank so many liqueurs at a French embassy do that he collapsed, and his heart briefly stopped. "I've been sober for twenty-two years," he says now.

His route has been via art college in Dublin, fire-fighting in Manchester, near-paralysis in a hit-and-run accident, traveling the world until washing up in Rhodesia. Broke, he answered an ad for police recruits. But unlike most white servicemen, Paddy stayed on after independence in 1980, and stayed and stayed. Until, by 2000, he was the last white officer in the Zimbabwe Republic Police (ZRP).

Some suspected he must be working for the CIO. In the end, says Paddy, he fell into disfavor for trying to investigate a drug ring, which involved senior police officers. Very senior ones. He was punished by being put in charge of the special constabulary, part-timers, who run neighborhood watches. When Paddy boosted the rag-tag force from one thousand to six thousand, as ordered, his superiors became uneasy, accused him of planning a coup, and relegated him to the Commissioner's Pool, to which were sent senior officers who had incurred the wrath of Chihuri, the chief of police.

"There were ten of us there, most suspected of MDC sympathies, only one desk and nothing to do. It was designed to humiliate you and make you leave." But Paddy stuck it out for two years, to reach his magic twenty years' service, in 2007, and collect his full pension as a chief superintendent. Now he has a Lithuanian wife, and runs a small team of Swiss-trained black Zimbabweans who repair antique watches, sent to them from all over the world. Paddy waves his large rectangular wristwatch, delicately spinning flywheels visible through its glass window. "Ingersoll 1920s repro," he says.

Jeremy Sanford is a regular here. He helped to hide Emmanuel Chiroto when he was on the run, after Abigail was murdered. "I thought, he's gonna get killed if he sticks around here, so I got one of my drivers to take him down to Bulawayo."

He is harsh in judgment of the remaining whites, especially himself. "I think we're like the dregs who didn't get out. Idleness and fear stopped us leaving. The caliber of my parents' generation was far higher. There are maybe 20k of us left, tops. It's a debate we used to have all the time—what the fuck are we still doing here? I've let myself down. I should have left in my twenties. But it's been so interesting—and horrifying too—watching a place melt in front of your eyes. I drive past the public pool in Avondale and have happy memories of swimming there as a kid. Now it's a cesspool. There's this continual sense of loss. And it's accelerating as the country becomes more degraded."

At fifty-four, he looks back and declares, "I wasted my life. I wanted to be a journalist, after studying law at Cape Town, I went to Israel and Greece to skip the army here. My mother said, 'There's no way any of my sons are going to get killed for this twerp, Ian Smith.' I started as a journalist on the *Diamond Field Advertiser* in Kimberley, and lasted six months. I hated it." After independence, he came back to Zimbabwe. His mother had cancer and was given six months to live—she lasted thirteen years. He became a public prosecutor, an accountant, and an antique-furniture restorer, flirted with Johannesburg, lost what money he'd made, had a nervous breakdown, saw his marriage disintegrate, lost his kids, and went into self-imposed rehab and came back.

He has a house in the Western Cape. "I built it with Shona border-jumpers—sixteen of them. It's a Kenyan colonial with a view of the Outeniqua Mountains, but unfinished. I ran out of money. Anyway, I won't retire there—I'll stay here. Why leave?"

Now he's a miner. "I've been reading Viktor Frankl. He says a man needs a passion. I've become quite passionate about mining. Mining's like a treasure hunt—shall we try here or there? I mine for gold, tin, and tantalite. The strike rate is one in ten. We have this guy, mad Mike, a black guy, a mental case, pretty much, a burrowing rabbit with this phenomenal ability to nose out gold and tantalite. I have seventy people working for me up there, in the Maramba-Pfungwe area, past Mutoko. The original prospector called it God's Gift mine. You can see why. I live on my own, in a wooden prefab house on the hill there, and it has an amazing three-sixty view. I have a local cook, and he makes the same supper for me every night—goat, *sadza,* and rape. There's no TV or electricity. I eat my goat and *sadza* and then I read.

"I have a right-hand man called Ishmael, who helps me run things. I built a house for him in town, but the police came and broke it down during Operation Murambatsvina. I had had quite a lot to do with the local community around God's Gift, helped them in various ways, employed them. I remember when I first arrived there, they were so welcoming. One old guy walked all the way up the hill to give me a watermelon.

"I had noticed before the election that the MDC seemed to be getting a foothold in our area, and I thought, this is too good to be true. Francis, my foreman, came into my office one day and sat down at my desk and said, 'I don't know if you have the stomach for this, but I want to show you what's happening just down the road from here.' He started showing me cell-phone pictures — they were horrific — of naked men so badly beaten they were just slabs of meat. When I drove out into the area, I passed house after house after house, burned to the ground. I was just appalled.

"What I saw there in Mutoko, if I had any balls, I'd be sitting in jail. Every aspect of my life is compromised now. It's the thing that fucks me up the most, that I've compromised my morality."

Roy Bennett is still on bail, waiting for his treason trial to begin. He has to report to the police station three times a week.

This evening, as I am leaving soon, we're having what we've been calling the Last Supper, and there is something about the atmosphere that feels final, that speaks of endings. His sister, Cynthia, has roasted a joint of beef, but Roy is kept late at an emergency meeting of the MDC executive, so John, Cynthia's husband, says grace and we start without him. When Roy arrives, he's fuming. At a meeting to resolve Roy's ministerial appointment, Mugabe is still refusing "point blank" to swear him in, because he is facing charges. When it was pointed out to Mugabe that Roy might be found innocent, he replied vehemently, "That will *never* happen."

"So that's me," says Roy, with a grim little laugh. "I never wanted to be in the damned government in the first place. I'll just go back to the party grassroots and help build them.

"Mugabe is totally intransigent," he explains. "He keeps saying he won the June election and he's President and that's that. On all issues — civil service permanent secretaries, provincial governors, farms, and about me. He doesn't even *consider* Morgan in all of this — to him, Morgan is nothing. He's not even allowed an official Prime Minister's residence."

After supper I ask Roy again about the incident in parliament which led to his jailing in Chikurubi and his exile. Cynthia rummages through a box and finds a tape of it, as parliament here is televised. We sit on the sofa while Roy cues it up, and watch it— with Roy commentating, and rewinding, like an action replay of a sporting move.

Chinamasa, the Minister of Justice, is at the podium. He says, "Mr. Bennett has not forgiven the government for acquiring his farm, but he forgets that his forefathers were thieves and murderers."

"*Wa kundi jairira!*" Roy roars at Chinamasa, and bears down on him. "You are really getting on my nerves!"

Roy shoves him. "I pushed him and he fell straight over, toward the Speaker."

Didymus Mutasa, Minister of "Anti-Corruption," sneaks up from behind and kicks Roy in the backside.

"Very brave man, attacks from behind."

Roy turns around and says to Mutasa: "You want to kick me— stand up and be a man, you are so used to sending other people to do your dirty work." And Mutasa falls back onto the bench and does a frantic bicycle-pedaling motion with his legs to keep Roy at bay.

"What made you snap?" I ask.

"That particular day," he says, "they had stolen the Lupane by-election, and there'd been a lot of violence there, and the guys had just been telling me about it. I had been kicked off my farm three months earlier and they had ignored High Court orders that I be allowed to collect my belongings from it. And now here was the Minister of Justice cursing out my forefathers and me, and yet he doesn't respect any laws."

Roy shakes his head at his former self, and grins. "I was cheeky like a snake then, man. It just all boiled over, you know. Mugabe probably watches that clip every night to keep himself angry with me!

"Afterward, the House was in uproar. Gibson Sibanda came to me, shook his head, and said, 'Roy what have you done? They're going to kill us all.'

"The sergeant-at-arms [the same man who ejected me from the Speaker's Gallery] marched me out the house. I got in my car but the guards wouldn't open the boom to let me out of the parliamentary car park, so I went back and sat on the veranda, outside the chamber, waiting to be arrested."

"Was it worth it?" I wonder.

"I felt better after I'd pushed him. I still feel good. It was worth it. Most definitely. You know, we've all got a threshold, and that was mine. Hopefully I'm a bit more controlled now."

At the time, the nation was agog, thrilled at the public spectacle of someone fighting back. "It was a missed opportunity," says Roy. "We could have mobilized around that."

We are now watching footage from the following day's ZTV news. Comrade Winston Zwayo leads a small demonstration outside parliament. "Rent-a-crowd," says Roy.

"Bennett hit all of us," says Zwayo. "He hit the President. He embarrassed our integrity in Zimbabwe. He won't go back into that parliament."

We switch off the TV and Roy walks me to my truck. "You know," he says, "Mugabe doesn't accept that this is a transitional government. There's no way he's going to leave voluntarily. I'm just gonna have to jack up my security for what's coming my way, and fight them. That's what it's gonna come down to—a physical fight. If I get put back in jail or I'm killed, what will I have achieved? Nothing."

We say goodbye. Roy gives me a bear hug, and promises I can be a guest of honor when the new era dawns.

"Maybe next time we'll actually get to the ceremony," I say.

thirty-nine

The Hook

WE ARE DRIVING THROUGH Highfields, to Mukai ("Wake Up!") High School, where Henry Chimbiri taught geography. Henry's explaining the different sections of the township: Lusaka, where Zambian migrants lived; Egypt, for former prisoners; Engineering, for railway workers; and Canaan, where many pastors resided. And here, in Canaan, at No. 4475, 89th Street, near the corner of Mangwende, sitting in a small garden, is the unremarkable red-brick house which was home to another Mukai teacher, Robert Mugabe.

Mukai was once a model school, and the grounds and buildings are robust and well laid out. But it has just reopened to find that most of its furniture was stolen and its classrooms vandalized; its lawns are overgrown, and the adjacent cemetery is now an informal garbage dump, which is spilling over into the school. Scum-scabbed pools of raw sewage line the road. But still, demand is so desperate for a place here that it "hot seats"—half the kids learn from 7:10 a.m. to 12:10 p.m., when the other half take their places until 5:10, effectively doubling its capacity. The siren wails and the grounds fill with children in green and gray uniforms, changing classes.

After his unsuccessful run for parliament, Henry returned to his classroom. He was explaining the intricacies of the Stevenson screen to his pupils when four CIO agents in dark glasses burst in and wrenched him away from the blackboard. "The kids were shocked," Henry recalls. "They cried out, 'Teacher! Teacher! Leave our teacher!'" The agents tried to bundle Henry into the boot of their car. "You can't load me in there," he shouted. "What do you think I am? *Groceries?*" and he hooked his legs and arms around a tree to prevent them from abducting him, so they began hitting him with the butts of their pistols. He was bleeding copiously now, a bib of red spreading down his crisp white shirt. The kids were crying and screaming.

"And I thought to myself, Chimbiri, you are dying here. So, in desperation, I grabbed one of the agents by the balls, and he yelled to the others to stop beating me."

After the riot police had been summoned, Henry was finally hauled off to the police station, and beaten so savagely that he lost consciousness. He awoke to hear a senior CIO agent admonishing his men: "Guys, you've gone and killed him. I told you — know your limits."

To DRIVE AROUND Harare with Henry is to get a conducted tour of the violent reality of Mugabe's rule. As we drive past State House, Henry points to the house opposite, another official government residence. A few years ago he was in a convoy of supporters on the way to a rally for Tendai Biti when his truck was passed by Mugabe's cavalcade, and the people chanted and jeered. Shortly afterward they were pulled over at gunpoint by soldiers and ordered in here. "They beat us so badly, using planks and sticks they had cut from the pine trees, one man had to have his arm amputated afterward, it was so badly injured," says Henry.

One of the policemen warned them that they were going to be killed, taken to the garden of that house and thrown into the *kugomba,* "the hole," a concrete-lined pit, like a septic tank, filled with a deeply corrosive alkaline solution, into which they throw bodies. Later they were herded into the central courtyard at the police station, where Senior Assistant Commissioner Ndou addressed them. "He said—'You guys are the ones making trouble at State House—you were lucky—you were going to be taken to the Hole.'

"I *am* one of the lucky ones," Henry admits. "I am still alive. But there are other people not so lucky, who didn't get word out to the party, who don't have Penny to call a lawyer. If no one talks about you, then no one will come to your rescue. Many of these cases haven't been followed up, cases of people being tortured, people being killed. The little people have disappeared and no one follows up."

Henry lives in a small house on the edge of Budiriro 5, with his wife, Patricia (who lost her job in the Attorney-General's office, due to Henry's politics), their two kids, and a cat called Merry, which he brought home after it hid behind him when soldiers were beating up patrons at the Speedie bar, where Henry was having a beer one Christmas Eve, hence the name. Patricia didn't take to Merry initially, until the night the stove was left on and caught alight, and Merry came into their room yowling and scratching Henry's leg until he awoke.

Now Merry sits with three kittens of her own, with blues playing in the background from PowerFM, and Patricia coming in from the garden with a yellow mitt of bananas. There is chocolate cake too, compliments of her sister, who has gone back to South Africa, where she and her husband, a science teacher, now live. The house is full of their furniture.

Patricia offers guava cocktail. "We boil the water," she adds, quickly. Penny remembers Henry coming to her, "really scared, saying there were mobile morgue vans coming round each morning to pick up the dead, and no one had any idea how cholera spread, how to prevent it or treat it." So she found a document online produced by the Center for Disease Control and printed out dozens and dozens of copies for him to hand out.

Neither is the Chimbiris' home as cozy as it seems. The house next door is occupied by the local ZANU chairman. At night fires are lit in his garden, and food cooked there for dozens of Mugabe's young militiamen. Often they shout insults across at Henry, and five times they have attacked, the last time at 4 a.m., when they hurled heavy rocks onto the roof, breaking the asbestos sheeting. One rock came right through and fell on his sleeping daughter's head, gashing it, so that she had to get stitches. The front door is shattered too, temporarily patched with cardboard.

Henry walks us out into the township. A youth, Morev Chamunorwa (it means "Why do you fight?"), is breaking rocks by the side of the road. He breaks big ones into little ones—prison hard-labor fare—and sells them for $2 a wheelbarrowful. He's been at it for two years now—the only way he can think of to pay his $30 monthly room rent.

At her street corner post, where she can usually be found, is Joyce Chihanya. She's sixty-five years old and used to work as a final checker at a textile factory that made Van Heusen shirts for export. Hers were those little pieces of paper with an inspector number you find in the pocket of your new garment. She's been a member of the MDC since its formation in 1999. Now she sits on the culvert wall, distributing party membership cards and T-shirts, and canvassing passers-by—telling them to support the MDC, "so we can see change." She's a Budiriro institution, the MDC Chairperson of Ward 43, the Masoja Branch. "ZANU-PF want to beat me, an old woman, they want to cut my head off. I was supposed to die for supporting the opposition," she says. "But this one"—she pats Henry on the shoulder—"he protected me."

In the presidential elections, ZANU-PF thugs threw bricks at her house too. "They climbed over my wall and smashed my windows. I switched off all my lights and closed my windows, and pushed my wardrobe against the door." She was also attacked in 2005, 2006, and 2007. The riot police threatened her too, she says. "'You, old woman,' they said, 'you are for the MDC, we will kill you.' But I said, 'You can kill me. I don't even mind. I am ready to die.' I would even give our party sign when the ZANU-PF passed by. Their fist sign is no longer just a fist, but it has now become a hammer to destroy the country. I don't fear anymore. Though they come in their dozens and I will be alone."

DRIVING HOME, later, we are talking about revenge and justice for torture victims, as we have done before, when Henry says, "It happened to me too."

"What did?"

"Torture." He is speaking so softly I can barely hear him.

"How?" I ask, hesitantly.

He rubs his eyes with the backs of his hands, and lets out a decisive sigh.

"The time I was arrested together with Raymond Majongwe, the head of the teachers' union—they said that I was involved in mobilizing teachers against the government.

"They handcuffed me and blindfolded me with a piece of black cloth, and threw me into the back of a vehicle." They drove fast out of the city, he says, and he tried to work out where they were going. He heard the clatter of expansion joints as they crossed a bridge, and the tar road turned into a dirt one, and they stopped. He could hear cattle mooing, the smell of pigs, so he knew this was some kind of farm. Then they threw him into an empty room and locked the door. After an hour, they removed his blindfold, and the interrogation began.

"I could hear Majongwe crying in the next room—I know his voice—and they were beating him there. I could hear the sound of big belts, those heavy army ones. They brought in a small blue enamel plate with a silver crochet hook on it, and a cotton reel with white thread. And they said, 'Tell us the truth. Only the truth will release you from this. Or else we will work on you the whole night, and you will not be a man when we are finished.'

"So I tried to tell them what I knew about the strike, that there were fliers floating round the school calling for the strike. They asked who distributed them—I didn't know. Then they blindfolded me again. I was sitting on a small bench. Again, I promised to tell them everything I knew. But they removed my trousers down to my ankles, and I started shivering, knowing that something terrible was going to happen. They called to someone, 'Skipper,' they called, 'get ready, we are waiting for you.'

"A person came in, this Skipper, and he got hold of my penis, and said, 'You tell us, there is a tape recorder, tell us.' I told him about Majongwe, and whatever I could think of. Then he said to me, 'You are a fuck-up!'—he said it in English—'And we are going to teach you a lesson.' He held my penis very firmly, and he pushed the crochet hook inside, and then he twisted it—that was when it was so terribly painful, I screamed with the pain—he had hooked it inside my penis—I could feel the blood spurting down onto my thighs—I fell off the bench and he punched my mouth repeatedly, telling me to shut up. I tried to pretend I was having an epileptic fit. He called his colleagues to bring some water. They came in running, and poured water on me, and then they removed the blindfold and said, 'Now tell us.'

"I looked down at my penis and saw the crochet hook was still inside it. Blood was everywhere. I looked at them, and I was weeping. And Skipper said, *Kusina amai hakuendwe*—Your mother is not here to listen. There is no one to help you.' Then he wrenched the hook out. Blood flowed even more. I screamed and screamed and screamed and there was blood all over. They all left the room, and I was remaining on my own, just looking at my groin. I tried to hold my penis, to stop the blood, but it was no good, the blood just kept on flowing.

"They came back a few minutes later, blindfolded me again, pulled up my trousers, took me outside, and threw me in a vehicle, saying to me, 'Shhhh. Shhhhh!' I was lying on the floor, in such pain. I was covered in sweat and blood. They drove me for a few minutes and then removed my blindfold, removed the handcuffs, but tied my hands again with the blindfold, and threw me out on the ground, and drove away. It was still dark. I could see lights and I started walking toward them to find help."

Henry is staring straight ahead, still speaking in a quiet monotone.

"My penis is still painful. Even now, it hurts when I try to have sex with my wife. There is a lump inside, I can feel it there. I am now disabled..."

I have pulled over to the side of the road while he has been talking. And now we sit there in silence for a moment while I struggle to respond. How does one—this is beyond all the clichés of empathy. There seems something ghoulishly intimate and premeditated about this particular torture—the pseudo-surgical instrument: the silver hook, like a sharp dental explorer, gleaming malevolently in its dish.

"Jesus, Henry, I'm so, so sorry. I had no idea." I pat his shoulder inadequately.

"About four months later," he continues, still looking straight ahead, "I had gone to the Star Bar at the Elizabeth Hotel, and was having a beer with a friend when I saw this guy sitting there, and I recognized those holes in his cheeks, from acne or chicken pox, and the big scar on his left hand, the cleft in his chin, and then I knew for sure that it was Skipper, the man who had tortured me. I heard one of his colleagues call him Sikovha. He looked up and saw me, and he knew that I had recognized him. Immediately he jumped up and left, even before he had finished his beer.

"I told my friend, 'That is the guy that tortured me, and one day I will take his photo and report him, in order to bring justice, for me to be settled in my whole life, because he disabled me.'"

forty

Men Without Knees

To get to the district of southern Bindura, Mugabe's hard-core heartland, you drive north on Borrowdale Road, past Hatcliffe township, where Emmanuel Chiroto's burnt-out house stands empty, and through the swelling granite outcrops of Domboshawa. On your left, painted in large white letters on a boulder, you will see the sign to the Rescue Club Shop & Bar, and a little later, the Chicago Drive-Inn.

Today is my second-last day in Zimbabwe; after three months here I am returning to my family in New York. But as we drive, Henry is still doggedly trying to rehab my Shona. "*Ndege*," he says, as a plane flies overhead. If you say it in a drawn out way and a falling pitch, it describes the noise of a plane flying high overhead. When the word was coined, that was about as close as most black people got to a plane.

"*Asine mabvi*." Henry grins, pointing at me. It translates as "Men without knees," which is what the Shona called the first white men, because we always wore long trousers so they could never see our legs.

"*Tambo ye magetsi*," Henry says, as we pass under power lines.

"String for the lights," I translate literally.

"*Magetsi*," Henry claims, is from the fact that when you switch on a bulb, it "gets(i) light"! I'm not sure I trust him, though—he and his friends at St. Albert's Mission School once convinced a Jesuit novitiate that the Shona word for a woman's genitals actually meant thank you, causing subsequent consternation in the staff room when the priest was trying to thank a female teacher for a cup of tea.

The road deteriorates sharply into a jagged colander, as we approach Super, a small group of trading stores at a crossroads. One of the abandoned stores here served as a base for Mugabe's militia— a combination of his youth wing, war vets, and thugs. "This place was very hot," says Henry. "Until recently you couldn't get anywhere near here, the militia had roadblocks all along these access roads."

He describes a running battle that took place when the MDC was trying to fight a by-election here a few years back. Seeking safety in numbers, Morgan Tsvangirai came down to campaign in a convoy that stretched nearly half a mile. But the CIO had prepared an elaborate ambush. They erected a police roadblock, which would let through only about ten cars at a time. Once the vehicles moved through in small batches, they encountered a huge force of Mugabe's militia, more than two thousand, he says, arrayed in the Nguni military formation of the "horns of the buffalo," with flanks ahead on either side of the road. They began stoning the cars and setting fire to them. "There," says Henry, pointing at the rusting, overgrown wreckage of a car at the roadside. "That's the Datsun Pulsar of Dr. Tichaona Mudzingwa, the Deputy Minister of Transport in this new government. They hit his doors with iron bars and then set fire to it and he was trapped inside, burning alive. I ran over and smashed the back window and pulled him out. A friend was in a VW Combi, which had stalled, and he panicked. I jumped in and we managed to get it started and reversed for more than two miles, while they chased us, throwing rocks."

"Don't you sometimes feel you've just had enough of all this?" I ask Henry. "Enough of the constant danger."

"My wife has pushed for me to go and get employment out of the country," he says. "I have many friends who have done that. We were going to teach in the UK once, and the British embassy gave us visas, but Morgan Tsvangirai convinced us that if we went we would be abandoning him.

"I'm so soaked into politics now and I've realized that sometimes you suffer for others, and it hardens you," he says. "For me to stop this, I would feel guilty. I would feel there's an incomplete project that I haven't finished. If I think of not doing it, I would be just empty. I tried to stop once, to avoid it, and I lost my self-respect, I felt I had walked away from the revolution.

"I know it's a dangerous thing, but at least I've done my part. Some day they will recognize that we did something for this country."

As we progress, Henry points out several more places where Mugabe's militias were based. Until finally, after a long bumpy stretch of dirt road and a river crossing, we reach Nyava, "Growth Point," where the militia used the council community hall as their base too.

"It looks quiet enough today," I say.

"*Chidziva chakadzikama, ndicho chinogara ngwena,*" says Henry. "The quiet pool is the one in which the crocodile lives." He points to the weeping *dwala* above. "That's where they took people to beat or even kill them," he says.

Chenjerai Mangezo's kraal is a couple of miles further, up a rutted track. It's very modest: some maize fields, groundnuts drying in woven baskets, clucking chickens, a couple of thatched mud-brick huts, and a rectangular building in a damaged state, one of its walls demolished.

Mangezo's decision to stand in the last elections as an MDC candidate for Bindura Rural District Council, a hard-line Mugabe institution, was brave to the point of foolhardiness. And in spite of all the chicanery and fraud, and intimidation, he won. Mugabe's ZANU-PF party officials were enraged.

Shortly afterward, deep into a starless night, a large posse of Mugabe's men surrounded this small house. "We have come to kill you," they chanted, and rained large rocks down upon the roof, preparing to burn it down.

Realizing that his wife and daughter were likely to be killed too, he ordered them under the beds. Then he burst out of the house, yelling and generally attracting the attention of his predators as he blundered down the hill, away from the house, hoping they would all pursue him, which they did, swarming after him, throwing rocks and spears, until finally one blade felled him, piercing his leg.

And as he lay on the ground, they loomed over him and smashed rocks down upon him, and they beat him with logs, lifting them high to get in good meaty bone-breaking blows, and he knew then that this was what it was like to be killed. He could feel his legs being broken, his arms splintering, his skull gashed and the taste of his own blood as it flowed down over his eyes into his mouth. Lying here among the fresh green stalks of maize that he had planted but would now not live to eat, he uncurled his arms from where they had been protecting his head, and he managed to hoist himself up a little so that he could look at his assailants, now lit against the newly emerging moon. And he said to them, "You had better be sure to kill me. Because if you don't, I am going to come after you, all of you. I know who you are."

I can't stop myself. I lower my pen. "Why? Why would you do that? Why would you lie there and provoke them like that? If it were me, I would be pleading for mercy, promising them I'd seen the error of my ways, begging to join their gang of goons. Why would you be so defiant, when they held your life in their hands, when they were about to kill you?"

Chenjerai listens while I vent my incredulity. He is a short, smiley man in his mid-forties, with wide-set eyes, and the sturdy back that comes of a life of labor. His head is cocked to one side, regarding me as though *I'm* the crazy one.

"Why?" He frowns, perplexed. "*Why* did I say such a thing? Because it was *true!* That's why."

And that is that, as far as he is concerned; it requires no further explanation.

He lost consciousness soon afterward and he was dragged by his feet over the rough ground to the base in Nyava, where he was saved by a disagreement among the hit squad. The militiamen were supposed to kill him there, at his house, in the dark, the CIO officers berated. Now everyone had seen them bring him here.

When Chenjerai eventually made it to hospital, he was barely alive. His legs were shattered and his body was pulverized by rocks. Penny visited him in Dandaro and was immediately struck. "He was one of the most positive, cheerful, determined people I've ever met," she says. "He was totally immobilized in plaster but never felt sorry for himself. In fact, the first thing he did was to get all his mates to write MDC slogans all over his plaster casts."

And when he heard that the swearing-in ceremony for Bindura Rural councillors was due to take place, he was determined to be there, defying doctors' orders. He insisted that Penny find a way of getting him there. His plaster casts meant he couldn't fit in a car, so she piled foam mattresses in the back of the pick-up and they loaded him onto them. Henry drove him out over the juddering road.

When he arrived, there was consternation among Mugabe's councillors. They had assumed that either he was dead, or at the very least that the attack would have rendered him too terrified to take up his seat. Yet here he was, in front of them, unable to walk, his plaster casts adorned with MDC slogans, taking great delight in telling the local journalists there for the opening how ZANU had attempted to eliminate him.

Once the meeting was over, Henry took him to see his mother. She hadn't heard from him since the attack, and thought that he was dead. She was beside herself when she saw him, thinking at first that he must be a ghost.

After three months, the doctors finally cut off his casts, and he immediately set about trying to rehabilitate his wasted legs, determined to walk again.

"Not long after he left hospital," says Penny, "a number of new patients arrived from his home area. A young gym teacher told me that Chenjerai had sought out people who had been beaten, but had been prevented from seeking help. He organized for them to get into town and seek assistance from CSU.

"He has only ever asked me for one thing, a bicycle. Unfortunately, I couldn't provide it."

And he continues to sit on the Bindura Rural District Council among councillors from Mugabe's party, including some of those who oversaw his beating. "I see those who tried to kill me, every day," he tells me now. "They are from my village, I walk past them on the road."

I still don't really understand it. The insane bravery of it, this man lying there in the hot dark night as his life ebbed away, taunting his own assassins rather than suing for survival. And yet, when against all the odds, he does survive, he hauls himself back and sits with them in council chambers.

Chenjerai's bravery is beyond doubt. But what is this other quality, the one that allows him to sit here with these venal people, his persecutors. Is it forgiveness? Reconciliation? I think not. At least, not yet.

Is it fatalism, a quality that Westerners see in Africans? Westerners often mistake African endurance, and the lack of self-pity, for fatalism. No, I think the other quality in Chenjerai Mangezo is patience, a dogged tenacity. He hasn't given up on getting justice. But he will wait for it. And when it comes, as I pray it will, I hope it is a dish that tastes all the better for being marinated in time, for cooking slowly on the stove of his resolve. He has that most unusual pairing of strengths, passion *and* persistence, and as such, he makes an implacable foe.

And I realize that people like Chenjerai are the real *asine mabvi*—the men without knees. Not only were his legs covered by plaster casts for months, but he has refused to kneel, refused to prostrate himself before the dictatorship, whatever the consequences.

forty-one

The Axe Forgets but Not the Tree

O N MY LAST DAY in Robert Mugabe's Zimbabwe, Henry drives me to the airport in his battered pick-up truck. The windscreen is patched with plastic where it has been stoned, and we list steeply to one side. Some of the street lights along the route still bear posters of Mugabe. They are old now, tattered and weather-beaten, his image faded and indistinct. But still people are afraid to be seen pulling them down.

On the way, we stop off at the wild grounds of a Catholic convent on the southwestern edge of the city. Among the boulders and trees, Gift Konjana sits in the "agreement circle," with eight other torture survivors, working out the rules of engagement by which they will share their stories. After this, they will each retreat to their own tree to reflect on their personal journeys, and pick out a totem for the exercise — it could be a pod, a seed, a twig, a leaf, a handful of earth — that they will use to represent themselves over the next three days. Then they will join the "trauma circle," where they will share their horror stories with one another. And finally, they will try to help one another wrestle to rebuild their shattered minds, their self-worth.

After what they have been through, most of them are suffering from a toxic residue of fear, anger and depression — undiagnosed post-traumatic stress disorder. How do you work to forget an experience like torture? How do you prevent it from defining the rest of your life? Montaigne said, "Nothing fixes a thing in the memory so intensely as the wish to forget it." Facing their memories like this helps to strip them of their malign power.

Konjana, thirty-nine, a handsome, muscular, former physical education teacher, is a facilitator for Tree of Life, a self-help organization trying to assist Zimbabwe's legion of tortured to heal themselves, as no one else seems interested in helping them. He has been tortured himself — all the facilitators have — it's a job requirement.

The idea for Tree of Life came to Bev Reeler, a Zimbabwean ecologist, when she was in exile in South Africa with her husband, Tony, who had run a human-rights NGO, Amani Trust, in Zimbabwe — before Mugabe closed it down. One day she found herself the only white woman on a protest march in Pretoria, and she was chaperoned by a group of young black Zimbabweans. Most of them had fled the country after being beaten and tortured, but they did not talk about it, even to each other.

Reeler began to work with Zimbabwean refugees living abject lives under the bridges of Johannesburg. She took a group of them to Groot Marico, to sit for three days and share their experiences, and in so doing, ease the burden of their trauma. (The first group was reported to the police by nervous Afrikaner farmers, who thought they were Zimbabwean insurgents training!) The people seemed to benefit from reconnecting with nature, and from being heard. It gave them a shot at recovery, at redemption, even. She used the tree as a metaphor for their lives. It wasn't about forgiveness, though; it was about healing. Forgiveness, she believes, has to happen on its own.

When she returned to Zimbabwe, she established the workshops there. In the last six months they have grown quickly, as the ranks of the tortured have swelled, and no formal counseling is available.

In order to establish the trust of the group, Gift must first share his own story with them — to enter "the trauma circle," and show them that they are not alone in their suffering.

As soon as he became MDC administrator for Mashonaland West in 2000, he drew the ire of Mugabe's enforcers. "They searched my office, took computers, party cards, pamphlets, and those red cards which said '*Mugabe must go*' — and they charged me for possessing those things." Then he was tortured. "They used *falanga* on me — beating the soles of my feet with batons, and tying my testicles in a noose and pulling it tight — and they also used the 'submarine' — they put me upside down into a drum of water up to my shoulders," he tells the group. He was arrested several more times, and tortured again. "The police used to take me from my cells and drive me to the bridge over the Hunyani River and threaten to throw me over into the river if I didn't tell them where our leaders were hiding, where arms caches were, who was funding us.

"Also, they drove me home, to Chegutu, at night and threatened to abduct my family. They would drive up to my house, where my wife and my new, two-week-old baby were. They would say to me, 'You see, we know where you live, you will never be able to escape from us.' They would knock at the door, and my wife would answer. I would be watching from inside the vehicle, behind tinted windows, gagged and bound. They would ask her, 'Where is your husband? Where is Gift?' She would say, 'He has been arrested.' And then they would come and say to me — 'We can take her any time, so tell us what we want to know.'"

On his next arrest he spent six months in police cells — this time accused of burning down ZANU-PF provincial offices. "The whole time — six months — I wasn't allowed clean clothes. My clothes became disgusting. They forced me to eat my own soiled underpants until I vomited. They tied me to a bench and beat my buttocks so severely that I could neither sit nor walk. They beat my back with batons until I was covered with wounds all over. The entire time I had no access to lawyers.

"I couldn't see my newborn second baby — when my wife visited me in prison, she had to leave him at the gate, she wasn't allowed to bring him inside. My wife named him Tinomuda—We Love Him—because he was born in my absence—I was arrested before I could see him."

By the time Gift was released, he had lost his job as a teacher. "No one else would hire me because I was a well-known activist. Even my friends—though some offered help—wouldn't give me a job, they said they would all get problems from the authorities. I couldn't support my family. By then, I was suicidal. I came to Tree of Life myself."

At the workshop, he says, "I began to see that, like a tree, I had been through all these things—droughts, fires, limb-cutting, and that I too could survive, despite all this. Like a tree, which still gives fruit and shelter to birds and insects and man. I can also do that, I can fend for my family. I am still *someone*. A human being. There is still a reason for me to live. I can still be *something* in my society.

"And at the end," says Gift, "we have a ritual—we discard our totems—burn them or bury them or put them in the river or throw them over our shoulder without looking back—it's about starting anew."

The group is singing now, in harmony, a song with the chorus "You are just like God," and each time, they add the name of a circle member. Their voices rise, soft among the balancing boulders, as they sit in their circle of hard-back chairs with their newly issued *koki* pens and their pads of paper, trying to draw away their suffering, struggling to heal themselves, because no one else will.

LIST OF ACRONYMS

CIO	Central Intelligence Organization
CSU	Counseling Services Unit
GNU	Government of National Unity
GPA	Global Political Agreement
IMF	International Monetary Fund
JAG	Justice for Agriculture
JOC	Joint Operational Command
MDC	Movement for Democratic Change
MDC-M	Movement for Democratic Change — Mutambara
NGO	non-governmental organization
SADC	Southern African Development Community
ZANU-PF	Zimbabwe African National Union — Patriotic Front
ZAPU	Zimbabwe African People's Union
ZBC	Zimbabwe Broadcasting Corporation
ZIPRA	Zimbabwe People's Revolutionary Army
ZNA	Zimbabwe National Army
ZRP	Zimbabwe Republic Police

RESOURCES

If you want to help the people of Zimbabwe, or just to follow their continuing struggle, please go to www.petergodwin.com for links to charities operating in Zimbabwe, and for news of the latest events there.

ACKNOWLEDGMENTS

I am indebted to the John Simon Guggenheim Memorial Foundation, whose fellowship enabled me to complete this book, and to the MacDowell Colony for a writing residence.

My thanks to: Andrew Wylie and his staff at the Wylie Agency. Judy Clain and Nathan Rostron at Little Brown. Charlotte Greig, Paul Baggaley, and Nicholas Blake at Picador, UK. Terry Morris and Andrea Nattrass at Macmillan, South Africa. And Cullen Murphy, Graydon Carter and Aimee Bell at *Vanity Fair*.

To my sister, Georgina Godwin, who is still the funniest, most observant traveling companion I know. My mother, Dr. Helen Godwin, whose fortitude is humbling. My wife, Joanna Coles, and our sons, Hugo and Thomas, who gamely tolerate both my lengthy absences, and my writing purdah.

In Zimbabwe (South Africa, the U.S. and UK) I relied on hospitality, help and advice from so many people. Three of them—Murelle Hayes, Mike Mason and Robin Watson—died during the course of this book, and are greatly missed. I am grateful to them, and to the following, whose inclusion here, however, should not necessarily imply that they agree with all I have written:

Kristen Abrams. William and Christina Anderson. Sara Andrews. Diana Anthony. Betsy Apple. Manuel Bagorro. Brett Bailey. Sebastian and Ruth Bakare. Jeffrey Barbee. Arthur Basopo. Richard and Penny Beattie. Roy, Charles, Heather and Casey Bennett. Rajiv Bhendre. Tendai Biti. Eric and Baila Bloch. William Brandon. Ed Byrne. Angela Campbell. Beefy and Lynda Campbell-Morrison. Guy Cary. Tonde Chakanedza. Takawira Chamauya. Godfrey Chanetsa. Hilary Cheinuru. Joyce Chihanya. Henry and Patricia Chimbiri. Emmanuel Chiroto. Edmond and Precious Chitawah. David Coltart. Paul and Marie Connolly. Laurent Contini. Albrecht Conze. Milos Coric. John "Paddy" Crean. Eddie Cross. Jumbo Davidson. Goof de Jong. Honorata Devlin. Esther Dewe. Miriam Dikinya-Chikoto. Lance Dixon. Tashi Dolma. Denias Dombo. Margaret Dongo. Elmon Dube. Georgie du Plessis. Raoul du Toit. Jonathan Elliott. Comrade Fatso. Grace Gambeza. Donnard Gambezi. Martin Ganda. Tichanzii Gandanga. Shepherd Geti. Zachariah Godi. Xanthe Godwin Summerfield. Lin and Jean Goncalves. Cedric Green. Peta Hall. Jeanette and Forbes Harvey. Rita Harvey. Simon Herring. Beatrice Hitschmann. David Hughes. David Hulme. Augustine Hungwe. Elias Hwenga. Brian James. Daiton Japani. Anna Kadurira. Thomas Kanodzimbira. Reason Kapfuya. Kerry and Iain Kay. Michael and Kim Keating. Shane and Birgit Kidd. Mike Kimberley. Paula Kingwill. Gift Konjana. Lynette Kore-Karenyi. Mike and Roxy Laing. Peter and Diane Lobel. George and Angie Lock. Frances Lovemore. Richard and Susie Lowe. Adrian Lunga. Chris Lynam. Trust Maanda. Lovemore Machengedzera. Owen and Fungai Machisa. Vincent Mai. Theresa Makone. Bright Makunde. Timothy Makwenjere. Jonathan Malikita. Andrew and Julie Mama. Chenjerai Mangezo. Sarah Mannell. Fideus Mapondera. Mlaga Maposa. Xavier Marchal. James Maridadi. Edison Marisau. Daffwell Marumahoko. Reason Mashambanaka. Sharon Mason. Godfrey Matanga. Mduduzi Mathuthu. Lawrence Mattock. Brian Maviso. Wilf and Trish Mbanga. Margaret Mbiriamowa.

Murray McCartney. Jim and Sheila McGee. Fraser McKay. Trish McKenzie. Dave and Irene Meikle. Roy Meiring. Brenda Meister. David Mhende. Sipho Mhlanga and all her orphans. Syma Mirza. Diana Mitchell. Joshua Moyo. Kundisai Mtero. Beatrice Mtwetwa. Tawanda Mubwanda. Pishai Muchauraya. Norest Muchochoma. Casper Mugano. Mudiwa and Julia Mundawarara. Tendai and Imelda Mundawarara. Godfrey and Killiana Mungwadzi. Prisca Muomo. Charity Murandu. Martin Murombedzi. Angela Mushore. James Mushore. Marcey Mushore. Pete Musto. Much Musunda. Happiness Mutata. Prosper Mutseyami. Carpenter Mwanza. Shine Mzariri. Isabel Ngenywa. Briarley Nicholson. Max Nkandla. Stanley Nkisi. Stephen Nkomo. Dominic Norman-Taylor. Alex Nunes. Mike Odendaal. Rick and Sally Passaportis. Tendai Pawandiwa. Gavin Peter. Darrel Plowes. Robin and Jennifer Plunket. Tyrone and Lucy Plunket. Andrew and Julie Pocock. John and Cynthia Pybus. Jan Raath. Kate Raath. Allen Radford. Bev and Tony Reeler. Ann Reid. John Robertson. Maud Samoyo. Jeremy Sanford. Weldon and Kathy Schenck. Ken Schofield. Kim Schofield. Dieter Scholz. Blessing Shambare and the congregation of Christchurch, Borrowdale. Belinda and John Sharples. Angus Shaw. Gabriel Shumba. Kurt and Laura Slight. Karl Snater. Irene Staunton. Sharon Stead. Trudy Stevenson. Clive Stockil. Roger Stringer. Paul Thistle. Tree Society of Zimbabwe. Morgan and the late Susan Tsvangirai. Doug and Tempe van der Riet. Leon and Mags Varley. Lester Venter. Paul Verryn. Heinrich and Amanda Von Pezold. Ellah Wakatama Allfrey. Pius and Winnie Wakatama. Glenn and Randee Warren. Sydney, Fiona, and Alasdair Watson. George and Tanya Webster. Hildegard Weinrich. Iden Wetherell. Lynne and Martin Wilkins. Pebbles Williamson. Spike Williamson. John Worswick. Paula Worswick.

I am obliged to these and all the people who were brave enough, in dangerous times, to talk to me.

Peter Godwin
New York, 2010

INDEX

ABOUT THE AUTHOR

PETER GODWIN is the award-winning author of *When a Crocodile Eats the Sun* and *Mukiwa*. Born and raised in Zimbabwe, he was educated at Cambridge and Oxford and became a foreign correspondent, reporting from more than sixty countries. Since moving to Manhattan, he has written for *National Geographic,* the *New York Times Magazine,* and *Vanity Fair.* He has taught at Princeton and Columbia, and in 2010 he received a Guggenheim Fellowship.